Endorsements

"Once a victim of this culture's disease—addiction, Kimberly rose from the pits of hell and has emerged a vessel of God's healing grace. As she honestly shares her stories of pain and shame, she gives us hope of a resurrected and transformed life. This study is a testimony to the power of His Word. If you are wrestling with destructive habits and want to be free then this book is for you. Read it and be transformed through the healing grace of God." –*Gregory L. Jantz, PhD, C.E.D.S., The Center for Counseling and Health Resources, Inc.*

"Kimberly has lived it and bled it. She knows the face of the enemy. She also knows where Redemption lives—and grace, and forgiveness, and peace. Kimberly doesn't just tell you where to find it, she'll take you there." –*Nancy, a writer, speaker, women's ministry leader and mentor from Oregon*

"Bravo for a book that gives a biblically sound frame of reference for addiction and treatment. I applaud the way Kimberly has addressed the biblical doctrine of sin and its connection with addiction. I have worked both in secular and religious circles in this field and in my experience *both* shy away from addressing the concept of sin and how it affects addiction." —*Sharon, MSW, a mental health professional from Kentucky, currently working in SE Africa*

"Kimberly writes from a place of personal knowledge. She is highly transparent about her experiences and deficiencies so others may learn how to deal with the pain that so often accompanies a hidden addiction. Her understanding of the specific struggles is obvious. She validates the realities of those struggling with addiction. I recommend this study, designed to provide a supportive pathway along the recovery journey. Each chapter is pointed and affecting. The format enhances spiritual growth and healing. Readers will witness the love of God and discover His amazing, limitless healing grace as they journey towards freedom from addiction. The book is an outstanding ministry tool." —*Doris, BSN, MS, PMHNP, a mental health professional and Bible teacher from Oregon*

"This book is different. Kimberly shares the only way to true healing: a relationship with God through his son, Jesus Christ. I've learned through this long journey that only God can fill those dark places in our lives. His Spirit will fill you as a substance never can. The result is peace and joy rather than shame and guilt. Read this book and let God speak to you through it." –*Jennifer, a wife and mother from Minnesota*

"This is an amazing, life changing book. I highly recommend this to any woman who has ever struggled with compulsive behavior, addiction or self-image issues. Be prepared for God to do a major work in your life if you'll be honest with him and yourself." —*Tanya, a wife, mother, and part-time realtor from Colorado*

SOMETHING HAPPENED ON MY WAY TO

HELL

BREAK FREE FROM THE INSATIABLE PURSUIT OF PLEASURE

KIMBERLY DAVIDSON

Also by Kimberly Davidson

I'm Beautiful? Why Can't I See It? *Daily Encouragement to Promote Healthy Eating & Positive Self-Esteem*
Emotional eating is an epidemic. Pastoral counselor and recovered bulimic Kimberly Davidson brings a clear message of hope and healing to anyone struggling with unhealthy patterns of eating and body image issues in this effective step-by-step 13-week devotional study.

I'm God's Girl? Why Can't I Feel It? *Daily Biblical Encouragement to Defeat Depression & the Blues*
What if the perfect depression medication wasn't a medication at all? Join Kimberly Davidson on a life-changing biblical journey and claim the same hope that many extraordinary women of the Bible found. In this 365-day devotional study you will find encouragement, wisdom, and practical help to defeat a depressed spirit.

Breaking the Cover Girl Mask: *Toss Out Toxic Thoughts*
There is no freedom without a change of mind. Research shows that approximately 87% of illnesses are attributed to our thoughts. Drawing from personal and ministerial experience, Kimberly Davidson will lead you on a life-changing journey where you will learn how to confront and conquer harmful thought patterns and behavior. Meet God in the pages of this book and experience powerful mind change.

Torn Between Two Masters: *Encouraging Teens to Live Authentically in a Celebrity-Obsessed World*
Kimberly explores the captivating and serious implications of this culture's obsession with celebrities and the effect it has on adolescents. Drawing on the latest research, the Bible, ministerial experience, and interviews with teens, parents, and leaders, Kimberly provides an eye-opening study.

SOMETHING HAPPENED ON MY WAY TO

HELL

BREAK FREE FROM THE INSATIABLE PURSUIT OF PLEASURE

KIMBERLY DAVIDSON

WestBow
PRESS
A DIVISION OF THOMAS NELSON

WestBow Press books may be ordered through booksellers or by contacting:

WestBow Press
A Division of Thomas Nelson
1663 Liberty Drive
Bloomington, IN 47403
www.westbowpress.com
1-(866) 928-1240

ISBN: 978-1-4497-7853-8 (sc)
ISBN: 978-1-4497-7854-5 (hc)
ISBN: 978-1-4497-7852-1 (e)

Library of Congress Control Number: 2012923310

Printed in the United States of America

WestBow Press rev. date: 1/8/2013

Important Note

This book is not intended to take the place of medical or psychological care. It is intended to be a spiritual component of your comprehensive care plan. Professional counselors can treat the difficulties of addiction with therapy designed to develop healthy habits while addressing underlying problems and trigger mechanisms.

If you are *suicidal,* seek help *immediately.* Call 1-800-273-8255 or 911 and ask for help. A professional will provide a safe place for you to talk and tend to your immediate needs.

Contents

A Journey to Radical Change

Most stories, books, and movies are about change. They embrace sagas of pain and torment which come from an outside force— life. In each story there is at least one monster and one heroine. When the monster attacks it is often unseen or ambiguous. And the heroine can't seem to see it. As the story winds up the heroine surrenders to a Person stronger than herself. She doesn't fully understand everything that is happening to her, but she can see the blazing light of victory peeking over the horizon.

We All Love Something Too Much
Prepare for the Journey Ahead

> You're addicted to thrills? What an empty life! The pursuit of pleasure is never satisfied. –Proverbs 21:17, *The Message*

Insatiable cravings. Nasty habits. Vices. Addictions. We've *all* got them. We *all* love something too much. We *all* want more. More pleasure. More love. More chocolate. More affirmation. More money.

Most of us know that an unquenchable desire for drugs, alcohol, nicotine, food, shoplifting, and gambling can destroy lives. However, multitudes of people are hooked on things that don't fit the addiction stereotype: love, work, sports, people-pleasing, shopping, exercising, dieting, watching television, even pain and chaos. Add to the list: technology, religious activities, risk taking, celebrity worship, gaming, tattooing, tanning, even love for pets and children.

It has been said that to be alive is to be addicted; that life in America is so stressful that it is impossible *not* to become addicted to some object. One Christian psychiatrist suggests "we are all addicts in every sense of the word."[1]

We live in the great age of excess which breeds an unsatisfied yearning for more and more. *You need. You deserve. You must have.* Misplaced affections and insatiable cravings often become addictions. Completely unaware, we harbor an infestation of hidden dependencies because they have silently invaded our lives. And they don't have to be grandiose or visibly evil to do great damage.

Behind every craving is a compelling urge to pursue pleasure— to feel terrific while avoiding pain, physically and emotionally. From the brain's perspective, whatever we do to produce feelings of euphoria, is worth repeating. Ultimately, we end up mastered by those things.

Surely you've noticed that the number of television shows developed around the topic of addiction and compulsive behavior has increased. Today we're restless, stressed, irritable, discontent, and obsessed. We distract ourselves and medicate our anxiety with activity, mood-altering substances, entertainment, and relationships, because we're unable to simply be present with ourselves. We may love God, but deeply rooted habits take control. Our focus rests on our objects of attachment instead of on him.

The church culture is not immune either. Christians, as well, hide and deny their behaviors. Many believe the church propagates addiction. The church, however, is in the unique position of becoming its own recovery center.

I have a message of hope: *We are not confined to or defined by our insatiable cravings and compulsive behaviors.* God is genuinely interested in your problems. He is in the business of changing lives. Turning to him empowers healing and transformation. We study the Holy Bible because it is God's personal Word to us, literally "God-breathed" (see 2 Timothy 3:16).[2]

Unlike what the pop culture presents, the Bible *always* tells the truth. It gives us exactly what we need. God intends for us to learn from the people portrayed in the Scriptures (the text of the Bible is referred to as *scripture*). We can see reflections of ourselves in their messy and troubled escapades. We share the same Father who declared, "I am the LORD, who heals you" (Exodus 15:26).

This 12-week healing study explores real issues of deep bondage that real women experience—both celebrated and condoned habits. This is not a self-help book. We need more than ourselves to be saved. *This is a God-help-transform-me book.* My intention is not to prescribe an antidote—the Word of God has already done that. I want to contribute to a changed paradigm. My objective is to paint a picture for you of human nature and divine efficacy, which most addiction-recovery models do not account for.

If we're going to be addicted, *let's be addicted to the power of the Gospel*, which not only heals and frees, but empowers; *let's be addicted to the Word of God.* Are you ready to begin a quest to find pleasure in him, and him alone? God is calling, "Come back to me and live!" (Amos 5:4)

Search and Rescue: Come Back Alive

For two decades I lived a secret double life. No, I wasn't a stripper by night or committing crimes or having an affair. By day I worked hard at making my outside sparkle, assuming others would think I had it completely together. I had the right job, wore the right clothes, and associated with the right people. Yet, behind the scenes I'd retreat into a dark, depressing dungeon where I fought the battles with my demons—with my hidden addictions. My specialty: trashing my own life. I held many secrets no one could know about. The humiliating behavior and degrading consequences I wore as my identity.

Skilled at walking in a counterfeit light, I donned a fresh new cover girl mask each day. The day came when I couldn't take living with these monsters any longer. Then something happened on my way to hell...I got saved. I said yes to Jesus Christ and stopped fighting God.

Jesus saved me from destruction—both present and future. To "save" in the Greek (*sozo*) means deliverance from danger and suffering; to heal, to deliver, and to make whole.[3] God knew everything, horrible things, about me; yet, he still sought, loved, and accepted me as his very own. How could I not say, "Yes, Lord, yes!"

I wish I could say the sky opened, the angels descended, and I magically changed into a completely new and different person, a person set free from the pull of addiction. Held hostage by lies for decades, I said yes to God and yes to Christianity, but I hadn't been set free from myself. A "saved" person, I was no longer destined to the hell the Bible speaks of. But I continued, by choice, to live in my own self-made hell. The same negative emotions and addictive behaviors that came out of a consumption-fixated culture still held my soul hostage.

Learning to break free of a multitude of negative and unhealthy coping styles has been a major challenge. Not until I asked Jesus to come and invade my life more deeply and I became hooked on the Word of God did I grasp God's healing grace. My life began to change positively, a direct result of God changing my desires and my mind as I developed a relationship with him and studied the Bible. I have learned to cultivate contentment, stop harmful practices, and challenge inaccurate beliefs. I am dependent on him every day because I know Christ in me is the only hope of ongoing positive change.

Why would anyone not want this? Missionary J. Hudson Taylor said, "There is a living God. He has spoken in the Bible. He means what He says and will do all He has promised."[4] Many people resist the Word of God because it feels too rigid and restrictive. It has been said, to be a Christian is to wear a straightjacket. My response is, "Not true!"

Think of the Bible as an owner's manual. For example, if your automobile's manual tells you to fill your car with unleaded fuel and you fill it with diesel fuel, the car will not run properly. It works the same way with us. God, our Creator, provides precise instructions on how to care for and protect his created. If we don't follow his instructions then there's usually a price to pay...as my life story will demonstrate.

We need to believe in the sufficiency of the Bible, trusting that Scripture has all the answers we need to run our daily lives. God's desire is for us to listen to his voice speaking to us through Scripture. The Bible says,

> The instructions of the LORD are perfect, reviving the soul. The decrees of the LORD are trustworthy, making wise the simple. The commandments of the LORD are right, bringing joy to the heart. The commands of the LORD are clear, giving insight for living. (Psalm 19:7-8, NLT)

I don't believe the saying that to be alive is to be addicted. We need to get away from the idea that only bad or weak or sinful or diseased people have problems with obsessive behavior. I have confidence in a God who won't let us ruin our souls. He can make something new out of our fragmented pieces. You may have had a rocky start but what's important is how you finish. There is no area in your life so painful, no offense so heinous, that God's grace cannot heal it. God can bring beauty out of your darkest secrets.

As I reflect on my life there are three threads that run through every chapter and each season—shame, addiction, and the need to be in control. I have spent a lot of time researching this topic for my own personal edification. Now it is my passion. I enjoy seeing how psychological and Bible studies come together to give us a clearer picture of what is going on in our lives. Psychological research repeatedly proves the themes of the Bible and confirms that God's Word can be trusted as a healing agent and transformation tool. It gives us courage and galvanizes us.

We all want to know that when we struggle we're not alone in our fears, our sorrows, our defeats, and our hopes. In this book I honestly share my painful experiences and my heart so we might connect; as well as integrate my education and experience as a pastoral counselor and spiritual development coach.

As you read my stories, believe God will bless you with a similar outcome. Chances are you will recognize in many ways my story and emotions are also yours—the transparency and the shame, the battles and the triumphs. I hope each vignette gives you inspiration, and you derive a greater sense of purpose and meaning from your own painful and challenging experiences. I can personally tell you that when the monster is defeated in your life, you will find joy, peace, and meaning, maybe for the very first time.

Make the Most of this Study

You will be inspired, with God's help, to identify and examine the things that keep you in a state of bondage. The greater your understanding of the dynamics of a behavior, the greater your ability to overcome it. Whatever you've been afraid to look at is not beyond the reach of God's touch.

This study is broken into twelve chapters or weeks. Each week covers five days of reading material. Each day concludes with *Reflect On It*—questions, exercises, and/or meditations to move your transformation process forward. *Meditation* is a process of reviewing, reflecting, thinking, analyzing, feeling, and enjoying Scripture. It is a relational, physical, intellectual, and emotional activity.

I suggest you write all your answers and personal thoughts in a journal or notebook. Try to be deeply transparent with God. You may be tempted to skip a week, assuming a particular chapter doesn't apply to you. Let me assure you, the material will speak to you in one way or another. Consider that God may put another person in your life who does struggle with the issue. You will be better prepared to befriend and minister to her.

Maintaining the daily discipline of devotional and study time is essential. Set your alarm, or calendar, or smartphone reminder; whatever tool works. Set aside at least 20 minutes each day to focus on study and prayer. Turn off your phone or any other device that tends to distract you. If you have young ones, you may have to shut yourself in the bathroom!

Prayer is vital. It is God's invitation to have an intimate relationship with him. It is also our measure of willingness to relinquish control. Prayer is simply talking with God. The psalmist wrote, "I love the LORD because he hears my voice and my prayer for mercy. Because he bends down to listen, I will pray as long as I have breath!" (Psalm 116:1-2, NLT). Don't be afraid to share your intimate problems with God. When you begin to open up he will show you things about yourself you would never have discovered any other way.

Begin to memorize and personalize verses. You will need them in the days ahead. The psalmist stated, "Those who love your instructions have great peace and do not stumble" (Psalm 119:165, NLT). As you look up Scripture, personalize it. Insert your name in place of the personal pronouns. Let God speak the verse to you. For example,

> This is what the LORD says—he created *me,* he formed *me:* "Fear not, for I have redeemed you *Kimberly*; I have summoned you *Kimberly* by name; you *Kimberly* are mine." When *I* pass through the waters, *God* will be with *me*; and when *I* pass through the rivers, they will not sweep over *me.* When *I* walk through the fire, *I* will not be burned; the flames will not set *me* ablaze. (Isaiah 43:1-2, *my personalization*)

I encourage you to discuss the material with at least one other person. Evaluate, question, and think about what you read. Dig for in-depth explanations. Take the time to look up the verses which are referenced.

Don't say, "Tomorrow," when God says, "Today!" You can do

this. Take baby steps, but at least move forward. You will discover who you truly are: a significant and secure woman who cannot be enslaved; someone who has the potential to be a loving, giving, and confident person. God's got your back: "Don't be afraid, for I am with you. Don't be discouraged, for I am your God. I will strengthen you and help you. I will hold you up with my victorious right hand" (Isaiah 41:10, NLT).

Pre-Study Exercise
Identify Insatiable Cravings

Anything I wanted I took and did not restrain myself from any joy. I even found great pleasure in hard work. This pleasure was, indeed, my only reward for all my labors. But as I looked at everything I had tried, it was all so useless, a chasing of the wind, and there was nothing really worthwhile anywhere. (Ecclesiastes 2:10-11, TLB)

Our objective is to examine everything in our lives that has taken on significant meaning—things we believe give us purpose, meaning and value; things we sense are "a chasing of the wind." I suggest you start to create a list of your habits. Putting your thoughts to paper will help you see the big picture.

1. Write down what you perceive to be the most frequent negative things you do. Think about the things that have become distractions from God. Note the obvious ones. Discovering the less obvious ones will require time.

2. Observe your habits closely. As you go about your day ask yourself these questions: "What activities take up most of my time?" "What do I think about most of the day?" For example,

- How many hours do I watch television or Netflix?
- How long do I exercise each day (or not exercise)?
- How much time do I spend on the Internet? List the sites you frequently visit.
- How often do I check my phone in one hour?
- How often do I eat? What types of foods do I eat?
- What else do I ingest beside food?
- Who do I spend most of my time with?
- How do I handle stress, worry, or chaos?
- How do I feel emotionally most of my day?
- How much time do I spend with God each day?
- What do I think about myself?
- What does God think about me?

This is a good start. If possible, ask your spouse, significant other, close friends, and/or family to share their observations. This requires honesty. They may not want to hurt your feelings. Tell them you desire an honest answer and won't get upset. Remain calm.

3. Make a commitment to regularly examine those things in your life that tend to take on enormous meaning. Then ask yourself, "Where is God in this?"
4. Lastly, it is important as you move through this book to pray and journal through your emotions:

   - What am I feeling? What am I reacting to?
   - How am I responding to my interpretation of the situation?
   - What are my options? Listen to God and to what others have taught you.
   - Weighing all options, I choose to…

Week One
It's Never Enough
Evidence of Addiction

Day One: An Earnest Attempt to Change

> We're a nation of addicts, and it seems like we ought
> to be talking about it. We pretend that addiction
> only happens to other people. That's not true. –David
> Hawkins, M.D., Ph.D.[5]

Life felt good. God had blessed me with a thriving ministry, a
good marriage, and health. Yet, it didn't take long for a new
daily ritual to begin.

I love to shop and I'm convinced it is part of almost every woman's
DNA. I also love a bargain. I got on a daily email list of an online
rack-type store. I couldn't resist opening each email and falling into a
magical trance as the daily sales flashed on my computer screen. Not
just fifty percent reductions, but sixty, seventy, even eighty percent
off name brand and designer merchandise. *I'm a kid in a candy store!*
Pinch me! The temptation to *not* buy was too overwhelming. *I'm too*
weak!

One day I said to my husband, "Leave the gate open tomorrow.

UPS will be delivering a package." In a tone of voice I hadn't heard in quite a while, he disgustedly answered, "Every day there are packages coming in!" Then he had the gall to state I was addicted to shopping.

My tongue paralyzed, I grappled with his allegation. *Hmm… Maybe he's right.* Then I turned to God. "Lord, through your power and by your grace I've already overcome a deadly eating disorder, my alcohol dependence, and addiction to nicotine, collecting, and tanning, as well as codependency. Am I still addicted, a compulsive shopper? Or is this merely a nasty habit?"

The next question to answer was, "Is this problematic?" No! After all I can afford the merchandise. I'm not hurting anyone. Never mind this was actually God's money I liked to spend. *No, it's not a problem. It's merely part of my impulsive personality, which if you really think about it, God gave me* (denial; rationalization).

The Bible explains, "Don't you realize that you become the slave of whatever you choose to obey?"(Romans 6:16, NLT) *Ouch!* The most important question was, "Is this habit hurting my relationship with God? What had become more important: spending time with him or shopping?"

"Lord, can I get off the merry-go-round once and for all? This is crazy. I've been to seminary and studied counseling!" After a great deal of self-reflection I admitted to God the shopping got out of control. If compulsive shopping gets out of control, it is likely an addiction.[6]

Consumer addiction or *oniomania* are terms for compulsive shopping or shopping addiction. "Shopaholics" experience a high—not from owning the item, but from the act of purchasing it. Experts say a brain chemical associated with pleasure is often released in waves as shoppers see a desirable item and then consider buying it. This burst of excitement can become addictive. Research supports that the act of shopping produces pleasure, or relaxation, or relief from stress, and is a way of coping.[7] These shoppers can't resist a special offer and accumulate items they don't need. *Guilty!*

I eventually took responsibility by removing myself from the source of enticement. What I've learned is if I pray for resistance from temptation, and then replace my thoughts with God's thoughts, I usually don't want the item. I ask myself, "Do I really need this?" The answer is usually no. "Could I be doing something better with my time?" The answer is typically yes. I resist by acknowledging my vulnerabilities and rely on the power of the Holy Spirit to guide me away from shopping. [In the upcoming weeks, I'll be sharing a lot more on defeating temptation.]

Our gracious God has given me an understanding of addictions and compulsive behavior. I will be sharing those insights with you. Knowledge is important because it can bring us into God's presence. Not merely intellectual knowledge, but a deep personal knowledge that enables us to accept God's grace.

When we speak of *God's grace*, we mean all the undeserved good gifts we enjoy freely in life. The list of gifts is endless, and there's no way we deserve them or can earn them. Grace is a force which can rise above hidden compulsions that seek to destroy us and our desire for God. It is where our hope lies.

Change Your Master

Are you tired? Worn out? Burned out on religion? Come to me. Get away with me and you'll recover your life. I'll show you how to take a real rest. Walk with me and work with me—watch how I do it. Learn the unforced rhythms of grace. I won't lay anything heavy or ill-fitting on you. –Jesus, speaking in Matthew 11:28-29, *The Message*

Too often we cope with distress in life through denial or a numbing activity. These activities often become addictions and impede the progress of our restoration. No wonder the apostle Paul told us to turn away from everything wrong and to give ourselves to God alone (see 2 Corinthians 7:1-2).

Every battle with addiction and compulsive behavior begins with an earnest attempt to change the behavior. We substitute constructive actions for destructive ones. I replaced bike riding for bingeing. Instead of smoking a cigarette I'd chew on two to four pieces of gum. Then I became addicted to the sugar! After receiving a diagnosis of gastritis, as per doctor's orders, I weaned myself off my daily wine intake. Instead I started collecting vintage teddy bears and dolls.

I call this musical addictions—anything to fill the hole in the soul; anything to not feel the feelings. As comedian George Carlin once said, "Just cause you got the monkey off your back doesn't mean the circus has left town."[8] The bottom line is, we can't get rid of our insatiable cravings or change toxic behavior by ourselves. We need the empowerment of God. We need help from other people.

The fight didn't start to turn around until I looked at my behaviors through a spiritual lens. I've won the battle today. How have I done that? Through *knowledge*—knowledge of God and his plan of redemption and recovery through Jesus Christ; knowledge of the human condition; knowledge of spiritual warfare, and applying what God teaches me through the power of the Holy Spirit. We can use knowledge to connect us with an all-powerful God. It is his power that changes minds and behaviors.

God Almighty is present and waiting to be asked into your life. His great desire is to empower you through your struggles. God promises, "Those who hope in the Lord will renew their strength. They will soar on wings like eagles; they will run and not grow weary; they will walk and not be faint" (Isaiah 40:31). By developing a real relationship with Jesus Christ and putting into practice biblical instructions, breaking an addictive cycle is highly possible.

Reflect On It

Are you ready to admit your plan isn't working? Are you ready to hear and accept the truth about yourself and your behaviors?

If you say yes it means you are willing, at least to some extent, for God to enter your life and transform your desires.

Day Two: Name Your Poison

> It is hard to understand addiction unless you have experienced it. –Musician Ken Hensley[9]

The sneezing, coughing, watery eyes, nasal congestion, sore throat; we all experience this nuisance—the common cold. This particular year I worked at a medical clinic which stocked sample drugs for anything that ailed you. Desiring a decongestant, I searched the drug closet. I hit the jackpot—several trays of mini Dristan bottles. *Snort...snort. Ah...instant relief! I can finally breathe again.* As soon as it became hard to breathe, *snort, snort.*

I concluded I had one of those long lasting colds. Ten days passed and I needed more samples. But there were no more Dristan bottles. I asked a doctor what else I could use. He questioned me, "How long have you been inhaling Dristan?" I replied "About ten days."

He firmly stated, "Stop now! Did you read the label?"

"No," I answered. He said my poor little nose had become addicted to Dristan.

This is an example of a chemical addiction. It taught me a great deal about the characteristics of the addiction process. What I didn't realize is by drying up my nose the artificial chemicals disturbed the natural balance. Trying to restore the balance, my nose adjusted by producing more congesting chemicals and less of its own decongestants. When the effect of the drops wore off, there were more natural congesting chemicals and less natural decongestants than there were to begin with. Therefore, I was stuffier and used more nose drops. Labels today still read, "Do not exceed recommended dosage."

This is a simplistic example of how our body can become addicted to substances. The substance alters a balance of natural body chemicals. The body then adjusts to the change by trying to reestablish the proper balance. In doing so, the body becomes dependent upon the outside supply of the substance. In the same way, I became addicted to caffeine, nicotine, laxatives, and alcohol.

If you don't drink, over eat, gamble or abuse drugs, you may mistakenly assume addiction doesn't apply to you. The same dynamics apply to non-substance addictions. If you spend hours on activities to the exclusion of everything else; even if it is a healthy activity, like bike riding or cleaning the house, it may be a sign of addiction. Everything in life can easily become an object of attachment. As one of my clients said, "Our objects are either a good poison or a bad poison."

Habit or Addiction?

Habit is a man's sole comfort. –Author Johann Wolfgang von Goethe[10]

In the Australian bush grows a little plant called the *sundew*—the black widow of the plant world. Although its attractive clusters of red, white, and pink blossoms are harmless, the leaves are deadly. The shiny moisture on each leaf is sticky and imprisons the unlucky bug that touches it. As an insect struggles to free itself, the vibration causes the leaves to close tightly around it. The flower feeds on its victim. It is hard to imagine God would create such a devious and deadly plant. I think this depicts how destructive behaviors silently invade our lives.

What exactly is the difference between a habit and an addiction? A *habit* is a pattern of behavior acquired through repetition. It can be moral, immoral, or amoral. Approximately 90 percent of what we do every day is governed by habits.[11] We rely on them to steer us through our daily routines. Habits create needed routines for living and patterns for loving.

Good habits keep us connected to our real self, to others and God. Bad habits isolate us from the world. Some habits become tendencies toward self-serving ends; others develop into addictions. Samuel Johnson said, "The chains of habit are generally too small to be felt until they are too strong to be broken."[12] They are difficult to break because they meet some need or desire.

Many professionals agree that a habit is something a person can generally stop if they choose to. They are not enslaved to it, contrary to the addicted person who is unable to stop their behavior without help because of the psychological and/or physical issues involved.

One dictionary stated a synonym for habit is *addiction*.[13] It's been said addiction is when you can give up your favorite thing (your object of attachment) any time, as long as it's next week. In Dr. Tim Clinton's book, *Turn Your Life Around,* he states that addiction is "embracing the gods of wrath" and feeling "wrapped in bondage with the stench of hell."[14]

With *addiction*, the desire of the heart is to habitually attach itself to a specific object or activity or person, which harms or deters our ability to function in a major area of life. Impossible to control, the attachment ultimately enslaves the person's will and masks their true feelings. It can be physical—to substances or food; or psychological—to compulsive behaviors.

Addiction is a form of emotional anesthesia; an escape from responsibilities; even an excuse to blame someone else. Addicted people feel the need to deceive themselves and others. They lie, deny, justify, or cover up their behavior; and rely on confused perceptions and misbeliefs. Life issues which need to be acknowledged and dealt with are not, thereby, enabling them to remain addicted.

Some people insist addiction is a failure of society, or a spiritual weakness called sin, or a state in which people simply won't take responsibility for their behavior. These moralistic understandings are usually rejected by American society. The most popular theory is addictive behaviors are diseases. What is clear is addiction is a complex interaction of psychological, biochemical, neurological, and spiritual influences.

Like other compulsive behaviors, addiction is driven by deeper emotional factors such as, overwhelming helplessness, failure, rejection, anger, depression, abandonment, criticism, anxiety, or even boredom. You can have all the willpower in the world, be working like crazy to stop, but you can't stop the behavior.[15] Founder of analytical psychology, Carl Jung, said, "Every form of addiction is bad, no matter whether the narcotic be alcohol, morphine or idealism."[16]

What I've learned is the difference between having a passionate desire towards something and an addiction is *freedom*. If you have been unsuccessful in your attempts to cut out or cut down on your favorite thing, it may be an addiction. If your favorite thing interferes with your relationships, your work and family responsibilities, or your worship of God, it may be an addiction. If it dulls your awareness of your true feelings, it may be an addiction. If you continue to use it or do it despite negative consequences, it may be an addiction.

The consequences of addiction are estrangement from God, habitual sin, health, and relational problems. Unbeknown to us, the heart of any addiction is the longing for the holy. The only way to heal completely, I believe, is to first fill the hole in our soul with God Almighty's healing grace made available through Jesus Christ.

Reflect On It

What do you expect to get out of this God-centered recovery book?

Day Three:
Substance and Behavioral Addictions

> In each of us there is something growing, which will
> be hell unless it is nipped in the bud. –Lay theologian
> C. S. Lewis[17]

In the world of addiction, there are two major categories: *addiction to substances,* which involves abuse of and dependency upon chemicals; and *addiction to patterns of behavior.* Many compulsive behaviors are hidden addictions. They are overlooked because they cause no harm and appear to be a positive influence on the person's life. They are celebrated—the super-woman, super-mom, super-athlete, and super-sheep. We are more apt to label them as obsessive or compulsive behaviors, not addictions. They may actually increase one's self-esteem versus tear it down. These compulsive "good" behaviors can wreak as much havoc on families, careers, and lives, as drug and alcohol addiction.

Behavioral addictions, often called *process addictions,* involve problematic repetitive behavior patterns, such as watching television marathons, Internet social networking, working, shopping, eating, reading, risk taking, engaging in sex, jogging, and religiosity. We can also become addicted to pain, worry, chaos, and stress. Many people struggle with both types of addiction simultaneously.

The following are socially sanctioned and usually perceived as healthy, essential activities with which the majority of the population has little concern or personal struggle. Yet, each of these activities has the potential to become an addiction:

- *Religion:* starting charities, helping, martyrdom, seeking a high from a worship service.
- *Health:* exercising, dieting, bodybuilding, feasting on vitamins.
- *Beauty:* ongoing cosmetic treatments, plastic surgery, tanning (termed tanorexia), tattooing, apparel and accessory shopping.
- *Professional:* over-achieving, over-working, pursuing multiple academic degrees. For a stay at home mom it may be cleaning, cooking, or homeschooling.
- *Investments:* stock market risk taking, hoarding money, collecting, couponing.
- *Recreation:* thrill-seeking activities, Internet social networking, watching sports, TV, gaming, listening to music, reading, gardening, cooking, writing.
- *Family:* worshiping children, a spouse, parents, or pets.
- *Relationships:* celebrity and hero (including pastors) worship, people pleasing.

My desire is for you to become aware of your behaviors and acknowledge you may have an issue with addiction and control. If you're not able to manage or stop an activity or behavior, there is a good chance you are addicted to it.

For example, you say, "I won't stop exercising. Physical exercise is important because it enhances fitness and overall health and wellness. God told me to take care of my temple!" True. But if you *must* exercise daily, for long periods of time, then you're out of balance. Doctors warn there is a fine line between a healthy exercise regimen and addictive behavior that can actually harm the body. No amount of justification will change the fact that an addiction exists.

As a compulsive runner, my knees took an intense pounding day in day out. Consequently, I had two arthroscopic surgeries on both knees. As my thinking began to change, my rigid regimen began to relax. I could see how compulsive my routine was. It is important to exercise, but it is also important to listen to your body and not take it to extremes. I still exercise daily, but I've learned balance—when to work out and when to rest.

If there's any good in any of these behavioral addictions it may be that they lead us into the arms of God. It also helps to remember that the destructiveness of addiction does not lie in the things we're attached to. They are simply part of creation and God made them essentially good. The destruction lies in our bondage to them. Temptation is everywhere and we all too frequently get sucked into its trap.

Addiction is a bad thing because it usurps and obscures our desire for the truest and deepest form of love and goodness—God himself. And no matter how religious or spiritual we think we are, our behaviors are always capable of sidetracking our love for God. The more we can understand how enslavement happens, the more we'll be able turn the opposite way—back towards God, the creator of freedom.

The Pleasure Principle

A fool finds pleasure in evil conduct. –Proverbs 10:23

My best friend in seventh grade boasted she had stolen several items from our local discount store. "Prove it!" I said. She laid them out: a lipstick, stockings, and two records. I desired the same things. She challenged me, "I dare you!" I went for the dare.

Like a panther I surveyed the entire area. Scared and nervous, I didn't weigh the consequences because I wanted the stuff. [The frontal lobe of the brain governs decision-making, problem solving and planning. It is not completed in the teen years. The adolescent brain is not capable of making mature decisions with respect to risky behavior.[18]]

I did it! I stuck a record in my shirt. Then I casually wandered over to the cosmetics area and shrewdly put a lipstick in my pocket. *What a rush!* I don't know which gave me more pleasure—not getting caught or the free items. As long as I didn't get caught, I kept stealing. It felt intoxicating.

Perhaps you've heard of the *pleasure principle*. The law of effect simply states that if a behavior is associated with an effect of pleasure or relief from pain that behavior will occur more frequently. This is a component of learning called positive reinforcement. If I do "x" which makes me feel good, I'm likely to repeat "x." Whether it's shoplifting or taking heroin or drinking coffee or having sex, if the pleasurable effect is immediate and powerful, my brain will make a strong association between the behavior and the experience. It will push me to repeat the behavior because of the association of pleasure or pain reduction, making me more likely to repeat the act again.

The fact is, once engrained I don't want anything to interfere with my new habit. My habit may become a source of stress, compounded with feelings of shame, guilt, and fear. So I deal with the stress by repeating the behavior. You can see what an ugly cycle it becomes.

How do you know whether your issue is a habit or addiction? Based on my research and personal experience I'd say if you find it easy to "stay clean," as they say, for seven days straight, then you probably don't have an addiction. On the other hand, if you feel depressed, angry, anxious, scared, paranoid, or edgy without "it," or find yourself really missing your attachment, it is most likely an addiction.

The bottom line is: we were created for God—for his pleasure. He is the definition of the pleasure principle. We are designed to find pleasure in him—him alone. The Bible says, "Delight yourself in the LORD and he will give you the desires of your heart" (Psalm 37:4). Notice the first thing God asks us to do is delight in him. To delight in God is to experience great pleasure and joy in his presence. This is why we must get to know him.

I have presented only a small snapshot of the dynamics of addictive behavior. If you want more detailed or scientific information I suggest you visit your local library.

Reflect On It

- Does your behavior involve secrets, lies, deceptions? Secrets can be poison and lying can become a habit. If you hide it, deny it, justify it, or lie about it when someone asks, that implies you probably feel bad or shameful. Your habit may be an addiction.
- Not sure? Ask people you trust. Approach friends, family and/or a professional, and ask their honest and discreet opinion. "Do you think [this] is a problem?" Remain silent. Listen carefully to their answer. Do not defend yourself. If they express concern, chances are this issue should be addressed.

Day Four: The Solution to Control

When a controller has the sense of life being out of control, he or she reacts with an even stronger need to 'get things under control'...usually with the negative result of alienating the people who matter the most. –Author J. Keith Miller[19]

Perhaps the deepest need human beings have is for control. Some people are addicted to it. "Letting go" is not in their vocabulary.

Things must be just perfect. They panic when circumstances change.

When we feel we've lost control, we experience a powerful and uncomfortable tension. One of the most disturbing things about, for example, having a terminal illness, or being abused, or losing a loved one, or being laid off, or moving, is the feeling of powerlessness.

Control is the common thread which seems to run through compulsive and destructive behaviors. We want to protect ourselves from pain. For two decades I lived as a "control freak" because my life collapsed. Many of our everyday habits are rooted in the need for control and affirmation. What we really seek is a *sense* of control. Many women seek authority or father figures whom provide this.

Un-entangling bad habits and addictions requires more than willpower. It may work short term but we'll usually return to our vices. Memorizing Bible verses is important, but it takes more. Healing begins with the understanding that God is sovereign and in control. Ask yourself, "Do I *really* believe God? Do I *really* trust him for my future?"

As believers we have the assurance we're not controlled by our addictions and sinful nature, but by the Spirit of God (see Romans 8:9). What we need is biblical faith—a personal trust in Jesus Christ; belief that God is near and our hearts are bound to him. You can take back your life by giving Christ the keys to pilot your life.

The Immenseness of God and Jesus

I must surrender my fascination with myself to a more worthy preoccupation with the character and purposes of God. I am not the point. He is. I exist for him. He does not exist for me. –Psychologist Larry Crabb[20]

How often have you thought, "Do I even matter to God?"
Our God is a personal God. He knows us, loves us, and has made

a huge commitment to us. God is not like most kings we're familiar with. He doesn't wish to live at a distance from his subjects. He made us so we might walk together forever in a love relationship.

Like any other relationship, our connection to God can only exist when both parties know something about one another. *The route to knowing God the Father is to know his Son.* Jesus Christ, in the flesh, came down to earth as an exact likeness of the invisible Father (see Hebrews 1:3). In the man of Jesus Christ we see the very face of God.

The paradigm offered through the life and work of Jesus provides us with deep insight, not only into how we should live in this world, but more importantly, into how to reap radical transformation and recover from our personal monsters. Those touched by Jesus walked away from their old lives of shame and fear into new lives of peace and joy. What Jesus Christ models is how to draw life from God the Father.

What is your opinion of Jesus Christ? Do you think he is the Son of God, the Savior of the world? Do you think he's overrated, inferior to God? Do you see him merely as a prophet, a wise teacher, and moral example to the world? Do you worship him as Lord and Savior?

It would not be unusual for you to know *about* Jesus, but not know him *personally.* Maybe you've heard the Jesus miracle and healing stories in Sunday school. Maybe all you know is the Christmas story. More than a teacher or a prophet or a healer or a miracle worker, he was, and still is, the Messiah—the Son of the living God. Jesus, the man, was radically different than any other ordinary man. Many were offended by his audacious claims. C. S. Lewis pointed out that "he was the Son of God or else a madman."[21] We too must decide—is he a liar or is he Truth and Grace (see John 1:17)?

Even though Jesus is holy and God, transcending time and space, he set aside his rights and privileges of divinity to become a human being. Jesus was God in human flesh. Not God dwelling in a man, or a man made to be God; but God and man—two natures combined in one personality, baffling every possibility of explanation, called the *incarnation*.

Jesus's reason for becoming God incarnate was to secure for us freedom from sin, guilt, death, and evil. He took on a role that brought intense and agonizing physical, emotional, and spiritual suffering, in order to reconcile us to God. I can almost hear him saying, "You think your life is hell on earth? Let me tell you my story!" This is proof that God cares compassionately.

A real person, Jesus had a distinct personality. Ordinary like us, he experienced similar physical pangs and raw emotions: hunger, thirst, fatigue, exhaustion, sadness, playfulness, anger, distress, laughter, loneliness, disgust, joy, agony. He learned obedience. As author John Eldredge said, "Those nails actually hurt."[22]

When I study Jesus's three years of public ministry I see one long period of intervention in multitudes of people's lives. He behaved and said what he did because he was on a mission to rescue his created—those who were completely deceived. Today he still intervenes. He doesn't throw the Bible at us, and then tell us to deal with the world and figure it out. Jesus Christ became a man to show us the way. He offers us a way out. Jesus makes peace between us and God, giving us access to God's immense presence.

This is how God chose to present himself to the world—his real self. As we grasp his humanity, we find a person we can approach, know, trust, love, and adore. Our existence is about Jesus's relentless pursuit of us—to the point of dying on the cross so we might be intimately acquainted with God the Father. This is a picture of God's grace.

God's calling us to bond with himself. Bond refers to a feeling of connection. Presently we're (unconsciously) bonded to an object of our affection, and certain emotions and beliefs. This means we're not drawing the essence of life from God. Our deepest desire should be to break the negative, toxic and deceptive bonds, and connect with the source of life.

Saint Athanasius said, "He [Jesus] became what we are that He might make us what He is."[23] Jesus is still on a mission to save his created. Let him rescue you.

Reflect On It

- What false hopes for change have you relied upon so far?
- Describe what your life might be like if you simply let go of the need to control?

Day Five: The Kaleidoscope

Our lives are in the hands of a skillful weaver who can use the roughest of materials to make the most glorious of garments. –Pastor Dr. David Jeremiah[24]

If you're like me, you probably wish you could edit out the not-so-nice chapters of your life. But remember, you are a beautiful unfinished project to God (see Philippians 1:6). Think of yourself like a kaleidoscope made up of bits of broken, colored glass, which are constantly and forever changing. Inside each kaleidoscope is a mirror which reflects the beauty of each piece of broken, colored glass.

God won't make the past disappear. Instead, he'll use the blows of hard circumstances of life to mold you into a beautiful kaleidoscope full of hope, faith, and love. Piece by meticulous piece, he fits them together in such a way as to form the likeness of his Son in us.

A kaleidoscope is a picture of Romans 8:28: "We know that in all things God works for the good of those who love him, who have been called according to his purpose." Paul is talking about our spiritual transformation. The "good" of verse 28 is explained in verse

29: "For those God foreknew he also predestined to be conformed to the likeness of his Son." When we give our broken parts to God, he will begin to restore our lives. He will use every circumstance in a mysterious way to transform us more into Jesus's likeness (see 2 Corinthians 3:18).

Every tiny, intricate piece of broken glass in a kaleidoscope comes together perfectly. As the pieces come together a magnificent and beautiful vision is created—you! I bet you never realized that broken glass could shine so brightly.

The Real Focus

Diagnosed with terminal cancer at thirty-three, Carly worked to maintain a joyful spirit. Weakened but hopeful, she asked her girlfriend Beth to go shopping with her for a new dress. After selecting a few dresses she called Beth into the dressing room. Donning a smart royal blue jersey wrap, she pointed to herself in the mirror and asked, "Do I look fat?"

Beth shook her head and grunted, "You don't have time for that!"

This story kicked me right in the gut. I realized whether we're ill or not, in the kingdom of God we don't have time for "that"—for worrying about our weight, or whether we're admired, or covering up the pain with a substance or activity, or… You know what your "that" is.

Jesus had something to say about this, "Do not worry about your life, what you will eat or drink; or about your body, what you will wear" (Matthew 6:25). I regularly remind myself of this woman's wise reply and Jesus's words. My desire is for my heart to be focused on the kingdom of God, not on myself—on my body size or wardrobe. As a child of God these things no longer identify me.

Through prayer and Bible study, God will put up a mirror and we'll begin to see our attitudes, beliefs, and motives from a very different perspective—his. One of the purposes of Scripture is to show us the truth about our own human nature. Self-examination is a light shedding process; the light of truth penetrates and exposes deception. Jesus said the truth will set us free (see John 8:32).

God gives us our experiences so we might be able to examine them under his light. We learn that his fingerprints have been on them our entire life...even before we were born. Even the worst chapters of your life are full of his presence.

God promises he will "bestow on you a crown of beauty instead of ashes, the oil of gladness instead of mourning, and a garment of praise instead of a spirit of despair" (Isaiah 61:3). Can it get any better than that?

Reflect On It

We can change our stories when we change our choices. Here are five ways you can begin to facilitate change and growth:

1. *Bring God into everything you do.* The ongoing presence of God can strengthen and heal as he nurtures your mind, body, spirit, and cleanses your soul. No addiction has a chance of survival. Work on continuously communicating with him until it becomes a regular habit. Set aside a specific time each day to immerse yourself in God's Word, even if it's only a couple of verses. He will provide the light so you can understand (see Psalm 119:130).

2. *Practice solitude and self-examination.* Find a still quiet place where you can meet with God to pray and examine yourself. Ask him to help you answer these questions as you move forward. Take your time and scrutinize your motives.
   - What do I think will truly make me happy?
   - What or who do I believe fills the hunger of my soul?

- What deep needs am I trying to fill?
- Do I fear God's plan for my life is not what I really want?

3. *List the personal traits you want to change first.* Go back to your answers from the "Pre–Study Exercise." Pray over the areas in your life where you feel enslaved. It helps to focus on changing one area at a time. Ask God to reveal the area he desires to begin working on first.

4. *Be patient and give yourself time to heal.* God's timetable will most likely be slower than yours. Depend on God for the power to change, but don't expect him to miraculously change your personality and behaviors. Changing engrained traits takes time.

5. *Keep directing your energies toward growth and healing.* Get a routine going, and an adequate amount of rest and sleep. Scripture tells us that rest leads to restoration, "The LORD… makes me lie down in green pastures, he leads me beside quiet waters, he restores my soul" (Psalm 23:1-3).

Week Two

Connect the Dots
Understand the Root Cause

Day One: The Hooked Brain

A healthy soul actually enhances brain function, and a healthy brain is essential to a healthy soul. The brain-soul connection is involved in everything we do. –Daniel G. Amen, M.D. [25]

Why is saying no to temptation difficult? Why can't we just turn-off our insatiable cravings? Depending on the field of specialty, answers will differ. Yet, we all agree the human body and soul is incredibly amazing, interconnected, and complicated.

My goal in this chapter is to lay out an overview of the facts and connect them as an encapsulated explanation of addiction from a biblical viewpoint. We need to explore the brain (which includes our mind), the nature of mankind, and the biblical doctrine of sin, to understand why we are an addicted people.

Let's start with the brain. Each time your smartphone rings does a voice inside your head scream, *Yay! Someone needs me. Something needs my attention. I must get to it now*! If you were to look inside your brain, chances are you'd see a surge of pleasure seeking chemicals which can drive us toward addictive substances and behaviors. I believe we're really not addicted to substances, activities, or people. We're addicted to the pleasurable feelings produced by these chemicals.

In our brain there are different types of chemicals or neurotransmitters. All of our emotions, behaviors, and moods are shaped significantly by these chemicals in our brain. The right amount helps us think clearly, feel well-balanced, and cope with both emotional and physical stress and pain. Improper balances of transmitters contribute to diseases such as obsessive-compulsive disorders, anxiety, and many forms of depression.

Depending on the part of the brain involved, our internal balance of neurotransmitters can cause our feelings to range from fearful and anxious to assertive and powerful. The majority of psychoactive drugs exert their effects by altering specific neurotransmitter systems.

Neurotransmitters are responsible for inducing euphoria. *Endorphins* are one group. No doubt you've heard the term "endorphin rush," which refers to feelings of exhilaration brought on by pain, danger, or other forms of stress, apparently due to the influence of endorphins.

Another neurotransmitter is *dopamine*, which plays a big role in driving human behavior. This chemical fires up the brain triggering feelings of pleasure, passion, adventure, motivation, and reward. When we do something exciting or rewarding, it produces a feeling of exhilaration or pleasure—the "I've got to have it" feeling.

Dr. Nora Volkow, head of the National Institute on Drug Abuse, said, "When a person is addicted, they get conditioned like Pavlovian dogs."[26] This is because dopamine rewards all substance and process addictions.[27]

When God created the dopamine response it was for survival.

Activities like eating, drinking, engaging in sex, and working, contribute to the survival of the human race. Therefore, our brains are programmed to encourage these behaviors by making them highly pleasurable (see Ecclesiastes 2:24-25). These activities trigger a dopamine response in the rewards center of the brain, resulting in feelings of pleasure. We get immediate gratification and find them hard to give up, which is a good definition of addiction.

Drugs. Food. Sex.

A television ad for a restaurant chain claimed, "Help yourself to happiness!" Wouldn't it be great if a helping of chicken n' dumplings quenched the need to feel perpetually happy. For millions of people, food or a host of other things like drugs and sex, are consumed in the quest for pleasure.

It is not just doctors who learn to tamper with the body's pain relief system. According to Dr. Steven Stiles, author of *Thorns in the Heart*, some people discover drugs, such as opioids, cause the release of the very transmitters which prevent pain, provide pleasure, and offer a sense of well-being. From the brain's perspective, this is worth repeating. But they soon discover these drugs have either depleted their natural supply of neurotransmitters or cause their bodies to quit producing the transmitters they need.[28] The pleasure seeker must now find new and different ways to increase the brain's production levels of dopamine in order to feel pleasure, even normal.

Today brain SPECT imaging can help with substance abuse and other addictions by identifying toxic exposure. For example, when the effects of drug abuse are detected by SPECT, patients can see how their drug use has damaged their own brain function. Brain images can help a person break denial, motivate treatment, help identify comorbid (pertaining to two diseases which occur together) conditions, and be used in prevention education.[29]

Most drug addiction specialists indicate much more goes into the making of an addict than the availability of a drug. Most significant are socio-medical factors such as mental health, a family history of addiction, alcoholism, or trauma, such as abuse.

Not only do drugs and alcohol alter brain chemistry, but so do the wrong foods. Most people, however, don't see food addiction akin to substance abuse. Dr. Mark Gold, chief of addiction medicine, McKnight Brain Institute, University of Florida, stated, food addiction is "eating despite the consequences, being preoccupied with food, feeling guilty about your eating habits, and overeating in the face of various health concerns."[30]

Scripture says, "All food is good, but it can turn bad if you use it badly" (Romans 14:20, MSG). For example, if you eat a fatty and/ or sugary food such as a doughnut, the brain releases dopamine. Most people walk away satisfied. But for some the desire to repeat the pleasure is too strong to resist. Dr. Nora Volkow said in an interview on *60 Minutes*, the more dopamine released, the more the person wants the food. Eventually, it takes more and more food to feel normal.[31]

To break the food queues and negative eating cycle we should:

- *Look at the role of food in our lives.* For example, do you eat because you are hunger and want to receive vital nutrients? Is eating a family ritual? Does entertainment and food go hand in hand?
- *Start an eating diary to identify unhealthy eating patterns and food triggers.* For example, when you crave chocolate write down what is going on around you. Did you just have a fight? Were you criticized? Are you afraid? Do you feel lonely? Look for patterns.
- *Change eating habits by developing a healthy view of food.* Ask a medical professional and/or dietician for resources and help.

24

- *Say no to dopamine triggering foods* by distracting yourself with a healthy activity like prayer or taking a walk.
- *Be patient.* It takes time, but evading problem foods allows your dopamine levels to return to normal. And your brain changes!

Similarly, when people have sex, it triggers the release of dopamine and rewards them for engaging in such an exciting and pleasurable act.[32] This is why infatuation is said to be similar to cocaine addiction. It impacts the same pleasure centers and reward circuitry. It is why some people seem "addicted to love," constantly seeking their next relationship fix.[33]

Sex is addictive because it provides pleasure, stimulates excitement, reduces tension, and burns up calories. It has the ability to either draw you closer to another human being, or leave you hungrier and more alone than before.

Scripture states, "Don't put your confidence in powerful people [*or drugs, food, sex*]; there is no help for you there...But joyful are those who have the God of Israel as their helper, whose hope is in the LORD their God" (Psalm 146:3; 5, *my interpretation,* NLT).

Someone said, "The one who puts God first will have happiness that lasts."

God and Science Meet

Research is increasingly making the connection between the dopamine system and one's experience of God. One particular study traced the activation of dopamine in Christians who prayed the Lord's Prayer. The study suggested the expectation of the person praying the prayer is one of receiving back both reward and relationship.[34]

Christian counselors who work with addicts have seen clients turn away from their drug of choice or object of attachment as their love and passion for God deepened. Most often it is their motivation to fight to replace their drug of choice with a longing to know and love God. As I spent more time with God and incorporated a daily devotional and worship plan into my week, I felt God touch and speak to me.

I have also learned we need to be extremely sensitive to expecting the Holy Spirit to give us a dopamine high or a feeling of magical supernaturalism. Religion and spirituality can provide a euphoria which is as potent as any mind-altering drug. The church and/or spiritual rituals can become the source of a fix versus a community for worshiping and serving God. The devil will tell you if you don't experience a transforming psychic event then you're unspiritual. It is not the job of the Holy Spirit to give us LSD types of experiences.

Transformation is a journey, a "steady as you go" type of walk. Some days you'll feel the outpouring of the Holy Spirit; other days you won't. Never forget, "The LORD himself goes before you and will be with you; he will never leave you nor forsake you. Do not be afraid; do not be discouraged" (Deuteronomy 31:8).

Reflect On It

- How does this information change how you see and think about yourself?
- Where might you begin to make changes in your lifestyle?

Day Two:
The Theological Nature of Addiction

> For I felt I was still captive of my sins, and in my misery I kept crying, "How long shall I go on saying, 'tomorrow, tomorrow'?" –Saint Augustine[35]

From the beginning, God has loved us and continues to long for us. Whether we realize it or not, we love and long for God. Throughout our lives, God desires to draw us toward fulfilling the two greatest commands: to love God with all our hearts, souls, and minds; and love our neighbors (see Matthew 22:37-39).

I am convinced it is love for ourselves, and lack of love for God and other human beings, which sets in motion insatiable cravings. The longing of our hearts is usurped by cultural, non-loving, often evil forces. The best explanation for this tragic condition is the biblical *doctrine of sin.*

Many see sin, or God to be exact, as a sour killjoy, shaking his finger at everything we label as desirable. *Why are you so mean to me God? Why are you always right and I'm wrong?* Even some pastors and pastoral counselors fear they'll be considered harsh and judgmental if they discuss sin in the context of addiction. Over time valid scientific, medical, and psychological models have been applied to human difficulties, and the concept of sin has been dropped completely.

I believe the problem comes from lack of clarity about the doctrine of sin. Sin is not about behavior. It is about our choice to alienate ourselves from God, and everything he represents. Theologian Derek Tidball wrote, "Sin is spiritual pollution that needs cleaning; willful disobedience that needs putting right; explicit wrong that needs pardoning, and manifold failure that needs forgiveness."[36]

Theologically, sin is what turns us away from our source of love, and away from loving others and valuing ourselves. We don't discuss sin anymore because it's not a popular topic. The concept of sin has become offensive and ridiculous to many. Yet, we cannot overlook it. Theology professor, Linda A. Merchadante wrote,

> Many people fear that talk of sin in connection with addiction will return us to an earlier age when alcoholics were often ostracized, viewed with no compassion, and finally given up as hopeless. Professionals in the addiction field often worry that any talk of religion or sin will underestimate the physiological aspects of addiction.[37]

27

We all have idols we must turn away from. There are hurts and losses we must grieve. But first, we must know something about ourselves. Sin is a big reason people go to counseling. Whether it's the sin of others, the sin of self, or the effects of a broken world, we must address the role it plays.

Habits are hard to change. Before we know it we're enslaved to them. A couple of drinks or smokes or shopping sprees is not an addiction. But if we derive pleasure and continue to repeat the behavior, in many cases, an addiction forms. Some repetitive actions form a habit, but others turn into a biological need for more due to changes in brain chemistry.

It is sin in the form of disobedience or separation from God which begins the process. I choose this substance or action over worshiping God. God is so holy that he cannot look at sin, which is why we're counseled to confess it and ask for forgiveness. Once God forgives us he hits "clear." The record of our failures is wiped out and we're back in harmony with him again.

This doesn't necessarily change the biology of our brain. Certainly God can do that if he desires, but often he doesn't. Most people will struggle and have to deal with biological and emotional withdrawal symptoms, in addition to changing their lifestyles.

Studies suggest people view spirituality as an important dimension in their recovery. *Spirituality* refers to our experience of God; to the devotional life and practices which provide the motivating power for transformation and action; and, therefore, is central to everything that revolves around our lives. It is a powerful healing tool and can sometimes do what no psychotherapist or formal treatment can do. Yet, often it's the combination of spirituality, therapy, and a solid medical and nutritional plan, which are the winning combination.

We can't fill up the real with the unreal. It won't work. Making changes on the inside—in our hearts, minds, and souls, with God at the center, is the only way.

In the Beginning...

The cause of sin goes back to the very beginning to the Garden of Eden (see the book of Genesis, chapter 3). It is the account of the very first temptation. The central theme in Genesis 1 and 2 is the interrelationship of the Lord God with his creation, Adam and Eve, our original parents.

Man and woman were created to have an intimate relationship with God. He never planned to force himself upon us. As his created, we can choose to love him or not, called *free will*. God had one requirement for Adam and Eve—to obey him (see Genesis 2:16-17). He foreknew they'd be free to deviate from his will. Consequently, he risked introducing evil.

One day an evil enemy slithered into the Garden—Satan, disguised as a serpent. [How he got there is another story.[38] We will get to know him better in Week Eight.] Satan suggests Eve disobey God and eat the forbidden fruit. She does and Adam follows (see Genesis 3:6). The motive: to become "like God."

Satan persuaded Adam and Eve that their disobedience would guarantee them an abundant life. Believing Satan's lie, they disobeyed and lost what they had—innocence. The joy of Eden was replaced with a wilderness of shame, with sin, and its consequences.

As a result, mankind lost their perfect relationship with God and their understanding darkened (see Ephesian 4:18). From that day forward, every baby inherited a sinful nature (called *original sin*.) Today Christians everyday buy into Satan's favorite lie: *There's more! You deserve to have every desire fulfilled. Go after what you crave!* He knows this lie is hard for us to resist.

For reasons only known to himself, God permitted humanity's fall from innocence. Theologians call it "the Fall." A pattern of temptation, sin, shame, and fear evolved. Every human being unconsciously strives for independent control over life, thereby, suppressing the truth and knowledge of God (see Romans 1:29).

Scripture says if we claim to be without sin, we deceive ourselves (see 1 John 1:8).

Speaking about the problem of sin, Pastor Timothy Keller wrote in his book *The Reason for God,*

> Sin is the despairing refusal to find your deepest identity in your relationship and service to God. Sin is seeking to become oneself, to get an identity, apart from him...[which] leads inevitably to deep forms of addiction...As in all addiction, we are in denial about the degree to which we are controlled by our god-substitutes.[39]

According to the Bible, sin is a failure to do something God has commanded us to do. It is more than doing bad things. It is taking the good things God created and making them into grandiose things, allowing them to define our significance, purpose, and happiness over our relationship with him.

The bad news is, if anything goes wrong with our good thing we end up feeling stressed and out of control. A life not centered on God only leads to desolation. The only solution is to reorient our hearts and minds, and focus on Almighty God.

Let us remember, the one who enticed Adam and Eve to sin was not God but Satan. Eve's mistake was trying to reason with the serpent. God is utterly opposed to evil. He created the world "good" (see Genesis 1). When Jesus walked this earth he said, "The thief [Satan] comes only to steal and kill and destroy; I have come that they may have life, and have it to the full" (John 10:10).

God is not the author of evil and sin. He is not the source of our pain. Although God is all-powerful, he sometimes steps back and allows the bad consequences of sin to run their course on this broken planet. We wait, knowing God is just. He will judge evil and bring about justice. We trust that more is going on behind the supernatural curtain. Faith reminds us something new will be born out of suffering.

Reflect On It

The doctrine of sin can be a great source of hope! When man broke the relationship, God did not cast off his creation. He put in motion a plan to restore that relationship. His plan included covering our guilt and shame with his healing grace. *Only* Jesus Christ is the perfect solution to this problem.

This is why Jesus came and died. He will do whatever it takes to save us, offset our guilt, and cover our shame. He will reconcile us to God and restore harmony to our relationships. This is God's character—he provides a way out in the midst of this horrific problem.

How does his mission give you hope today?

Day Three: Filling the Soul-Hole

Blessed are those who hunger and thirst for righteousness, for they will be filled. –Jesus, speaking in Matthew 5:6

Why do we feel bad in the very era where we have more than what we could ever ask for? We have got the latest and greatest of everything, yet we're no nearer to discovering real meaning in life.

A self-confessed nicotine addict, psychiatrist M. Scott Peck, offered his perspective in his lecture, "Addiction: The Sacred Disease." Dr. Peck believes at birth humans become separated from God. Everyone is aware of this separation, but some people are more attuned to it than others. They report feeling empty, a longing, and refer to it as "a hole in the soul." They sense something is missing, but don't know what it is. At a point in their lives these sensitive souls stumble across an object which makes them feel better—a soul stuffer. Dr. Peck pointed out the alcoholic is really thirsty for the Holy Spirit.[40]

Whether we realize it or not, deep inside we all feel "something" is missing. Our need to be filled up is God-given because God created us to be overfilled by him. We are designed to hold him as the object of our deepest affections. When we don't, a hole in our soul is exposed. We can't stand for the hole to be empty so we stuff it with all sorts of things. Those things become the Lord of our lives. Yet we are never satisfied because only God can fill us sufficiently. I believe this may be God's definition of hell—living perpetually unfulfilled; living in increasing denial, delusion, isolation, and self-absorption.[41]

Society has us believing that only more of what it offers will satisfy: a bottle of booze, a cheesecake, a couple of pills, the perfect man, designer accessories, a pack of smokes, breast implants, access to Facebook. Some people have an "Apple-shaped hole" in their heart that only a new iPhone® or iPad® can fill. Our view of life says everything is to be evaluated on whether it satisfies *my* desires and makes *me* whole. We devour the bait because *we are spiritually hungry.* What we humans really desire, and long for, is a connection to God, an alignment with the Holy Spirit, and a union with Jesus Christ.

There are consequences to choosing not to seek a relationship with God. When we center our lives on anything but him, the anything becomes an enslaving dependence because we have to have it to feel satisfied. Therefore, recognition of the role of our spiritual life is an important aspect of addiction and recovery.

Time and again, the Bible speaks about God's promises to the hungry—to those of us with a huge soul-hole. God "satisfies the thirsty and fills the hungry with good things" (Psalm 107:9). God Almighty wants you to enter his promised land, but that may feel like a risk to you. Step out in faith when he asks you to bury your other gods—those things that rival his rightful place in your soul. The truth is, only he has the power, and the desire, to give you a better life.

God Knows You're Hurt

> The problem isn't that God has abandoned us in our pain, but that sometimes we refuse to face it with him. –Pastor Mike Wilkerson[42]

Pain is everywhere—the pain of betrayal, the pain of a miscarriage, the pain of being single, the pain of being married, the pain of being broke, the pain of cancer, the pain of the lost child, the pain from childhood abuse and neglect. We can't get away from it…and we don't like it. Derek Tidball wrote, "The world is so shattered by sin that suffering is the background music of our existence."[43]

It seems our world has been driving head-on into an abyss of addiction and compulsive behavior in order to relieve some kind of inner pain. Therapists say when pain is denied it results in maladaptive behavior such as substance abuse, eating disorders, compulsion, depression, anger, and the inability to maintain healthy relationships. Human beings gravitate towards either stimulating or tranquilizing themselves in an effort to cover up pain and hurtful emotions. Then they become addicted to a temporary fix which provides momentary relief.

Many areas of the brain are involved in the experience of pain. Findings published in the *Proceedings of the National Academy of Sciences* indicated the brain cannot distinguish emotional pain from physical pain.[44] One researcher wrote, "While everyone accepts physical pain is real, people are tempted to think that social pain is in their heads, but physical and social pain may be more similar than we realized."[45]

We have all experienced it—rejection. Words can hurt as much as sticks and stones. Rejection is one of our most powerful and destructive emotions. It may cause as much distress in the pain center of the brain as an actual physical injury.[46] Literally, a person's words can either intensify or relieve stress. That is why the Bible says, "Pleasant words are a honeycomb, sweet to the soul and healing to the bones" (Proverbs 16:24).

The melancholy poet, Edgar Allan Poe, said,

> I have absolutely no pleasure in the stimulants in which I sometimes so madly indulge. It has not been in the pursuit of pleasure that I have periled life and reputation and reason. It has been the desperate attempt to escape from torturing memories, from a sense of insupportable loneliness and a dread of some strange impending doom.[47]

Every person hurts different. Taking prescription medication for a real illness, such as clinical depression or severe anxiety, is appropriate. Taking a pill to heal the body is commendable. But taking a pill to merely deaden emotions is both tragic and inappropriate. Emotional and physical pain, at the hand of God, has a precise and necessary impact in our lives. God knows what kind of pain and how much we need, and how much we can actually handle.

Emotional pain is like an alarm. When we push it away, deny or medicate it, we are in reality pushing away important warning signs of stress. I don't think it was God's intention when he created us that we ignore or medicate emotional pain. Jesus suffered, not to save us from suffering, but to teach us how to bear suffering. He knows there is no such thing as a life free from it.

Scripture says Jesus, the night before the crucifixion, being in agony prayed more earnestly (see Luke 22:44.) As he hung bleeding to death on the cross, bearing immense pain, Jesus rejected the painkiller (see Matthew 27:34). He chose instead to pray and drink from the cup of suffering his Father had given him.

In speaking of the purpose of pain, Dr. Steven Stiles wrote,

Pain may be bitter medicine, yet the destruction it prevents is far more distasteful. Whether we like it or not, we need the constant influence of physical and emotional pain to keep us alive and healthy by keeping us in touch with our vulnerability as we walk on earth.[48]

In times of angst, we are like a city under siege, attacked by fear and doubt. Our pain and suffering tends to separate us from God. This is the worst part of pain—the damage it can do to our view of and relationship with God. Feelings of abandonment or disfavor creep in. *Why did God let this happen?*

Do not fold under hardship or lose hope. Faith is the fort we take refuge in. No matter how desperate the situation becomes, genuine faith will not fail. It cannot fail because it holds on tight to Jesus, and he doesn't fail.

Reflect On It

We all have pain and we need to let our wise God take care of us his way. How are you medicating emotional pain?

Day Four: Dr. Jekyll, Mr. Hyde

I have had more trouble with myself than with any other man I have ever met! –Evangelist D. L. Moody[49]

Most of us struggle with one form or another of stress, control, anger, submission, love of money, fear, self-pity, perfection, approval, disordered eating, or the need to be number one. We say, "Do you think I really want to do this? I've sinned. I've repented. I've tried to change and obey, but I can't!" We have all felt it—that desperate longing to find a thread of hope and free ourselves from bondage.

Compulsive habits and addictions split the will in half—one part desires freedom and the other desires to continue with the behavior. We feel like we're living a double life, a sort of Dr. Jekyll, Mr. Hyde existence. We struggle against forces we really don't understand. I am convinced Christians often feel uncomfortable admitting to obsessive thinking or compulsive behavior because we mistakenly believe our faith should automatically eliminate it.

Whatever our vices, we all have a war on our hands. Maybe it's people pleasing, or lack of self-control over alcohol, sweets, sexual sin, or the need to control every situation. Because sin affects our minds, we're unable to think God's thoughts. Because it affects our hearts we set our affections on ungodly desires. Because it affects our feelings, we're in emotional turmoil. Because it affects our wills, we don't choose well. Inevitably, it erodes our self-esteem and self-worth.

The great apostle Paul too felt tormented. His description comes close to that of an addiction. We identify with him when he said, "When I want to do good, I don't; and when I try not to do wrong, I do it anyway. Now if I am doing what I don't want to, it is plain where the trouble is: sin still has me in its evil grasp" (Romans 7:19-20, TLB).

Paul speaks as one helplessly torn between the desire for good and his rebellious will. His anxiety emphasizes a kind of bondage which comes out of an inherited sinful nature. Internally, Paul the Pharisee battled with Paul the Christian. His solution: a relationship with God (defined in Romans 8).

Freedom is defined as being free of restraints, having the capacity to exercise choice, and to do as one desires. Freedom according to God also means we are dependent on him. The fact is: our new Christian self and mind (guided by the Holy Spirit) and our old self and old mind (guided by the flesh) exist side by side.

When we are born-again sin doesn't reign, but it remains. It is always trying to get back on its throne. This is why we still do what we don't want to do, like over indulge in our favorite vice. Likewise, what we want to do, like pray and read our Bible for one hour every morning, we can't seem to make a regular part of our lives.

Paul knew his weaknesses and recognized the necessity to yield his life to Christ daily. He didn't get discouraged like many of us. He chose to move closer to God. Paul proclaimed that Christ, "is able to do immeasurably more than all we ask or imagine, according to his power that is at work within us" (Ephesians 3:20).

Paul is talking about the power of God working deeply and gently within us. It is also power *for* us, to empower us in this life; to rise above so others can see the healing power of Christ. In the gospels Jesus never quit. He hung in there and pushed through every awful circumstance. As a believer, Jesus has imparted his nature and power into us. Therefore, we cannot quit.

Lured into a Web of Idolatry

> Whatever feels good, what seems to give us an immediate experience of life, we decide *is* life; we decide it is food for our souls, and we chase after it with all the excitement of a street person in the back alley rummaging through the fine restaurant's garbage. —Psychologist Larry Crabb[50]

Hard, cold facts reveal that we tend to set our sights on godless promised lands and people who assure us of every good thing. In what's been called "the parable of the rich young ruler" (see Mark 10:17-31) we find Jesus about to leave town. One man knows it is his last chance to ask his question to Jesus face-to-face. The young man kept all the commandments, but still sensed incompleteness. A picture of urgency and humility, he ran up to Jesus and fell on his knees before him. He asked, "Good Teacher, what must I do to inherit eternal life?"

Jesus addressed the young man's real point of need, "You still lack one thing. Sell everything you have and give it to the poor, and you will have treasure in heaven. Then come, follow me." Scripture then says, "At this the man's face fell, and he went away very sad, for he had many possessions."

Imagine how devastating Jesus's words were to this young man. The young man clutched an idol. Money and processions can be horrible masters. Jesus said, "Where your treasure is, there your heart will be also" (Matthew 6:21). Let the idol go and follow me. My desire is for you to join me, but I will not force you.

Of all the people who came to Jesus, this man went away worse than he came. The thought of giving up his possessions, his way of life, his security and status—his pleasure, was too much. He declined Jesus's offer. The hole in his soul would remain eternally unfilled.

When we repeatedly worship worldly treasures instead of God, they become an obsessive addiction. This explains why we can't "just stop." This is idolatry: the practice of ascribing absolute value to things of relative worth—things other than God. Idolatry elevates pleasure in things or people above pleasure in God, which God considers a sin.[51] He doesn't want to share his throne with anything or anyone else.

The idols in themselves are not actual sin, but can lead to sin. The danger of idolatry is it usually goes undetected. At first the idol seems exciting and it makes promises. Before we know it we've become its slave. Anything we use to soothe our stress or pain, and boost pleasure, may potentially be made into an object of our devotion.

Pray: "Lord God, You are God Almighty. Yet, sometimes in ignorance and arrogance I try to take your place. I ask for your forgiveness and submit my life to you. I acknowledge that all glory, honor, and praise belong to you alone. In Jesus's name, Amen."

Addicted to Busyness

See how important I am because I'm so busy! Busyness can too be an idol. We have come to believe in this culture, and in the church, if we're not busy then we're not significant.

What lies behind busyness apparently isn't simply ambition and drive; it's the dread of what we might have to face in its absence. This is because "busyness serves as a kind of existential reassurance and hedge against emptiness."[52] It fills the soul-hole—temporarily.

- Are you addicted to busyness, feeling you need to be constantly doing something?
- Do you do it all: work, run the house, raise the children, take care of the finances, volunteer at the PTA and the church, go to Bible study?
- If you lose electrical power to your home do you feel you will go stark raving mad because your activities have been subverted?

If we choose to spend more of our time looking to God, most likely we'll soon forget our idols. The starting point is here, "Apply your heart to instruction and your ears to words of knowledge" (Proverbs 23:12). God's holy Word has the power to transform the human personality and fill the soul-hole.

Pray: "Lord, your Word says to guard myself from idols. Search my heart and help me to understand the intent of my thoughts. You know the idols in my life which compete with you. Show me and help me to turn from them and serve you only. In Jesus's name. Amen."

Reflect On It

What has a hold on your heart today? Are you living separated from God? Answer these questions:

- What am I living for? Who am I living for?

- Finish this sentence: "My idols promise life but lead to …. They promise sight but end in…"

Day Five: Recover God's Plan

Recovering God's plan "requires an active participation in following Jesus as he leads us through sometimes strange and unfamiliar territory, in circumstances that become clear only in the hesitations and questionings, in the pauses and reflections where we engage in prayerful conversation with one another and with him." –Pastor and author Eugene Peterson[53]

"Lord, why can't I stop?" After following the culture's formula for decades I finally learned that a person cannot free herself by merely heightening her willpower and self-control. Our nails can only be driven out by Jesus Christ—the one who already took the nails for us, and every insatiable worldly craving.

Someone once said, "It's time to give up all hope of a better past." Stopping poisonous behavior must be our goal and can be called *recovery*. Recovery simply means "change." Most of us don't like change because it takes effort and usually requires learning new skills.

The U.S. Substance Abuse and Mental Health Administration defines recovery as "a process of change through which individuals improve their health and wellness, live a self-directed life, and strive to reach their full potential."

As a Christian I define it: "Recovery is a process of transformation through which individuals improve their health and wellness, live a Christ-directed life, and strive to recover God's plan for their lives."

Recovery isn't something that automatically happens when we pray and ask God to heal us. God's plan is to restore us to our real selves and to heal our soul-holes (see 1 Corinthians 2:7). Yet, we are active participants in the process. Recovery means partnering with God. He will never give up on us. The Bible's vocabulary makes this clear. *Renew. Repair. Regenerate. Reconcile. Redeem. Restore. Recover. Resurrect. Return.*

One of the most dramatic personal changes that happens early in the recovery process is an increased self-awareness. God opens our eyes and we begin to see patterns and self-destructive tendencies which need to be changed. There is also a new awareness of the pain we bear and have thrust on other people. Be aware: it is very easy to avoid confronting our issues because of the fear of change and losing what we've got. That is Satan's strategy.

Recovery is a journey, not an endpoint. A word of caution: For some the recovery process becomes a god or a new addiction. As a process, healing doesn't happen in one big "aha" moment, but through small, almost imperceptible shifts the Holy Spirit makes every day making us more and more like Jesus.

God promises you that he has "plans to prosper you and not to harm you, plans to give you hope and a future'" (Jeremiah 29:11).

Our Treatment Plan

> I will instruct you and teach you in the way you
> should go; I will counsel you and watch over you.
> —God, speaking in Psalm 32:8

By the grace of God there is still a great deal of good in us. After all, we are made in God's image. Saint Augustine said, "God's image is not broken entirely, but our righteousness and true holiness were lost by sinning, through which that image became defaced and tarnished."[54]

We all wrestle with negative emotions, such as shame and guilt. We need some way to protect ourselves. So, we put up defenses. We create and hide behind a false self that gives us the illusion we are better off than we actually are.

There is only one solution—being in a love relationship with Jesus Christ and meditating on his self-sufficiency. In time, he softens our hearts, begins to melt the false masks, and gives us the courage to risk becoming honest with him and ourselves.

In the Gospels distressed people: the diseased and the wealthy, both men and women, young and old, came to Jesus for healing and counsel. He guided his disciples through emotional and spiritual problems. He even gave life-changing counsel to the repentant thief on the cross. Today he still counsels us through his Word and by his Spirit.

How do we develop a close connection with a spiritual being? The same way you develop intimacy with another person. You spend time together. You share thoughts. There are no risks in entrusting our thoughts and secrets to him. Remember, he already knows your innermost thoughts and feelings. God is a confidant we can trust and love.

Spiritual growth is not an easy journey. We often find ourselves fleeing back to what is comfortable, to our object of attachment because we're seeking that "normal" feeling. We will usually find prayer and Bible study becomes more difficult in these times. We have a choice: avoid God's call. Or, tap into the power of the living God, and in time replace the object with his Spirit.

Personal change generally comes through studying the Bible. A positive attachment to the Bible is worthwhile to develop. D. L. Moody said, "The Scriptures were not given to increase our knowledge but to change our lives." The truth of the Word of God must renovate our head and heart if it's going to change our lives. When God sends out his word he heals and rescues his people from the grave (see Psalm 107:20).

No one is changed by an unread Bible. Spend time reading the Bible every day, both the Old and New Testament. Study it. Memorize it. Saturate your thoughts with it. Immerse your soul in it. Drink deeply of its truth. Allow it to run through your veins. Don't look at it as adding one more thing to your already busy schedule. When we make time for God's Word, it has a way of putting all of our activities into perspective.

Real spiritual transformation, and breaking the power of habits and addiction, is possible when we're submitted to Almighty God and guided by the power of the Holy Spirit.

Pray: "Dear Lord God, help me to treasure every word in the Scriptures and use them to lead me to you. May your words be stepping stones to knowing you, to finding freedom and peace. Steer me away from false teachers. Help me to love you and the Word as Jesus, Moses, David, the apostles, and so many others did. In Jesus's name. Amen."

Reflect On It

Your beliefs will govern whether you move near to or away from God. Ask yourself:

- Do I acknowledge, believe the teachings, trust the promises, and desire to follow God's commands?
- Will I allow the Word to convict me of sin and assure me of forgiveness?

Week Three

"Fat"—A Fate Worse Than Death
Addicted to Food and Body Image

Day One: Beauty is a Full-time Job

Society's Myth: I must be thin and beautiful to be accepted and/or loved.

The reflection in the mirror illuminates a grossly unattractive, unfit, fat person. One night I purge in the restroom after eating an enormous dinner with friends. Later, I sneak potato chips and cookies into my bedroom and eat both bags when everyone has gone to bed, and then carefully hide the wrappers. The next day I starve myself by ingesting only a couple hundred calories. I think constantly about my body and diet regimen.

This is a story about a monster that sneaks up on the struggling princess. It covertly and subtly destroys her. It began as a diet and a battle with the mirror. Decades later she realizes who and what the monster is…and who and what her Prince is.

Seventeen years old, at five feet, four inches, and 140 pounds, society labeled me "chunky." As women, we're vulnerable to competitive standards and comparisons. We compare ourselves all the time and come up feeling inadequate. After seeing a photo of myself I agreed, "I look like a whale! I'm going on a diet." From that day forward I chose what I put inside my mouth. I worked towards a goal weight and lost a healthy two pounds per week.

My parents were proud of me. I was proud of me. Boys noticed me. It seemed I had power over others when they'd ask me how I managed to lose weight. Like millions of other dieters, I liked receiving compliments and praise in my search for approval and love.

My soul craved acceptance. I didn't have anything in my life I excelled at. I failed at playing a musical instrument. I didn't date. My grades were average. I didn't belong to the popular girls' group...but I excelled at dieting. This kind of admiration is hard to give up. Soon my weight and number of consumed calories became my identity... and an obsession. I'd wake up each morning looking forward to manipulating that day's diet plan. And I started smoking cigarettes in an effort to cut my appetite.

Then something snapped. Conscious of our weight, my friend and I felt miserable, physically and emotionally, after gorging on left-overs from her parent's dinner party. She said, "I know how we can feel better and not gain any weight. Stick your finger down your throat until you throw up all the food." *Nirvana! Now I can eat anything I want and stay skinny!* This is bulimia. From that day forward, life spiraled out of control. Eventually I reached my revised goal weight of ninety-eight pounds.

After five agonizing years, I graduated from college and landed a coveted sales position in the pharmaceutical industry. My life looked great on the outside. But inside, the battle with this life-zapping monster raged on. Completely powerless over this parasite, my friendships, my work, my entire life, continued to unravel. I held a secret no one could know.

Isn't it interesting that the very desires which lead to our ruin start as healthy longings? Pure desires such as the need to feel joy, love, approval, security, to eat and enjoy sex, can become polluted. This is what the power of sin does. We can look at our motives and see bliss, when, in fact, destruction is lurking in our blind spots. Think about your desires. Could they be manifested in some type of harmful behavior?

Excessive dieting, in this culture, is a metaphor for social acceptability. It is also an attempt to manage an uncontrollable life. The root of disordered eating is a need for control, for some kind of order. The person uses their obsession with food as a means to gain back control and order which they somehow feel has been taken from them or lost. It may also be a distraction because they feel inadequate or have low self-esteem or suffer from severe depression, anger, anxiety, or loneliness.

We develop a need to control in order to protect ourselves from pain. If you were abused in any form, constantly rejected, experienced a great loss, or had an addicted and/or controlling parent, you probably felt unable to manage your circumstances. In an effort to curb the frustration and deaden the pain you turned to food, a substance, exercise, or another outlet. I figured since I'd already experienced betrayal, loss, and disappointment, why risk more? A relationship with food or a substance is safer. A personal prison is safer.

We believe we're calling the shots, but we're not. Temporary fixes only hide the truth about the source of the pain. When we finally recognize we're imperfect and desire power over each situation, we can begin to release control back to God. Then we're less likely to use food, or any other substance or behavior, to plug the hole in our soul. Try it. Pray about it. A huge burden will be lifted off your shoulders. Over time, balance and stability can be restored to your life.

Captivity and Self-Abuse

Somewhere and somehow, in a past time, the forces of darkness took hold and I gave in to a faceless captor. Every time I purged I swore. "This is the last time." It never was.

On some days my gag reflex didn't cooperate. *I have to purge this food. I'll die if I can't get rid of it. I'll keep trying, even if I scrape and bloody up my throat, and burst the blood vessels in my eyes.* A nightmare of unbound terror, I'd eventually purge the food, but the battle wounds ran deep.

Like a junkie taking a hit of heroin, I had my food binge, followed by a gruesome episode of self-induced vomiting, and then a smoke. The cigarette would burn my freshly irritated throat. Lastly, I'd ingest eight or more laxative tablets to ensure I'd eliminate absolutely everything from my body. Can you imagine living for seventeen years with chronic diarrhea and stomach cramps? I did—all in the name of "body beautiful."

This is self-abuse. Millions of other males and females do the same thing. Why do we self-inflict damage? Aside from the psychological distress in our lives, toxic behaviors are often a result of adhering to a set of self-imposed rules based on misbeliefs and lies:

- If you're not thin you are not attractive, therefore, not loveable.
- If you're not attractive you will be rejected.
- Being thin is more important than being healthy: ingest appetite suppressants, smoke cigarettes, or worse, meth.
- If you eat a fattening food, punish or harm yourself afterwards: run six miles, purge, take a handful of laxatives, or starve tomorrow.
- What the number on the scale reads and/or the number of calories you ingest each day is your identity.

The pursuit of thinness is an epidemic ruining our health and identity. Millions of human beings, through internalizing the culture's standards of success, beauty, and love have sacrificed their souls. We need to see how beautiful, special, and unique we are without resorting to self-destructive behaviors. God wants us to find pleasure in him alone. He said, "Open wide your mouth and I will fill it" (Psalm 81:10).

Eating disorders are serious with severe medical, nutritional, and psychological consequences. For more information on the causes, red flags, dos and don'ts, and other valuable information on eating disorders, visit *www.OliveBranchOutreach.com*. If you want to know if you or another person has an eating disorder, you can take a free survey at Caring Online: http://www.aplaceofhope.com/evaluations.html. After submitting the confidential survey, you will be given a score which indicates the likelihood an eating disorder is present or not.

Reflect On It

The biblical doctrine of creation teaches that God made everything good—including the bodies of the creatures he made in his own image.

- How do you view your body? Would you describe your body as belonging to God?
- Ask yourself: When I diet or exercise excessively, is my goal to gain human or self-approval, or to please God by improving my health?
- Read 1 Corinthians 6:19-20. What is God telling you in these verses?

Day Two: Abducted

In a condemning voice I tell myself, "You're disciplined and smart. Stop it!" Blind to reality I answer myself, "I can't. The captor gives me acceptance, pleasure and relief. It demands my loyalty, devotion, and service. It won't release me."

You may remember the story of 11-year-old Jaycee Lee Dugard who was kidnapped in 1991. Abducted from a school bus stop, she went missing for over eighteen years. During this time Jaycee had two daughters by her abductor. Most people wonder why she simply didn't run away when she had the opportunity. Psychologists have a term to help explain this phenomenon: the *Stockholm syndrome.*

Stockholm syndrome is a psychological response that occasionally occurs in people who have been abducted and held hostage. The abductee doesn't resist and actually shows signs of loyalty or caring for the person who took them. They do so despite the dangerous and harmful things the abductor does to them. Instead of hating the abductor, the person befriends and, at times, actually believes the captor is protecting them instead of harming and dominating them. Some people believe this may have happened to Jaycee.

We can use this term, Stockholm syndrome, to also understand how a person becomes abducted by addiction. Using an eating disorder as the example, the disorder takes hold of the person's mind and won't let go despite the fact the eating disorder is harmful, even potentially lethal. The abductor (eating disorder) makes the person do many things: starve, binge, purge, take laxatives, or exercise until exhaustion. In return, the abductor offers her a false sense of protection.

The woman held captive believes she controls the power of the eating disorder because she chose it. As a result, she befriends the eating disorder and creates an identity around it. She will even defend it when other people show concern or try to medically treat her; similar to the abused woman who defends her abuser. Over time she actually believes the eating disorder is trying to help, not hurt her. It gives the message, "If you are thin, all your problems will disappear. I'm your savior!" It promises you life, but ultimately robs you of your very soul.

There is a good chance that right now you feel stressed. You promised yourself you wouldn't engage in a negative or self-destructive behavior. But somehow the abductor baited you with those familiar promises. The liar he is, he starts the process of churning out negative self-talk. You find yourself doing what you don't want to do.

Sin deceives. It whispers, "The abductor will give you what you want. It will take care of you. God won't. He's angry at you." The abductor promises to relieve your pain and fill the hole in your soul. Christians have a name for this captor, Satan—and his goal is to silently seduce us, infect our minds, and destroy our lives.

The good news is: healing and transformation often occur smack in the middle of life's adversities.

Spiritual Vision

> Better to be blind and see with your heart, than to have two good eyes and see nothing. –Activist and author Helen Keller

A few days before my thirty-first birthday, I abruptly lost the vision in my left eye. The diagnosis: optical neuritis. The ophthalmologist indicated I could even lose the sight in my right eye. *Blind! Impossible!* I couldn't fathom it.

I tried to imagine what life would be like as an invalid. How could I handle that sort of deterioration? Anguished, I waited days, and then weeks, for dozens of test results to come in. *I must have done this to myself. If only I wasn't bulimic…if only I could start all over…*the torment dragged on. Deeply depressed, I bargained with God: *If you make everything better I'll be good. I'll stop bingeing and purging!* Every test came back negative. *Thank you God!*

Other professionals and I are convinced, due to pressure I put on my optic nerves when I purged, the eye didn't receive an adequate supply of blood and/or it suffered a stroke. Eventually part of my sight was restored. Today I am legally blind in that eye. There are always consequences to self-destructive behavior…and I didn't hold up my end of the bargain. I continued to binge and purge because of the grip of addiction, and God wasn't the foundation of my life.

I believe God allows consequences because they serve as instruction. My physical vision may be lacking, but the good news is my spiritual vision gets clearer each day. It is less clouded by self-serving desires and goals. I keep my spiritual eyes fixed on God. As we turn our eyes to God in times of pain and struggle, we experience his comfort and hope. He helps us to see more clearly each day.

Reflect On It

- Describe your abductor. List the promises it has made you.
- What precious gifts has it stolen from you?
- How have you been deceived? Pray for spiritual vision and clarity.

Day Three: The Road to Perdition

God often uses the pain we fear the most to save us from our self-made hell on earth. –Psychologist Tim Clinton[55]

Many people have asked me how I ended up on this self-destructive road to Perdition or hell. According to the *National Eating Disorders Association*, the causes of disordered eating are numerous: cultural and social (includes the media), genetic, environmental, psychological, and biological factors.[56] I believe my eating disorder was caused by a combination of all these factors. What I clearly see is a gradual accumulation of feeling the emotion of shame which budded in the second grade and continued to mushroom.

When I was seven-years-old we moved from America to London, England. Unbeknown to our family, the boys and girls had gym together. Each kid undressed exposing uniform underwear—dark navy blue "knickers," or underpants, and a thick, stark white undershirt. On my very first day of school, I slithered into the gym wearing a flimsy undershirt, and a pair of worn out flowery underpants with a big hole along the elastic line. Kids pointed and laughed at me—at my underwear. *Shame!*

Schoolmates teased me because I didn't fit into the British culture. They considered me weird because I had an accent and dressed differently. I felt stupid because I needed a tutor. *Shame!*

When we moved back to America, again my peers labeled me weird. More rejection and teasing from schoolmates only made the previous toxic messages deeper. The pain of rejection and *shame* became part of my normal thought process.

From grade school to high school, I dreaded gym class. When it came time to choose up team players it simply hurt too much to stand and wait, only to be picked last or next to last. The *shame* of not being chosen felt awful.

Our family relocated several more times. Moving can be painful because it is a loss. The loneliness and loss of friendships hurts. Feeling the pressure to fit into the junior high world, I fell in with the wild crowd. This group gave me a sense of belonging and a means to shove the pain away.

Then I began to gravitate into a new world of worshiping celebrities and models. Teen magazines said, *Kimberly, don't worry about being smart and good, worry about looking good and being socially accepted!* I believed the lies and set my sights on being a model. A few boys in my class laughed, "You'll be a model for MAD Magazine." *Shame!*

In high school no guy ever found me worthy enough to ask to a prom. *Shame!* Then I got fat, falling below this culture's standard of beauty. Rejection and demeaning words by people who were supposed to care for me brought on more *shame.*

The disordered eating thought process exploded when I entered college and joined a sorority. [Sorority girls are more likely to be burdened with negative body image and disordered eating.[57]] My assigned sorority mother didn't have any interest in spending time with me. When the other mother-daughters' connected I felt rejected and *shamed.*

As a bulimic, I did things only bums did—steal food, eat discarded food, and mess up toilets. *Shame!* Guys treated me like an object and sexually violated my being, fueling more *shame.*

I started shoplifting food and laxatives. Eventually I got caught and taken down to the local police station. *Shame!* The same month I applied for a part-time job at a jewelry store. The humiliation was awful when the manager told me to my face that she discarded my application because I was a thief.

My pharmaceutical representative career came to an abrupt stop when I got fired. Being fired from a job happened a couple more times. More *shame!*

Many Christian women have alleged that living in a legalistic (meaning over-emphasis on discipline of conduct, an ignorance of the grace of God, and/or emphasizing the letter of law) family, and/or belonging to a legalistic church, brought on condemning, shameful messages.

Perhaps you remember the saying, "We don't drink, smoke or chew, or go with boys that do." *Stop talking to that boy—you're flirting!* In other words, "You're bad!" *You can't buy that short dress.* In other words, "Good girls wear conservative clothing." *Sit quietly in your room and read your Bible for one hour in the morning and again before you go to bed.* In other words, "You'll only be accepted in this family and church if you read your Bible constantly. Bible reading makes you a good girl."

Shame can either bring us to God or keep driving us away from him. It should not cripple or make us fearful. To the shamed

I say, "Remember, the perfect Jesus was condemned, mocked and rejected too. Yet God said, "This is my Son, whom I love; with him I am well pleased" (Matthew 3:17; 17:5). He said to *me,* and he says to *you,* "This is my daughter, whom I love; with her I am well pleased."

There is only one way out: knowledge that leads to belief—belief that leads to trust in God, his Word, and his promises.

> "Fear not; you will no longer live in shame. Don't be afraid; there is no more disgrace for you… For your Creator will be your husband; the LORD of Heaven's Armies is his name! He is your Redeemer, the Holy One of Israel, the God of all the earth" (Isaiah 54:4-5, NLT).

Pray, "Lord, search my heart and show me the damage shame has done. I ask you to cleanse my soul of it with your amazing grace. I look forward to the day when you return and those who are first will be last, and those who are last will be first (see Matthew 19:30). In Jesus's name. Amen."

We will revisit the subject of shame in Week Eight.

Reflect On It

To begin identifying pain and shame, and possible triggers which set off your addictive behavior, answer these questions:

- What do I want to hide? What makes me feel worthless?
- What memories cause me to feel shameful? Identify who, what, where, when, and if you can, why.
- What areas of my life am I embarrassed about, such as, status, appearance, family, children, or possessions?

Day Four: From Deception to Redemption

> I'm happy from the inside out, and from the outside
> in, I'm firmly formed. You canceled my ticket to
> hell—that's not my destination!" –David, speaking
> in Psalm 16:9-10, *The Message*

Wallowing around in the cesspool of this eating disorder, it was beginning to look like a life or death situation. I needed to be rescued from this road to hell. I agree with Pastor Timothy Keller's definition of hell: "hell is one's freely chosen identity apart from God on a trajectory into infinity."[58]

What my soul really craved was an introduction to Jesus Christ—the Savior who is called a friend of sinners. Sadly, bondage is what ultimately leads us to seek the Savior. I cried out to God for help. To be honest, my cries didn't come out of conviction over sin, but out of fear for my life. I knew I was in trouble and needed God's help.

In his mercy, God sent that person and he took me to church. Then Jesus walked into my messed up life. A couple months later, in faith, I committed my life to God Almighty through his Son Jesus Christ. Then a miracle happened. I no longer had the urge to binge and purge every day. This was an example of supernatural or extraordinary grace.

Some mental health professionals call these rare events natural change or spontaneous remission. "Spontaneous remission" is somewhat misleading, as it fails to convey the intensive effort required to make lasting behavior changes. Grace empowered me to stop my compulsive behavior of bingeing and purging. This was wonderful, *but* my thinking remained the same. Dr. May explains,

> Deliverance *enables* a person to *make* a change in
> his or her behavior; in my experience deliverance
> does not *remove* the addiction and its underlying
> attachments...there is still a role for continued

55

personal responsibility. Considerable intention and vigilance are still necessary.[59]

Research shows many addicts who fail traditional treatment programs are able to free themselves from their addictions when they develop a connection with God. If he chooses, God can set someone free instantly, although we usually see the more traditional path of lots of hard work.

I can't answer why he doesn't do more miraculous healings. All I know is when they happen our belief is strengthened. Our worship becomes stronger because of the awe and wonder.

I stopped bingeing and purging but remained deceived because I didn't take personal responsibility. I neglected to feed myself truth. I believed the bulimia ended through my own willpower until God took me to the truth of his Word. In the New Testament it says,

> On a Sabbath Jesus was teaching in one of the synagogues, and a woman was there who had been crippled by a spirit for eighteen years. She was bent over and could not straighten up at all. When Jesus saw her, he called her forward and said to her, "Woman, you are set free from your infirmity." Then he put his hands on her, and immediately she straightened up and praised God…."Then should not this woman, a daughter of Abraham, whom Satan has kept bound for eighteen long years, be set free on the Sabbath day from what bound her?" (Luke 13:10-13,16)

Immediately I saw this as a word-picture of my life: crippled by bulimia, bent over the toilet for hours a day, for seventeen years. Then Jesus, my Savior, set me free from Satan's bondage. It had nothing to do with personal willpower. Jesus is the great transformer.

For almost two decades this unnamed woman had been tethered to her deformity and clinched tight by Satan. She took her seat in the synagogue and Jesus noticed her. He doesn't recoil or flinch. He knew the story of the last eighteen years. He recalled her suffering and pain. His heart must have broken to see her like this, just as his heart broke when he saw all the damage and destruction I endured.

Then he called her over to him. Surprised and embarrassed, all eyes were riveted on her deformity. Jesus healed her and instantly she stood up straight. Was she pain free from then on? I don't know. Although she rejoiced at her immediate physical healing, the process of healing her heart and mind had most likely only just begun, as it did for me. My body healed, yet I was still messed up emotionally and spiritually. I had a lot of issues and shame from my past which needed to be acknowledged and disposed of.

This story is for all of us. In some way, we all feel disfigured and afflicted. Jesus said the kingdom of God is within us (see Luke 17:21). The Holy Spirit invades our spirit and slowly permeates our life and begins to transform it. Nothing can compare to being found by the Savior of the world. No more wandering and wondering which way to turn!

Often, the only way we receive these benefits is to be humbled by the realization of our weaknesses and problems—our insatiable cravings, our obsessions and compulsions. I am not grateful for the tragic circumstances I experienced, but in hindsight I realize the insight, character, and strength I've received I couldn't have acquired elsewhere. With time and perspective, many of us will find good reasons for at least some of the tragedy and pain.

Deliverance is about moving from slavery to freedom, from bondage to life with Christ. Jesus will always meet us right where we're at. We don't have to be good enough, smart enough, or religious enough to earn an audience with him. Jesus is not about religion. He is about relationship. As John Eldredge wrote in his book *Beautiful Outlaw,*

> More words about Jesus are helpful *only* if they bring
> us to an experience of him. We need Jesus himself.
> And you can have him. Really. You can experience

Jesus intimately. You were meant to. ... A simple prayer, at the outset... *Jesus, I ask you for you. For the real you.*[60]

Where Truth Collides with Self-Deception

Our greatest illusion is to believe that we are what we think ourselves to be. –Unknown

Psychologist Diane Langberg stated that addicts are, "addicted to the narcotic of deceit."[61] The spirit of deception is thriving in our world today. The same lie Satan used to tempt Adam and Eve is still alive: "You can be free. Do whatever you want. It's your life! There are no divine laws; no absolute authority; no judgment."

Self-deception occurs when you are both the deceived *and* the deceiver.[62] I unknowingly become deceived because I believe an untruth and then perpetuate the untruth. The human heart and mind are sensitive to any kind of influence. We buy into the "I can't deny myself" lie. Our minds are constantly receiving input from our surroundings, shaping our thoughts. Misbeliefs say, "If I want something I should have it—no matter what or who is involved."

Humans have emotional attachments to beliefs, or biased truths, which in many cases are culture based, and flatly false and irrational. Every person has his or her own perception of truth. We are deceived when we choose to believe messages that don't line up with the Word of God.

Here is a test: Can you support what you believe using the Word of God? When false doctrines are presented, how will you know they are false unless you know what is true? Paul told the Roman Christians if they desired to experience freedom they needed to apply to their life what they knew about God. He essentially said, "Think against your feelings; unmask the unbelief. Let God correct your errors in emotional thinking. You have the Spirit and the Spirit has you!" (See Romans 8)

The road to healing begins when we start to identify patterns of impaired thinking and begin to reprogram them. This often begins when someone close points them out and suggests that we, as the Bible phrases it, renew our minds with the truth. In time we can begin to accept and then change faulty core beliefs.

Perhaps you picked up this book because a glimmer of truth has broken through the shell of deception. You realize what you've been using to numb or hide the distress simply doesn't work any longer. You've decided to turn to God. It is not a quick process. We all need to overwrite faulty mental tapes and replace addiction rituals with healthy rituals. It is a journey you'll never forget because God is the counselor and guide.

Reflect On It

- John Eldredge wrote, "We've all grown accustomed to committing dozens of little white lies about ourselves every day."[63] List three lies you say to yourself each day.
- Ask God to pour his wisdom into your perceptions: "How does this look to you, Lord?" The Bible and, for example, a Christ-based step program such as Celebrate Recovery, will illuminate your value and worth, as well as help you move through the process of trauma repair and forgiveness.
- Ask God to bring in several people you trust—shepherds who will speak truth and walk alongside of you in love.

Day Five: The Power of Mindholds

Don't be misled, my dear brothers and sisters. Whatever is good and perfect comes down to us from God our Father. –James, speaking in James 1:16-17, NLT

Crazy thoughts. Consuming thoughts. Unrelenting thoughts. Infected thoughts of lust, anger, fear, sorrow, and hopelessness. Someone once said, "My own thinking is a neighborhood I should stay out of!"

What we fill our minds with will largely determine what type of thoughts we have. We all make audio and video tapes in our head. These tapes are part of our learning process and help us solve problems. Far too many tapes contain negative messages. In stressful times they play over and over. Add to this, Satan, the granddaddy of liars, consistently bombards our minds with falsehoods. He manipulates us into reviewing the faulty tapes repeatedly.

Beliefs, attitudes, and choices make us who we are. Over time, our habits and thoughts shape who we are. As we nurture them, we choose to bend our will until we can no longer choose a different route, becoming a slave to the compulsive thought and habit. "My mom is addicted to exercise and so am I. I can't change." This is a stronghold. Like a slave, we submit ourselves to its wicked demands. It may even end up destroying us.

A *stronghold* is a thing which has a strong hold or powerful influence on a person. It is a mindset resistant to change; a deeply entrenched pattern of thought, ideology, value, or behavior burnt into our minds through negative repetition. Synonyms are stranglehold, vice-like iron grip, cancer, and infection.

Learning specialist, Dr. Caroline Leaf, author of *Who Switched Off My Brain?* states a stronghold looks like a cancer or abscess on a brain scan.[64] I call these mental strongholds *mindholds* because harmful thoughts and emotions are literally embedded in our minds. Mindholds temporarily make us feel good by filling the hole in our soul. They can also be God's way of telling us we have serious issues to deal with.

It has been said, "If you always think the way you've always thought, you'll always get what you always got." I have exciting news: thoughts come before feelings and feelings before actions. This means we have control over what we do once we learn to think in new godly and positive ways. It is possible to change our actions and our brain with healthier thinking.

For Paul, winning the war for freedom and joy is considered transformation through renewing the mind (see Romans 12:2; Ephesians 4:23). The word *transformed* in Greek is *metamorphosis*, meaning a change in form. Our minds have to be changed in such a way that old values, beliefs, and practices are replaced by those which conform to the mind of Christ.

Through the power of the Holy Spirit, God will lead our thoughts in the right direction. To renew your mind is to involve yourself in the process of allowing God to bring to the surface the lies you have mistakenly accepted, and then replace them with truth. If our minds are filled with the Word of God, then they can't be filled with toxic thoughts.

Knowing it and doing it are two different things. We must make a commitment to know God and pray every day. I suggest:

Pray: "Lord God, I ask for victory. Enable me to bring every negative thought into your obedience. Help me to refute the enemy's words which have been repeatedly playing and stealing my victory. In Jesus's name, Amen."

Bible study: The prophet Isaiah told the people to joyfully draw water from the wells of salvation (see Isaiah 12:3). God provides the living water, but we must draw it out. When God's Word penetrates our minds and hearts transformation into the likeness of Jesus Christ begins. Start by simply selecting one verse, one which is relevant to what's going on in your life today. You may want to select one from this book, or one which is universally helpful and inspiring. Use the concordance in the back of your Bible as a guide. [The *concordance* is an alphabetical index of the principal words in each book of the Bible, with a reference to the passage in which each occurs.]

Meditate on God's personal message to you: For example, "God who began the good work within you will keep right on helping you grow in his grace until his task within you is finally finished on that day when Jesus Christ returns" (Philippians 1:6, TLB). Read the verse slowly and then out loud several times. Pause briefly. Spend three to five minutes on the verse, until you feel God's message has sunk in. Your life will begin changing.

Take Every Lie Captive

> Nothing others do is because of you. What others say and do is a projection of their own reality, their own dream. When you are immune to the options and actions of others, you won't be the victim of needless suffering. –Don Miguel Ruiz, M.D.[65]

My story reveals that a God-given natural desire for love and acceptance changed into an abnormal desire for attention of any kind. When temptation promised I could lure attention with my body, my innate desire gave way to sin. So began the downward spiral. Praise God, today I am recovered from an eating disorder. Yet I still admit I hate to gain weight.

There is a certain amount of tension in every Christian's mind concerning our biblical walk. In one compartment of the brain there is a pull to live up to all the standards of Christ, but on the other side, there's a war to measure up to society's standards. The day came when I knew I had to relinquish control to God and devise a plan to change my thinking once and for all.

Disordered eating and addiction are disorders of the mind. I believe restoration is limited by treating the physical symptoms or behavior alone, such as focusing only on diet or abstinence. Once a stable food and medical regimen is established, and the person is safe, then the priority is to get to work on the mind, replacing the lies and toxic thinking with biblical thinking.

The enemy works relentlessly to destroy the people and work of God. Therefore, we must wage warfare! Paul wrote:

> For though we live in the world, we do not wage war as the world does. The weapons we fight with are not the weapons of the world. On the contrary, they have divine power to demolish strongholds. We demolish arguments and every pretension that sets itself up against the knowledge of God, and we take captive every thought to make it obedient to Christ. (2 Corinthians 10:3-5)

Taking every thought captive to the obedience of Christ means we must not yield any ground in our minds to the world or Satan. Only the right weapons will subdue and capture this abductor. Our weapon is the gospel of Jesus Christ. Only the Word can make that which sets "itself up against the knowledge of God," namely rebellious unbelief, obedient to Christ.

The *New Living Translation,* which I've personalized, reads, "*I will* destroy every proud obstacle that keeps *me* from knowing God. *I will* capture *my* rebellious thoughts and teach them to obey Christ" (2 Corinthians 10:5).

Our mission is to quickly capture those intrusive, flatly false thoughts before they become compulsive, negative acts, and then replace them with scriptural truths. We give our toxic thought to Christ, praying for it never to rise again. Every behavior begins with a thought, so by bringing our negative thought into submission to Jesus Christ, the right actions follow. We move from slavery to liberty.

"The only thing to do," Oswald Chambers said, "is to maintain a vital connection with Jesus Christ, to see that nothing interferes with that."[66] Only when we are connected to Christ, our Master and Savior, can we successfully take negative thoughts captive to him. How do we do this? By loving and obeying him; by submitting more and more of ourselves, including our thoughts, to him each day.

I acknowledged what had happened wasn't my fault. I had been baited and abducted. The Serenity Prayer, "God grant me the serenity to accept the things I cannot change, the courage to change the things I can, and the wisdom to know the difference..."[67] challenges us to focus solely on changing those things which can be changed.

Real healing began when I shifted my thinking from guilt and shame to grief and sadness. In other words, toxic emotions gave way to healthy emotions. I had lost my worth and dignity, my health, and precious time, which God highly valued. Allowing myself to be genuinely sad broke the strongholds that guilt and shame constructed. Through the enlightenment and direction of the Holy Spirit I began capturing the toxic thoughts and separated these emotions. I strongly encourage you to do the same exercise.

Our desire is to capture false beliefs and perceptions—the parts of our minds which have been infected with irrational and illogical notions. This will require you to begin challenging both your thoughts and feelings. For example, when a thought like, *If I eat this sandwich I'll gain weight which means I will not be attractive*, comes up, you can replace it with truth: *If the sandwich contains lean meat and a light spread of mayonnaise, I will not gain weight. And my weight has nothing to do with my value as a beautiful daughter of God.*

After being captured, every negative thought must be sifted through our brain's filter system. If we build our mind with Scripture and godly thinking, then every thought that goes through the sifter which is not truth will set off our mental alarm. We reject it and toss it into the trash bin. This is a life-long exercise and we won't win every battle. Prayer and persistence is the name of the game.

Pray: "Jesus, Please enable me to capture and bring every negative thought into your obedience. Help me to sift out the lies and deceptions, and purify my mind. Amen."

Reflect On It

Even though you can't always control a situation or other people, you can change the way you think about yourself and the situation. Practice these suggestions:

1. *Dispute your self-talk.* This means challenging the negative or obstructive aspects of your thinking. Ask yourself:
    - Is my thought factual or just my interpretation?
    - What evidence supports my thought is true?
    - What proof is there that my thought is false?
    - Does thinking this way help me feel good and/or achieve my goals?
    - What other ways can I look at this situation?
    - What can I learn from this to help me think clearly in the future?"

2. *Reverse condemning messages.* Catch each judgmental thought you have about yourself. Say, "This is not who I am. This is not what God says about me. He loves me. In his eyes I'm extremely valuable. I'm a good person. I'm lovable. I'm God-approved!"

3. *Clarify faulty thinking.* For example, if your mind tape begins, "I am damaged," quickly add a "but..." "But, I'm a kind person." "I have issues I'm dealing with right now, *but* I'm also strong and courageous." Likewise, if it is hard for you to accept compliments work on simply answering, "Thank you."

Week Four

The Quest for Perfection
Addicted To Flawlessness

Day One: Seared to Perfection

Society's Myth: I must be painstakingly perfect in order to consider myself valuable. I must be a super-woman, therefore, I will forever work on improving myself. Perfection is attainable.

"The very fact you are in graduate school says you probably have a bent towards obsessive-compulsiveness." Speaking to our class, a pastoral counseling professor at the seminary I attended alleged this. I laughed and then agreed. My thinking patterns remind me of a '60s song the Rolling Stones made popular, "Can't get no satisfaction...I tried and I tried."

Perfectionism, often defined as *anxious slavery* or *slow suicide*, makes us loathe ourselves when we spot inadequacy. Then we try harder to be perfect. We feel we need to prove our value to avoid the threat of rejection. The Twelve Step program calls perfectionism a character defect.[68] It shouldn't be confused with obsessive-compulsive disorder or narcissism.

If there is a single quality which characterizes perfect people it is a powerful, unconscious need to feel in control.[69] It often starts by attempting to master or restrain our self, but quickly develops into a desire to dominate and influence what others think, feel, and do. Perfectionism creates a negative paradoxical effect: the harder you work at doing everything perfect, the more you see what is wrong. Come to my home, comment on how nice the house looks, and I'll show you the cat fur balls under each sofa.

This is pride—the denial of our inherent limitations. There is a cost. Having standards so high you can't live up to them leads to stress and guilt, depression and anxiety—angst over past issues you can't change or angst about the future which you cannot control. This is bondage.

If you are a perfectionist, understand the culture and the devil have baited you into believing that if you can control your environment and please everyone, then you can compensate for feelings of inferiority. Being perfect is a real burden. It means always coming up with the right answers, never making mistakes, and constantly reprimanding oneself for falling short. It is no wonder perfectionists are so discontent. They seek to be sinless. It is impossible to be perfect. Only Jesus was perfect…and we aren't Jesus.

There is a correlation between perfectionism and addiction. Psychotherapist Anne Wilson Schaef wrote,

> It may be hard to picture addicts as conscientious, concerned people with high aspirations and high expectations of themselves, but that is what most of them are. Alcoholics, drug addicts, anorexics, compulsive overeaters are perfectionists. They are convinced that nothing they ever do is good enough, that they are never good enough, that they don't do as much as they should, and that they can be perfect if they figure out how.[70]

There is good news for those of us who want to rub out the rough

67

edges. God will use our strengths and our defects for his glory. Thus far I have relinquished a good deal of that rigorousness to God. I am fully aware I still hold onto some of my obsessive perfectionist tendencies. I have learned I need to intentionally carve out relaxation and fun time.

It is important to take regular relaxation breaks, to use laughter to diffuse stress, and listen to calming music. A word of caution: do not substitute a stress-inducing habit with a lot of television. Watching television has a tranquilizing effect and can become an addiction.

We all make mistakes. This is why pencils have erasers!

Addicted to Work

> We are not built for ourselves, but for God. Not for service for God, but for God. –Author Oswald Chambers[71]

We live in a society which defines a person's value and worth by productivity and appearance. How much we get done, how well we do it, and how it looks are the benchmarks of a successful day. We are a people obsessed with meeting and surpassing goals, staying ahead of the pack, and working on weekends.

This is a challenge because the Bible tells us we were created to work (see Genesis 1:26). Work is part of our divine image, for God himself is a worker (see Genesis 2:2). Yet, for many people work is a curse. In the beginning, work was not a curse or a mountain to be conquered or an obsession. It was a calling. People worked for the glory of God.

Maintaining a frantic schedule, being consistently preoccupied with work and performance, and being unable to relax, are symptoms of work addiction (called *workaholism*). Workaholism in America has become an all-consuming obsession. Mental health professionals say it needs to be treated as an addiction.

What we learn from the creation account is the various activities of human life were never intended to be ends in themselves. We were made to work, but not become enslaved by it. When this balance is broken, work can become an idol and a source of agony. God created the seventh day for rest for a reason. Our work must be managed within the context of a healthy relationship with God, marriage and family life, church and community.

Given my personality type and history, it isn't too hard for me to take the work God gives me to do and focus on it excessively. After all, it gives me great pleasure. Doesn't Scripture say what I reap, I sow? Often, that didn't seem to happen. Many days I've whined to God, "Where is the fruit of all my hard and laborious work? What did I do wrong?"

The prophet Habakkuk's response is what I believe God desires from us:

> Though the fig tree does not bud and there are no grapes on the vines, though the olive crop fails and the fields produce no food, though there are no sheep in the pen and no cattle in the stalls, yet I will rejoice in the LORD, I will be joyful in God my Savior. (Habakkuk 3:17-18)

What did God want from me? To have him, not success, be my source of joy. To break the culture's definition of achievement. To live by faith and not sight. To learn to be content with the blessings he'd already given me.

God tells us, "For my thoughts are not your thoughts, neither are your ways my ways" (Isaiah 55:8). In other words, our definition of work is quite different from his. I have had to learn to find a balance between contentment and ambition. Anytime we take the focus off of Christ and put it on ourselves in an attempt to dazzle others with our accomplishments, the enemy wins.

I have to constantly remind myself that numbers and success are not that important to God. Success was not Jesus's ambition.

Submission to his Father was. As Pastor Paul Scherer said, "You are not likely to be sent out under the will of God to do startling, impossible things. You are likely to be sent out to do the quiet, unspectacular things that matter, precisely where you are and with what you have."[72]

Reflect On It

Answer these questions with more than a yes or no. Pray for quietness and clarity. Talk to God about your answers. Ask him to show you how certain misconceptions about him may be connected to your brokenness.

- Do you believe God loves you based on what you do?
- Do you find it hard to believe God loves you?
- Do you feel like you are always disappointing him?
- Maybe you know he loves you, but do you feel disengaged from him, as if he is ignoring you, possibly even mad at you?
- Do you feel he wants you to work harder to be better?

Day Two: The Perfect Controller

Those who think they can do it on their own end up obsessed with measuring their own moral muscle but never get around to exercising it in real life. Those who trust God's action in them find that God's Spirit is in them—living and breathing God! Obsession with self in these matters is a dead end... Anyone completely absorbed in self ignores God, ends up thinking more about self than God. That person ignores who God is and what he is doing. And God isn't pleased at being ignored...Even though you still experience all the limitations of sin—you yourself can

experience life on God's terms. —Paul, speaking in
Romans 8:5-8,10, *The Message*

The need to be perfect and in control can manifest itself in these
ways. How many of these apply to you? Solicit the opinion of a good
friend or spouse:

- Fear of making mistakes or wrong decisions.
- A very strong devotion to work or ministry.
- A need for order or a firmly established routine.
- Frugality and stinginess.
- The need to know and follow the rules.
- Emotional guardedness. Cautiousness.
- Tendency to be stubborn and oppositional.
- Inclined to worry, contemplate, or doubt.
- A need to be above criticism—moral, professional, or
  personal.
- Chronic pressure to use every minute productively.[73]

How did you do? If it makes you feel any better I checked them
all. The measure of our life is not our image—where we live, how we
look, or how well we do. If God doesn't use a performance system,
then we needn't either. Instead we take these thoughts captive and
throw them in the garbage.

You have been *chosen* by God. You are his *special treasure* (see
Deuteronomy 7:6). In the mind of your Creator, there is no
questioning your value. It is like winning the God lottery! You
don't need to work or struggle to become good enough. This truth
should rock your world.

If we truly desire change we look towards Jesus. His life flowed
out of his relationship with the Father. He listened and obeyed his
leading. Take the first step toward submitting to God. Admit it has
been your will which has been the driving influence in your life. Ask
for help to listen for his voice. Then follow.

The Perfect Church Member

> Next to faith this is the highest art—to be content with the calling in which God has placed you. –Priest Martin Luther

During the pursuit of my degree in pastoral care to women, it became clear to me that far too many Christian women feel they have to be perfect in order for God to love and accept them. They tend to struggle with rulebooks, sense of duty, responsibility, and fairness. They rarely feel the joy of the moment. The present hardly exists. They may have heard Scriptures quoted which emphasized works or put them down. Following rules and laws doesn't work. All it does is make us feel worthless because our sin nature is repeatedly exposed. When we mess up then we feel condemned.

Some churches breed stereotypes of what the perfect woman must be, like the "Proverbs 31 woman" (see Proverbs 31:10-31). It is easy to get caught up in the comparison game: *She has more faith than me. She's got so many spiritual gifts. Her children are so well-behaved.* There will always be others who are at a different place in their growth, responsibility, and maturity. Someone said, "Jealousy is counting someone else's blessings rather than your own."

As a ministry leader I often find myself falling back into the perfection rut, feeling I have to meet some high expectations. What freed me was the realization that when God called me to ministry he knew what he was getting. A couple months down the road he didn't say, "Bad decision. I shouldn't have called her!" Companies say that. People say that. Not God. This is the freedom of grace.

James 3:2 states we all stumble in many ways. We will make mistakes, even humiliate ourselves. We must remind ourselves that God's grace is greater than any old imperfection. Jesus Christ became the curse, freeing us from all perfectionistic law traps (see Galatians 3:13).

Reflect On It

- Do you recognize that when you don't accept yourself you are contradicting God's image, because our rejection of ourselves comes out of faulty human perception and not God's?

- Give yourself grace. *Grace is God's acceptance of me just the way I am—a flawed human being.* Repeat: "God accepts me, therefore, I accept me exactly the way I am!" Say it again—and believe it.

Day Three: Hooked on Physicality

In "Beauty and the Beast," it is only when the Beast discovers that Beauty really loves him in all his ugliness that he himself becomes beautiful. –Author Frederick Buechner[74]

A woman was looking for a church to accept and love her. She had a recent facelift and her doctor released her with this advice:

My dear, I have done an extraordinary job on your face, as you can see in the mirror. I have charged you a great deal of money and you were happy to pay it. But I want to give you some free advice. Find a group of people who love God and who will love you enough to help you deal with all the negative emotions inside of you. If you don't, you'll be back in my office in a very short time with your face in far worse shape than before.[75]

Today, more than ever, we are hooked on *physicality*—a preoccupation with the body and satisfaction of its desires; an intense physical orientation usually at the expense of the mental, spiritual, or social.[76] Far too many women over forty are hooked on anti-aging treatments and are being treated for eating disorders and depression, a sign, experts say, of society's pressure to stay young.

The anti-aging business is booming. Plastic surgery, bioidentical hormone replacement therapy, body building, nutraceuticals, and extreme cosmetic and dental makeovers are common place. We've been made to feel we must uphold society's definition of perfect: to be flawless and defect free.

Like it or not, in this society how we look and what we wear is a part of who we are. Our "image" reveals not only our social, economic, and educational levels, but also our moral values. We all know first impressions count and play a major role in determining the course of a relationship. A person's face is one of the first things we notice, particularly the mouth and teeth.[77]

Research indicates consumers are becoming even *more* appearance conscious.[78] *Packaged Facts* projects U.S. retail sales of cosmeceuticals will reach $11.9 billion by 2016.[79] We all understand the lure of cosmetic treatments, and hormonal and vitamin therapies. We understand the desire to want our outside to look the way we "hope" to feel inside; the desire to step back in time and recapture our youth.

Sadly, women's bodies and their hunger for love and meaning are on a collision course. Most of us have days when we're disgusted by the face or body in the mirror. Usually this feeling doesn't linger very long and we're able to regain confidence. But for some, seeing an unfit, unattractive reflection staring back is a skewed perception which occurs daily.

I can tell you personally, no matter how many cosmetic procedures we have, we still end up searching for our real selves. I learned that in the quest for physicality one can *easily* get caught in the addiction trap. First, the professionals dangle the bait. Walk into an office and you will be greeted by an attractive receptionist. Then you will notice strategically scattered photographs and brochures of ideal, beautiful and flawless women throughout the waiting room.

Then the doctor pulls out the hook—the carefully planned, subtle sales messages: *We can take ten years off you!... You don't really want a nose that looks like a golf ball?... Liposuction will reduce your total body fat... Eyes which look like basset hounds won't get you a promotion!*

"I'm sold! When can we do this?"

These professionals prey on our insecurities and we purchase costly procedures all in an effort to obtain, or retain, youth and beauty. Many women are completely satisfied with their "work." Others know the pain of a broken promise. Let me tell you "the rest of the story..."

In my early forties I was convinced *everyone* else was younger than me. The crow's feet and turkey-neck were only accented by this realization. I said, "It's time to battle a new monster: lines, wrinkles, and saggy skin!"

A cosmetic dermatologist promised I could wake up each day with confidence, looking and feeling my absolute best. I began investing thousands of dollars in lunch time laser treatments. At one appointment I learned about a simple non-invasive mini-lipo-suction treatment for the neck. The doctor would suck out some of the fat through a small cannule. I asked, "If you suck the fat out, what happens to the excess skin?" He said it will tighten up on its own within six months. "Okay, let's do it!"

Months later I looked in the mirror in horror. The skin didn't tighten up. It just hung there. Years later, it's still hanging there! I have bought turtlenecks in every color, but they can't camouflage this mess. I hear the turkey gobbling every day when I look in the mirror. My new attitude is: *You don't have time for this. Move on! Off to the turkey thought farm for you!*

Despite cutting-edge cosmetic procedures available today, there's no guarantee of a perfect procedure. In my book, *Torn Between Two*

Masters, I describe the debacle with my rhinoplasty (nose) surgery which took place fifteen years earlier. One would have thought I had learned my lesson. Like multitudes of other women, I've had a hard time dealing with the societal pressure to look young. Many psychologists say it is a myth that how you feel about yourself is related to how you actually look.

Today I have a new kind of beauty, the kind which radiates from within. I think of myself like a red-hot coal, fired up from within by the power of the Holy Spirit. If I choose to leave the Spirit out of my life I become a cold, black coal devoid of any warmth. "Those who look to him are radiant; their faces are never covered with shame" (Psalm 34:5).

Does this mean when I look in the mirror I no longer see those ugly footprints of aging? No, but I try to limit my exposure to the media's messages. I remind myself that I am not God. I cannot reverse the effects of the Fall, no matter what I do to myself. And I work to refocus my thoughts with biblical thoughts such as,

- "Don't become like the [*plastic*] people of this world" (Romans 12:2, GW).
- "For the wisdom of this world is foolishness in God's sight" (1 Corinthians 3:19).
- "He [Jesus] must become more important, but I must become less important" (John 3:30, ISV).

Is Participating in the Anti-Aging Movement a Sin?

Many Christian women have struggled with this question. When the Bible was written, there were no plastic surgery or cosmetology centers. We need to answer this question based on what we know about God. It is a sin if these treatments and procedures take your focus off God and are put solely on yourself. I can personally attest that with every anticipated procedure it is very difficult to *not* focus on oneself.

I believe the issue isn't whether we have plastic surgery or wear makeup or go on a rampage of diets. The issue to God is whether it is an idol and we are in bondage to it. My cosmetic procedures were idols. We are a vain people. We need to realize we can't reverse the effects of the Fall. We all age. We all die.

Secondly, the Bible says one day we all will be accountable to God for what we did on this earth (see 2 Corinthians 5:10). I will have to explain why I frivolously spent so much money (God's money; see Romans 11:36) on my appearance and body. *Ouch!* We forget that our time on earth is limited, and we are to use it wisely.

What I know now is if you allow God to control your inside, you'll be genuine and beautiful on the outside. Look at how Jesus interacted with people. Notice how they changed the way they saw themselves when God himself looked at them. They felt loved, valued, competent, and a sense of belonging. They felt beautiful! It is impossible to spend time in the powerful presence of God and not emerge a beautiful person.

If you're struggling with negative self-image, the ultimate makeover isn't done at the cosmetic counter or the gym, or by wearing couture, or being remade by a plastic surgeon. It is done by God—from the inside out. Never forget you are *his* work of art, *his* masterpiece (see Ephesians 2:10). You may look in the mirror and see flaws. God sees excellence!

Reflect On It

- When God created you, he said, "very good" (see Genesis 1:31). Do you feel "very good?" Why or why not?
- What part of your body do you need to give to God today?

Day Four: Biblical Perfection

> As for God, his way is perfect; the word of the LORD
> is flawless. It is God who arms me with strength and
> makes my way perfect. –David, speaking in 2 Samuel
> 22:31,33

The Bible tells us that God did not create the world to have evil, disease, hunger or death. His original design was that every person live in a state of perfection with him. When Adam and Eve disobeyed God they lost the perfect setting, perfect experiences, and the fulfillment of perfect expectations. Since then we've been yearning and thirsting for the flawlessness that's been lost.

This explains why Jesus said, "I have told you these things, so that in me you may have peace" (John 16:33). Jesus didn't say, "You blew it again!" No, he said we don't need anything else to complete us—only him.

Maybe you've wondered, "If God wants me to be perfect like Christ, then why am I so imperfect? Maybe I'm not even a real Christian?" When we believe this, invariably the only solution is to keep striving to be faultless. Let's look at two texts many perfectionists misunderstand.

The first text is Matthew 5:48, "be perfect, therefore, as your heavenly Father is perfect?" The word "perfect" is the Greek word *teleios*, which means "mature, fully developed." It doesn't refer to flawless or moral perfection, but to the kind of love which is like God's love—mature, complete, holy, and full of blessing. To be perfect is to, one, seek to love others as wholeheartedly as God loves us; and two, fulfill the purpose for which we were made.

The second text is Romans 6:2, "We died to sin; [*through our union with Christ*] how can we live in it any longer?" When Paul wrote this he was not referring to the act of committing sins, but to continuing to live under the authority of sin. The word "live" means to continue or abide in. We must differentiate between the *activity* of sin, which every believer lives with, and the *power* or *dominion* of sin, which defines how we lived before Christ.

Paul's words "died to sin" mean as a Christian we no longer live under the reign of sin. When we are born-again God sends the Holy Spirit to live in us, to give us a new life, and begin the process of reversing sin's effects—remaking us from the inside out.[80] We will still succumb to temptation, either from our own fleshly desires (see James 1:13), or from the world (see 1 John 2:15-16), or the devil (see Ephesians 2:1-3). This is entirely different from a settled disposition. To paraphrase John Owen, our sin becomes a burden that afflicts us rather than a pleasure that delights us.[81]

The Real You

When the writer of Hebrews spoke about perfection he said, "…he [Jesus] has made perfect forever those who are being made holy" (Hebrews 10:14). God has already written our story. When we meet him in eternity we'll be completely perfect forever. Only God knows what the definition of eternal perfection is. What I do know is it will be utterly captivating!

The writer also tells us we are *presently* being made holy. It is like God is saying, "I'll make you absolutely perfect at a later time but I'm going to start the process right now. I'm going to invest in you because you're worth it and I love you so much." Growing up, no one, other than my parents, ever invested in me long-term—no teacher, no big sister, no mentor. I've had certain people flit in and out of my life, but no one stuck by my side for the long haul...not until Jesus.

The Holy Spirit won't stop his work until we are perfected in eternity. Then every one of his children will be fully redeemed and healed. Yet, today Jesus has an amazing plan and wants to invest in us.

Get ready for a paradigm shift: *You need not change yourself as much as you need to begin to understand how God has wired you.*

At the beginning of our lives, we may be born into a family or community environment that is either supportive or not supportive. But, we also bring our own personal way of reacting to our surroundings. Our temperament as an infant develops throughout our lives and transforms into our *personality.*

Personality tests reveal I have what is termed a *powerful choleric* plus *perfect melancholy* temperament. The other two temperaments are the *popular sanguine* and the *peaceful phlegmatic.* There are strengths and weaknesses to all temperaments. Our temperaments were designed by God. I have also inherited my temperament from my parents.

In my opinion Paul was a choleric. Prior to his conversion on the Damascus Road, he used his temperament strengths to advance the cause of Judaism and terrorized Christians. After Paul's salvation he soon became the apostle to the Gentiles. Through the power of the Holy Spirit I too now channel my choleric temperament into the Lord's work.

It is important to recognize these are tendencies only. We must take into consideration our relationship with God, learned behavior, even birth order. Parental norms also have a big influence. Many women have confessed that conforming to family and church rules became more important to their parents than what they thought, felt, wanted to do, and even feared. Many "good" kids try hard to meet their parents' expectations, only to find lack of consistent appreciation, or worse, criticism.

You share a personality type with millions of other people. Embrace who God created you to be. Celebrate your differences. This is part of discovering who you are.

Our job is to get up every day and do our best using the gifts and opportunities God has provided. I call this a *spirit of excellence* (versus a spirit of perfection). We do the best we can and expect God to do the rest. Have patience with all things, but more importantly, have patience with yourself.

Reflect On It

- Ask God to help you begin to learn flexibility and acceptance, to teach you how to calm your mind down, and to develop the courage to be imperfect.
- Make a commitment to begin to override negative self-talk with God's thoughts about you.
- Reassure yourself, "This is not a perfect world. People are not perfect. I am not perfect. I must accept this and ask God to show me positive ways to overcome my perfectionism."

Day Five: Healthy Perfection

Who else has held the oceans in his hand? Who has measured off the heavens with his fingers? Who else knows the weight of the earth or has weighed the mountains and hills on a scale? Who is able to advise the Spirit of the LORD? Who knows enough to give him advice or teach him? (Isaiah 40:12-13, NLT)

These are the words of the prophet Isaiah. Guess what? He isn't talking about us! God is God and we are not. He is the only one capable of running the universe and running our lives. When we get on an airplane we don't insist on being in control of the cockpit. We trust the airline and have faith in the pilot's experience that we'll get from point A to point B safely.

God is absolutely sovereign. He is the pilot. We are his passengers. He is the creator. We are his creatures. He is eternal. We are finite. He is all-powerful. We have no power of our own. He is autonomous, just, independent, and self-existent. He needs no one and nothing.

We are completely dependent on him for our next breath. The supreme rule of God is non-negotiable.

On earth, Jesus recognized success is secured by God alone. He operated within the limitations of humanity. His humility represented complete dependence and submission to God and the Scriptures.[82] He didn't take up a sword or wave his banner. He didn't dash around trying to get more done and help everybody. He carried a cross. *Father, your will be done!*

Billy Graham, in his book *The Secret of Happiness*, wrote, "Happy are the meek. Happy are the yielded. Happy are those who trustingly put their lives, their fortunes and their futures in the capable hands of their Creator. Happy are those who "let go and let God.""

Even when we try our best we will still be imperfect. Can you accept this? Your well-being will be determined by whether or not you can accept this fact.

Love and Grace Conquer Perfection

> The greater perfection a soul aspires after, the more dependent it is upon divine grace. –Brother Lawrence

Little Gracie decided she wanted to help Mommy. She scooped out the kitty litter and exclaimed, "See Mommy! See what I did. I helped you!" Mom walked into the litter box room and found litter scattered all over the floor. She noticed the litter clumps had been scooped out and asked, "Gracie, what did you do with the scoops?"

She responded, "I put them in the laundry cuz they need to be washed."

Mom responded with a special tenderness, "Thank you Gracie." She didn't respond in anger or disgust to the child's actual behavior, but to the simple, childlike love which motivated the behavior. Parental love often expresses a likeness of God because it's unconditional and steady. But it's also prone to selfishness, pride, and distractions. Our choices can be wrong and destructive. Whereas God's love remains perfect, solid, and unchangeable.

There is a dimension of God's grace which is interactive. God and his created have the ability to mutually respond to each other's love. Yet, for some people God may seem unloving, cruel, or simply absent. There may be four reasons for this thinking. One, we are blinded by and preoccupied with our dependencies. Therefore, we cannot hear God's voice.

Two, our image of God from childhood is faulty. It is easy for us to define God in terms of our own expectations and history with our own earthly father. We have a tendency to project onto God the unloving characteristics of the people we esteem. In doing so, we make God man-like, thereby; we may not be experiencing his almighty love and grace.

Three, if you have a shattered self-image then you may have a shattered God image. What do you think God thinks of you? You will discover what you actually believe about God when you come to terms with what you believe he thinks of you.

Four, we believe God's promises are for someone else. "If God really loved me and is good why did this horrible thing happen?" The Bible teaches us that we have an enemy whose sole desire is to separate us from our loving Papa. We must look at the world the way Jesus did—as a brutal and cruel battle with evil. And for now, God has chosen to work on this broken planet mostly from the bottom up, rather than from the top down, as Jesus did when he was on earth. God often allows circumstances to play out naturally.

We tend to interpret God through our brokenness. These reasons are why it is imperative we get our information about God straight from the Bible. God is love. God is good.

Reflect On It

If you recognize you are struggling with perfectionism, consider the following:

- What is wrong with being imperfect?
- Why does failure and my personal blemishes devastate me?

Week Five

Fatal Attractions
Addicted to Relationships
and Religion

Day One: Love Me!

Society's Myth: Love is all you need. The right person will make you complete.

The weekends are spent in bars looking for Mr. Right. The mornings are consumed nursing hangovers and her dignity. How many times has she laid there with a strange man, staring at the ceiling, pretending to be loved and needed and desired?

Will he want to get to know me; perhaps ask me to spend the day with him? Or is he simply another "smooth operator?" Will he, like the others, promise to call only to dismiss me? Might he actually want to start a relationship—a meaningful love relationship my soul craves?

Then her mind switches tracks. *I can't believe I fell into this predicament again. I feel used, abused, and embarrassed. I hate myself.* Being rejected yet again fuels cynical and destructive feelings. *This keeps happening because I'm contaminated.*

Have you ever made a promise to yourself not to have sex with just anyone because you know how dirty and unworthy you'll feel afterwards? Yet, the feelings of pain, emptiness, and aloneness are just as horrible. So you go out to a bar with a friend, have a couple drinks, and meet who appears to be Mr. Perfect. *Wham. Bam. Thank you ma'am.* You thought you felt like dirt before. Now you feel cheap, used, and revolting.

Society portrays sex as something fun without consequences. Society is wrong. As Dr. J. I. Packer said, "Sexual laxity brutalizes you, and tears your soul to pieces."[83]

I wasn't a sex addict looking to meet my sexual needs (although sexual addiction affects many Christian women). Each encounter represented a potential mate. I believed the lie I'd only be a whole happy person if I was attached to a guy. Deep down, I hoped "true love" would soothe the ache of my deep need for love and acceptance, and bind the wounds of rejection and betrayal.

In the quest for intimacy, I confused sex with feelings of love and felt I owed it to men. Aren't I supposed to give into his needs in order to keep him wanting more of me? The plan backfired, causing my self-esteem to plummet further into a dark pit.

These men violated my boundaries, my personhood. So, the cycle of deceit and abuse continued. Now I understand why God warns us, "Never offer any part of your body to sin's power. No part of your body should ever be used to do any ungodly thing" (Romans 6:13, GW).

Generally, problems with lust are a male issue, while addiction to romance and intimacy is more often a female matter. Males get more attached to the sexual novelty while females get addicted to bonding. Unconsciously I believed, "If someone truly loves me then I can believe I'm not damaged." *Love me, even though I don't love myself.*

God eventually brought a godly man into my life and we married. He gave me the attention I craved. For years I found satisfaction in him alone, not Jesus. Only after I committed to spiritual transformation did I come to love Jesus and allow him to fill my soul-hole first. Today, Jesus is the glue that keeps the love in our marriage cemented.

The Damaged Gift

> The beginning of love is to let those we love be perfectly themselves, and not to twist them to fit our own image. Otherwise we love only the reflection of ourselves we find in them. –Unknown

In 1986 Robert Palmer made these words famous: "You're going to have to face it, you're addicted to love." Our culture is addicted to love. Sentimental love songs, enticing ads for romantic getaways, hordes of romance novels, and sappy movies are evidence. The yearning to be cherished by a special someone is a God-given desire. But for some women, this poses a significant problem. Because of insatiable cravings for love, they will do anything to find it and ultimately land in destructive addictive relationships.

For me, Russian roulette was the name of the game and worth the risk. I eventually got pregnant and chose to have an abortion. Then I had another demon to deal with. In a search to fulfill my deep, unmet needs, I was sexually assaulted numerous times. The shame, confusion, guilt, and breakdown of personal boundaries left numerous scars which carried over into later relationships.

God's Word says the person who lives for pleasure is dead even while she lives (see 1 Timothy 5:6). My soul died. If you were to take off my mask, there'd be no face. If you empathize with my story I want you to know: you're not damaged. You can't be damaged because you're made in the image of God Almighty! For this reason, you have great dignity, not because you're so good, but because you're made up of his essence which is capable of making God's goodness visible through you to others.

Healing requires we break the invisible bonds of deception,

shame, and fear; such as, *All men want one thing only. All men are alike.* I had become calloused to any endearing qualities in men…until I met Jesus. Jesus showed me there is a kind of love so pure it can wash away all my sins, no matter how unsightly the stain and permanent the scars.

Daughter, receive the love of God! The thought that anyone could really love me like this—unconditionally, no strings attached, overwhelmed me. I fell at his feet and pleaded for forgiveness. He forgave. The Savior gave me what no hustler could—genuine love; love that would be mine forever, not just for one night.

Listen to God and refute the lies you've come to believe. Believe in the goodness of who you are and what you're becoming. You're not a victim. You're God's child—*already complete in Christ* (see Colossians 2:10; Ephesians 2:13-14; the term "in Christ" refers to the vital spiritual union we have with Jesus Christ which produces peace).

When you are in Christ you have direct access to God Almighty (see Ephesians 3:12). When you are in Christ, Satan has no power over you. You can break the chains of bondage and claim genuine freedom! When you are in Christ you can't stay in turpitude for very long. It becomes a place of discontent. Regardless of what the culture or enemy tells you, keep focused on the goal of becoming a healthy victor in Christ.

Love Gone Wrong

Why couldn't my story end like Cinderella's? Cinderella didn't take her clothes off to win her prince. When the clock struck midnight and she returned home, she didn't lose anything she couldn't get back the next morning. And…she got the rich, handsome prince, living happily ever after. *Why her and not me?* Cinderella's life is a myth.

From the time we were little girls we've been encouraged to find true love. The messages we received from fairy tales were we cannot survive without a man. This is not true love. As I look back I recognize, like a junkie, I needed another person to fill the hole in my soul. Instead of allowing God to meet my needs and desires, I expected another human being to do it. I didn't know how to set boundaries. The word no wasn't in my vocabulary. I ended up hopelessly addicted to every relationship I had with a man.

This isn't God's intention for a man–woman relationship. People are limited when compared to God. They can be unreliable, selfish, and shortsighted. Yet we put our lives and futures in their hands rather than the all-knowing, forever-loving God. "For the LORD is good. His unfailing love continues forever, and his faithfulness continues to each generation" (Psalm 100:5, NLT).

Addictive relationships are not uncommon in our society. According to psychologist Gregory L. Jantz, relationship addiction occurs "when a person enmeshes self-identity with an unhealthy need for connection and relationship."[84] How do you know if you are a relationship addict? The focus on the partner is obsessive and fear of abandonment drives the obsession.

Did you experience abandonment, neglect, or inattention in childhood? If so, there's a good chance you allocate too much time, attention, and value to another person, while neglecting to care for or value yourself. Relationship or "love addicts" can be addicted to a lover, spouse, friend, parent, or child.

Addictive relationships are very powerful, seductive, and hard to resist. Each person feels they cannot live fully without the other, nor could they walk out on the person. *Isn't that the definition of true love?* Not when each person encourages the other's dependency out of fear of being left alone. Often, both people are reluctant to act independently for fear of threatening the relationship. They don't dare rock the boat.

Healthy love, in contrast, knows where appropriate boundaries begin and end. It knows when to detach and allow the person to be their real self. Healthy love doesn't try to solve the other person's problems. Healthy interdependent people can open themselves up to be vulnerable. They have a strong sense of self and don't expect another person to complete them.[85]

The Bible says, "God created man in his own image, in the image of God he created him; male and female he created them...Then the LORD God made a woman from the rib he had taken out of the man, and he brought her to the man" (Genesis 1:27, 2:22).

This is a statement of absolute equality. Both male and female are created in God's image. The female is made of the same stuff as the male. Whatever is true about the image of God in man is true about the image of God in woman. You too deserve to live a joyful and fulfilled life!

Reflect On It

- When it comes to love, what do you feel deprived of?
- First, list three false beliefs, such as: "I must keep everyone I love happy," "Giving (i.e. my body, my time, my stuff, or my money) to a man is how I feel good about myself."
- Second, list three truthful affirmations and commit to practice them, such as: "It's okay to ask for what I want," "I don't have to be attached to this person to be accepted and loved," "It's good for me to take time for myself."

Day Two: Addicted to Enabling

I give and give to him. Everything I do is for him. He never appreciates anything I do anymore.
–Unknown

"If I do what he wants me to do, I will be valued. If I don't, then I'm a bad person." This was my belief system for decades. American society has developed an increasing awareness of enabling and codependency. An *enabler* is a person who makes it easier for their loved one to continue their self-destructive behavior, usually by either criticizing or rescuing. Their self-worth is based on their ability to meet the needs of the other person.

We enablers get pulled into these kinds of relationships because our nature is to control pain, even in others. We want to help because it makes us feel better about our own image as girlfriend, wife, mother, or God's servant. We tend to attach ourselves to problems and problem people.

The term *codependency* refers to a relationship where one or both parties enable the other person to act in certain maladaptive ways. The word codependent literally means "dependent with." The opposite of codependency is *interdependent*. An enabler abandons their interdependence because they are obsessive about meeting the expectations of the other person. They live out their lives as incomplete selves; failing to become all God intends for them to become.

Codependents are attracted not just to other people but chemical substances or things or behaviors. Most people think of the companion of an alcoholic as being solely the codependent. Not so. The alcoholic is actively codependent. He or she is dependent on alcohol. We forget many partners of, for example, exercise-aholics, tanorexics, obsessive dieters, are enablers.

It is near impossible to live out God's plan for our lives if we're addicted to another person. If we give another person this much control over us, then we can't also give God control over our lives. Jesus said no one can serve two masters (see Matthew 6:24). We can only be satisfied when we're in a love relationship with God first.

Religious Addiction

In essence we have become addicted to the certainty, sureness or sense of security that our faith provides. It

is no longer a living by faith, with hope and growing
in unconditional love. –Reverend Leo Booth[86]

Addiction to religion is not uncommon. And it is a difficult subject to discuss openly. Religion can become so distorted and counterfeited that it becomes an addiction (also called *religiosity*). Some people seek a relationship with God simply to experience euphoria. Others immerse themselves in the church in order to escape reality and/or impress others.

Brittany spent thirty to forty hours a week at her church working in various ministries. It gave her a high. People would comment, *Brittany is amazing!* Long story short, Brittany felt trapped in her marriage. By attaching herself to the church she relieved the discomfort of her feelings. It wasn't a genuine expression of devotion to God or a love for her neighbor.

Calvin Miller, in his book *The Taste of Joy,* warns that many Christians are only "Christaholics," not disciples. He points out real disciples are cross bearers; they seek to follow the real Jesus Christ, not make a fetish of him. Christaholics on the other hand, are avoidants who are looking for a shortcut to happiness. They want "the joy of the Lord" without any responsibility.[87] The Bible makes it clear that the way to get our needs met is to develop a relationship with the person Jesus Christ; not a dependency on a particular image or aspect of following him.

Rianna came very close to ending her life by suicide. Then God pulled her out of her hell. She developed an incredible zeal and hunger to learn the Word of God and know Jesus Christ himself, to the point of spending all her spare time doing so. This is not an addiction. Religious fervor is not the same as religious addiction. Rianna's enthusiasm was a large component of God's recovery plan.

Most Christians do not understand the addictive process. It has been said that religious addictions are harder to break than addictions to substances because they're the hardest to see. This blindness may be reinforced by the church culture and authorities, certain Bible passages, or personal divine experiences. Satan's ploy is to subtly turn people away from Jesus, and this is one of his most popular tactics.

Christian Codependents

Diane was raised in a strict Christian family. She rarely ventured outside her home or the church. In either place when she came alive—when Diane was happy, singing, noisy, play-acting, energetic, and exuberant, they called her a "bad girl." Whenever she was studying and quiet, even ill—not living out her desires and feelings, they called her a "good girl." She learned that to be alive and to be herself is bad. To be accepted in her world she unintentionally practiced powerlessness and codependency. Many psychologists believe this is one of the most powerful addictions many Christian women have.

Countless Christian women do whatever it takes to be accepted and liked. The church culture is the perfect breeding ground. Christian codependents are good martyrs. They suffer and sacrifice. They set aside their own emotional, physical, relational, and spiritual needs for the sake of others. They are the servers, the volunteers who hold the church together. "You have to direct the women's luncheon. Nobody else can do it like you can!" Since they want to be good, liked, included, accepted, and loved, they say yes time after time. They end up overburdened and exhausted.

These motives are so powerful they take precedence over discernment. Only when we see ourselves as God sees us can we accept love, create boundaries, and take responsibility for ourselves.

Reflect On It

Much of recovering God's plan for our lives is finding and maintaining balance in every area. Pray God will enable you to begin putting steps in place to find balance in your life.

• Ask yourself, "Is my search for self-pleasure or for pleasure of God?" "Do I love the culture of my church more than I love Jesus?"

- Ask God to help you balance your emotional needs with your physical, mental, and spiritual needs; to balance giving and receiving; to find the dividing line between letting go, saying no, and doing your part; to find a balance between solving problems and learning to live with unsolved problems; to balance letting go of your idealistic expectations.[88]

Day Three: Unmet Needs

Remember: not getting what you want is sometimes
a wonderful stroke of luck. –Unknown

Lord, why do I find myself hopelessly captivated by the wrong things, wrong guys, and destructive influences? The time came when I understood I had deep, repressed unmet needs—needs that were presently affecting my relationship with others and with God. When we repress a need we try to keep it out of our conscious mind. We focus on other things which feel safer. Psychology calls this *displacement*. We may displace our need with an object like food, but the need that's been repressed is still there. Every now and then it reminds us of its presence.

Most of us know the difference between needs and desires. Needs are necessities so we can function in life and fulfill God's plan. What about the addict who says they *need* their drug of choice? In this case because of changes to the brain there are people who feel that they need the drug of choice to function normally. With an addict, he or she no longer has the same freedom they once had to choose whether or not to use the drug of choice.

Desires (or wants) are things which produce enjoyment. Often what we think is a need is really a worldly desire, like a phone app— something we want but don't actually need to thrive or survive. Without even realizing it, we treat worldly desires as a godly desire or need. There is nothing wrong with desires, as long as they fit into God's plan and purpose—the enjoyment of him and his definition of a good life.

Addiction starts as a desire—a desire to attain euphoria, tranquility, or to reduce stress or pain. For some it becomes a deep need because it enslaves them to certain behaviors, things or people. The object becomes a preoccupation, then an obsession, and then comes to rule their lives. Ask yourself:

- What occupies my attention most of the time?
- Has my focus shifted from what I have to what I don't have?
- Am I grateful God has met my needs, or am I always thinking about what it would be like to have more?

Break the Power of Unmet Needs

If the Lord is your shepherd, He is sufficient for all your needs. –Pastor Tony Evans [89]

Unbeknown to millions of Christians, they have significant unmet needs. As little girls we want to feel captivating. We want to know, "Am I beautiful?" I sought an answer to that question by starring as the beautiful queen in my own play productions as a kid. Sadly, advertising, the media, and our celebrity culture, has a way of chipping away at our soul-hole by implying, "There's nothing about you which is attractive."

My friend Nancy wrote, "Born to bond, we arrive into the world longing to belong, longing to love and be loved. Babies die for lack of it. So do we." This is where we unlock the secret to living a life of authenticity versus a life of slavery. Addictions sprout for many reasons. Knowing how one gets in can help one get out.

Recognize there are five essential deep needs every person has:

1. To have my love tank filled.
2. To feel I belong.
3. To feel I am worthy and valuable.
4. To feel I have a sense of purpose.
5. To feel I am spiritually secure.

These needs are universal for people of all ages. We cannot *not* have these deep needs met. We *will always* find something to fill the void.

We will finish this week's work by talking about our need to have our love tank filled. Next week we will study the other four deep needs.

Reflect On It

Have you asked God to meet your needs? Jesus and James said we don't have because we don't ask God (see John 16:24, James 4:20).

You may feel, "I'm not worthy of asking. Look at what I've done." You are worthy because you are his child. We have this hope and promise: "The LORD will guide you always; he will satisfy your needs in a sun-scorched land and will strengthen your frame. You will be like a well-watered garden, like a spring whose waters never fail" (Isaiah 58:11).

Day Four:
I Need to Have My Love Tank Filled

> Many people seeking professional counseling are emotionally and relationally stuck because they keep hoping that a valued parent, spouse, or other important person in their life will finally love them the way they wish. –Psychologist Robert Whitcomb[90]

We all seek an answer to, "Am I worthy of being loved?" When the cry of our hearts is ignored or abused the potential for any addiction or distressful behavior springs up because it distracts us from the pain of feeling unloved. Love makes us vulnerable to being hurt. The word *passion* comes from the Latin root *passus,* which means "suffered." We have all experienced the suffering which comes along with love.

Perhaps you now realize you're trying to cope with prolonged and unresolved feelings stemming from your need for love and affection. Since love is learned by being loved, it is difficult to experience it if you've grown up in an environment with barriers to giving and receiving love.

Those feelings may have started as a child because a parent or caregiver was absent for any number of reasons. Or, it may be a spouse who is uninvolved in family life. It may be a divorce or a death. Or, perhaps the heartbreak of a shattered love relationship. It may be the effects of a rape or emotional abuse.

Many of us deal with these kinds of losses by detaching. For decades, unconsciously, I put up barriers to letting others in so I wouldn't be rejected, hurt, or abused. I blocked my capacity to love and be loved. I turned my back on God, avoiding his subtle nudging to love him. Yet, he never gave up on me. He patiently waited because he loved me so much. We can continue to repress our desire for God but it will haunt us. God's cry is, "Need me! Choose me!"

There are many in the mental health field who refer to our need for love as a need to fill our *love tank.* Love tanks help us understand our basic love needs. When our love tanks aren't filled, life tends to be a struggle. There are several entities required to fill the tank.

1. *Spiritual:* We are designed to be satisfied by connecting with God. Only then can he fill our love tanks. God wants to be

loved by you![91] Our tanks fill up when we worship and serve him. Though there is little research on how God fills the hole in our souls, it has been found those who believe they have a relationship with a stronger, wiser nonphysical deity report higher levels of happiness.[92]

2. *Parental:* We are designed to be filled with love and support from our parents. If the parents aren't keeping each other's love tank replenished, they usually can't fill their child's tank adequately. For many women, their father didn't fill their love tanks. Consequently, these women spend their lives searching for the missing love. Since none of their male relationships can sufficiently fill the parental part of the love tank, the search is doomed. They often become "addicted to finding love."

3. *Romantic love:* We are designed to be loved intimately and tenderly by another person for a lifetime. From the time we're little girls we have our hearts set on finding our Prince Charming. Yet this kind of love can be one of the most painful to endure.

4. *Family, community, and peer support:* We are designed to connect and be loved by other people. If we choose to isolate we can't be filled sufficiently.

5. *Self:* We are designed to love ourselves, not as in narcissism. Loving yourself isn't selfish because love, truly expressed, isn't selfish or self-serving. Rather, loving yourself serves as a model to love others. It is to take care of your God-given needs and desires.

Every person's heart cries, "Love me and never leave me." It is not uncommon for our love tanks to be running on empty. It is no wonder we feel like dying plants on a vine when our relationships go wrong. We cannot make each other 100 percent happy. Only God can. The Christian story is about God coming into our lives and filling our love tanks with his unconditional love and grace.

Evaluate True Love

I have loved you with an everlasting love; I have
drawn you with loving-kindness. I will build you up
again and you will be rebuilt... –God, speaking in
Jeremiah 31:3-4

In this media-based society love is a feeling. "True love" means
two people are perpetually infatuated and devoted to one another.
William Shakespeare's tragic characters, Romeo and Juliet, and
Anthony and Cleopatra, killed themselves for love. Today we hear
about the distraught ex-significant other who kills the love of his life
and then himself.

Why do these stories end this way? We want someone to love
us so much we are willing to die for that person. Isn't it ironic this
is what Jesus did for us? God listed love as the first fruit of the Spirit
(see Galatians 5:22).

Let us educate ourselves on the true nature of love and throw out
the fairy tale and Hollywood versions. It is highly possible you have a
distorted view of God's definition of love. From a biblical perspective
there are different types of love. The Greeks had a different word for
each kind of love:

Eros (air-ose) comes out of Greek mythology. Although this Greek
term does not appear in the Bible, eros, or erotic love, is portrayed in
the Old Testament book, The Song of Solomon. Eros was the god
of sexual love and beauty. We refer to eros love as intense passionate,
emotional, and physical love.

Storge (storgē) is expressed between family members (also
called *familial love*). It is the desire to care compassionately for one
another.

Phileo (fil-eh-o) is a warm, brotherly heartfelt affection someone
has for close friends. Any time you see the word "brethren" in
Scripture, it is referring to phileo love.

Agape (ah-gop-ay) is the love of God for mankind. It represents divine, unconditional, self-sacrificing, active, volitional, and thoughtful love. This type of love delights in giving, and keeps loving and giving, regardless of the other person's response. "God demonstrates his own love for us in this: While we were still sinners, Christ died for us" (Romans 5:8).

The problem we have in America is we don't distinguish between these types of love. The Bible talks about agape love, and we think it means eros or phileo love. Human love changes and is conditional. God's agape love is unconditional and never changes—no matter what we do.

When God says, "Husbands, love your wives, just as Christ loved the church and gave himself up for her" (Ephesians 5:25) he is referring to agape love. Understanding and staying in agape love requires a commitment. It is the key to a successful relationship.

Reflect On It

We are renewed and made whole when we allow God to fill our love tanks. We also choose the extent to which we are willing to invite him in. How far are you willing to open your heart, to become vulnerable, and go deep with God? Explain.

Day Five: Accused of Adultery

So if the Son sets you free, you will be free indeed.
–Jesus, speaking in John 8:36

The apostle John wrote about Jesus's encounter with an adulteress woman who desperately needed her love tank filled (see John 8:2-11). The Pharisees discovered a woman in an unlawful affair. They grabbed her, then threw her to a large crowd for sentencing since Moses' law said to stone her to death.

> Then Jesus stood up and said, "All right, hurl the stones at her until she dies. But only he who never sinned may throw the first!" The Jewish leaders slipped away one by one until only Jesus was left in front of the crowd with the woman. Then Jesus stood up again and said to her, "Where are your accusers? Didn't even one of them condemn you?" "No, sir," she said. And Jesus said, "Neither do I. Go and sin no more." (John 8:10-11, NLT)

Who is this woman who was dragged, mocked, and thrown into this public square, her indiscretions laid out for everyone to hear? What thoughts ran through her mind? Scripture is silent. We have all walked in her shoes, worried others might find out our indiscretions. Or maybe we've had others publicly accuse us. I have. I hated them for the venom they spewed.

"Adulteress. Caught in the act!" The accusers threw her at the feet of Jesus. Trembling with fear, she looked into the face of her judge, the only one qualified to condemn her. But he didn't.

Unlike the other men, Jesus looked right through her to her very soul—not her breasts, nor her nakedness and shame. He saw her differently. He vividly remembered her as a tiny embryo in her mother's womb. He peered straight into her brown eyes recollecting her innocence as a young girl. His love, kindness, and grace pierced through the shame. She felt a warmth and peace like nothing she'd ever felt before. Jesus filled her love tank.

When Jesus looked into the eyes of this woman he didn't give her a sermon, only words of grace. In essence he said, "My precious daughter, your past is not your present. Don't give in to that masked woman who betrays you. Say no. Build boundaries. Stand up for yourself. You're made in my image. You have immense value. Stop seeing yourself as an adulteress and see yourself as my daughter. I love you and forgive you. Now forgive yourself. Go child and stay pure."

You forgive me Lord? It's almost too much to take in. You actually love me—me with all of my faults and failures? How can that be?

We can blame others or condemn ourselves for our circumstances. Throwing stones only hinders transformation. There is only one solution—Jesus. He fills our tanks with cleansing words of love and forgiveness, "Neither do I condemn you."

Move Closer to Love

If life is a river, then pursuing Christ requires swimming upstream. When we stop swimming, or actively following Him, we automatically begin to be swept downstream. –Pastor Francis Chan[93]

A drowning boy struggled to survive in a river as his mother stood watch, gripped with fright and grief. A well-built man walked up seemingly indifferent to the boy's fate. "Save my boy. Sir please save him!" cried the terrified mom. But he made no move.

Losing strength, the boy's thrashing began to diminish. He rose to the surface, weak and helpless. Then the man leaped into the river and brought the boy in safely to the shore.

"Why didn't you go after my son sooner?" cried the mom. "Madam, I couldn't save your boy as long as he struggled and thrashed around. He would have dragged us both down to certain death. But when he grew weak and ceased to struggle, then it was easy to save him."

To struggle to save ourselves is to hinder Jesus Christ from saving us. Why does God allow us to struggle in these mighty rivers? I believe he does this to overwhelm us with our own sense of inadequacy. He permits trouble and perplexities to ensure we fill ourselves with him and accept his grace.

In the Gospels, a picture emerges of the close communication Jesus had with the Father. God the Father was always available, supportive and affirming.[94] The Son sought his Father's approval, trusted him instinctively, and knew he could count on him to meet his deep needs.

When you're in a rough place, God desires you hold on to him. He won't drop you! As you get to know God through the Bible, you will find he is a strong rock, a sustainer, a rescuer, and refuge for the weak. No doubt this is why he brings us to the edge of the raging river.

Reflect On It

- What do you feel in your heart God is telling you to do right now to begin moving closer to him?
- Take an inventory of how much time you're spending with him (called *worship*)—in prayer, reading his Word, participating in church services and studies. Are you including him in every part of your day? If not, set three goals and write them out. Then stick to them. For example,

   1. I will get up 20 minutes early each day to pray. I will read and meditate on a few verses in my Bible.
   2. On my way to and from work, I will shut off the radio in my car and imagine the resurrected Jesus Christ sitting in the passenger seat. He wants to know what's on my mind and I will tell him.
   3. I will start attending church regularly and seek to get "plugged in."

Week Six

Anxious to Please
Addicted to Approval
and the Internet

Day One: An Ophelia Existence

Society's Myth: I must depend on others for my value. I must be loved or approved by every significant person in my life.

Young Ophelia in William Shakespeare's classic play *Hamlet,* is a typical girl, footloose and fancy-free, unaware of the harsh realities of life. Easily molded by the more powerful opinions of the men in her life, she loses herself in adolescence.

Ophelia falls in love with Hamlet and lives solely for his approval. She gets caught between her obedience to her father and her love for Hamlet. Ophelia is the quintessential submissive daughter, a role demanded of all young women in that century. Even though her love for Hamlet is strong, when her father orders her not to see Hamlet any longer or accept any of his letters, she obeys. As long as Ophelia is unmarried, she must live by daddy's rules. She has no control over her choices.

Ophelia's familial obedience leaves her vulnerable to the abuse of

Hamlet, who accuses her of being unfaithful and deceptive. When Hamlet rejects her, she clings to the memory of him treating her with love, respect and tenderness. Incapable of defending herself she defends and loves him to the very end, despite his brutality. Ophelia is crushed by Hamlet's unforgiving behavior, especially when he says, "I loved you not." She is devastated. The man who once spoke to her with "words of so sweet breath" turned on her.

Ophelia's value was determined by these men's approval. Hamlet causes her deep emotional pain. It appears she doesn't have a relationship with God and the insight of the Holy Spirit to guide and direct her. So when his hate is responsible for her father's death, she comes to the end of herself. Torn apart, she goes mad with grief. Tragically she drowns in a stream filled with flowers. It appears she accidentally fell into the water and then simply neglected to save herself from sinking. This seems to be a metaphor for the way she lived.

We feel the unfairness of how Ophelia was treated. Despite changing times and the feminist movement, far too many women today live an Ophelia-like existence. I did for twenty years. I was engaged to a Hamlet. Without Jesus Christ at the helm guiding my life I followed my deceived heart and multitudes of erroneous sources. Always put together, yet torn apart, I went mad with grief. In the search for significance I drowned in a stream filled with food, alcohol, diet pills, cigarettes, and men.

One enduring attribute of most human beings, particularly women, is we obsess about how people view us and our family, and our general appearance. We characteristically seek the approval of others. *I can't do this or wear that…What would they think of me!* Most often we don't realize it is an obsession, but it is. We are approval junkies shaped by other people's opinions, real or assumed. The bad news is this obsession affects more decisions than we realize.

The desire for approval begins when we're toddlers. Every child seeks recognition. "Look! See what I can do!" Most everyone has been caught in the trap of approval addiction, which is to live in bondage to what others think of us. *Approval addiction* is when a person compulsively seeks the acceptance and favor of others.

When a person has an excessive need for approval, they constantly seek out validation from others. This can take the form of always agreeing with or doing things for others, while at the same time ignoring their own feelings and needs. Personal boundaries become blurred and they aren't able to prioritize what is truly important in their lives.

Being addicted to approval is not the same as having a healthy need for praise. There is nothing bad in applauding someone for a job well done. In fact, it is important in building self-esteem. Everyone needs to feel valued. We all search for significance, but some not always in a positive way. And, what I've learned is that most people are not sizing you up. They are too busy thinking about themselves, thinking what they're going to say next to impress you or the other person!

Are You An Approval Junkie?

One day, in eastern Turkey, while shepherds ate their breakfast, one sheep mindlessly walked off a 45-foot cliff. The rest of the flock followed. According to *The Washington Post*, 1500 sheep mindlessly stumbled off the cliff; 450 sheep died. The rest were cushioned by the woolly pile of those who jumped first.[95]

The Bible often refers to human beings as sheep.[96] Easily distracted and susceptible to group influence, we'd rather follow the crowd rather than the wisdom of our Good Shepherd. "What will you think of me?" is an extremely powerful motivator.

Our longing for positive self-worth and self-esteem may lead us to do things that are equivalent to jumping off a cliff. For example, engaging in unhealthy relationships, morphing into a person someone else wants us to be, chronic dieting, searching for applause in volunteer work, or seeking attention by wearing designer labels.

Pastor John Ortberg, author of *The Life You've Always Wanted*, says if we live with a nagging sense we aren't important or special enough; if we're envious of others' success; if we keep trying to impress important people; if we're worried someone might think ill of us, then we're probably approval addicts.[97]

I can't recall a time I didn't seek others approval. Truth be told, today, it surfaces its ugly head on my Facebook fan page. If you "like" my post I feel approved of, possibly even admired. If few people "like" my posts it's tempting to believe no one likes me. A fact of life is we won't always be liked by everyone. It has been said that ten percent of the people you interact with will not like you, no matter how nice you are.

The devil tempts us to seek the approval of man above seeking the approval of God. It is a bondage trap. Once we yield, we become blind to obeying God. We put up all kinds of defenses to justify our actions. Psychiatrist David Burns asserts it is not another person's compliment or approval which makes us feel good; rather it is *our belief* there is validity to the compliment.[98] John Ortberg wrote,

> We are not the passive victim of others' opinions.
> Their opinions are powerless until we validate them.
> No one's approval will affect us unless we grant
> it credibility and status. The same holds true for
> disapproval.[99]

The gaping hole in our soul gets bigger when we substitute another person's approval for God's. Ask yourself, "Who am I following?" and "To whom do I belong?"

Are You A Digital Junkie?

With just one click of a key on a smartphone, iPad®
or laptop, you can access a source of pleasure that is
so powerful it can create any number of addictions
now being linked to the cyberworld. –Drs. Archibald
Hart and Sylvia Frejd[100]

We have all been part of a gathering where at least one person is
constantly checking their phone, email, and/or texting. Aside from
it being annoying and rude, it is a cultural obsession. Technology has
become our master. Far too many people are controlled by it.

Using social media and networking sites, Internet role playing
games, chat room use, stock trading, gambling, and watching delayed
television programming, can become an addiction if not moderated.
Images are also important. Anyone setting up a social networking
profile is encouraged to put up a picture they believe represents
them.

Why the lure? We seek intimacy and relationship. According to
Parenting magazine, lonely mothers are the new Internet junkies.[101]
One study stated Facebook addicts are more likely to be women.[102]
Psychologist Linda Mintle stated that social media environments
provide the temptation to those hurting in a relationship because
it can boost one's ego, makes one feel appreciated, and satisfies
temptation. She said, "The rush associated with the attention feels
good and can become addictive."[103]

Secondly, we are addicted to the need to be entertained. Addictive
online entertainment products are rampant in our lives. Third, we
can hide our addiction behind a computer in the privacy of our own
rooms. Surfing pornography or gambling or pro-eating disorder
websites in secret merely enables the cancer of addiction to spread.

If you get anxious or depressed when you don't have access to
the online world, you may be suffering from Internet addiction.
Internet addiction is used to describe excessive online computer use

which begins to interfere with daily life. Most psychologists agree anyone can get a high from simply going online. In addition to it changing our behavior, manners, culture, and customs, there is a growing body of evidence which shows that Internet addiction can literally change, even damage, the brain.[104] The change is similar to the effects of cocaine addiction.[105]

Children are at the greatest risk. In 2012 when Hurricane Sandy hit the east coast leaving thousands of families without power for days, children and teenagers did not function well without their electrical gadgets. Most complained, "I cannot live another day without the Internet and my phone."

We all are immersed in the digital frontier. Therefore, we must understand, prevent, and respond to the dangers associated with the compulsion to be online. Here are some red flags:

1. *Relationships begin to suffer*: Face-to-face personal, marital, and working relationships are deteriorating.
2. *Time distortion*: A few minutes checking emails or Facebook messages quickly turns into hours without any awareness. Regular activities are falling at the wayside.
3. *Being secretive*: You feel guilt or shame about the amount of time spent online, so you attempt to hide the extent of your usage.
4. *Physical problems*: Hours spent in front of a computer screen may result in stiff necks and shoulders, back and head aches, distorted vision, carpel tunnel syndrome, and weight gain.[106]

Digital addicts have to learn to exercise strict discipline in their usage. Experts in addiction suggest taking one day a week or month and unplug for 24 hours (the biblical term is *fast*). Unplug from your digital life and plug into real life. It is not easy which is why you need to immediately plug into God. Plug into a Bible study or devotional.

It is important to your overall health to connect with God and real people in real face-to-face settings.

Reflect On It

Consider how deep your natural longing to be liked and admired runs. Do you place others above yourself and God? If you regularly say these things to yourself then most likely you do:

- It's wrong to think of my own needs. If I don't give, give, and give, I'm not a "good" Christian.
- Approval from everyone else is essential to my feeling of well-being and peace of mind.
- I know God doesn't want me to be happy until everyone else is happy.

Take every people-pleaser thought captive to Jesus. This means refusing to allow other people's approval or disapproval dominate your life. As John Ortberg says, "Resign from impression management… One of the wonderful gifts of this practice is to begin to see how silly the whole enterprise of impression management is."[107]

Day Two: Whom Shall We Fear?

Always be yourself because the people that matter don't mind, and the ones who mind, don't matter.
–Unknown

The first step in dealing with an out-of-balance need for approval is to understand fear. Proverbs 29:25 says, "Fear of man will prove to be a snare, but whoever trusts in the LORD is kept safe." Many of our motives come out of fear—fear of man.

The word *fear* has two meanings. "To be afraid of" is what we normally think of. The other meaning is "to have a reverential awe of." Biblically, "to fear the Lord" means we hold him up in reverence and with respect because he is so awesome and holy; therefore, we obey him.

To "fear man" can go either way. One, we can become so obsessed with another person we're in reverential awe of them, possibly codependent. This type of fear is idolatry. Or two, the person's opinion of us is so important we become afraid of the consequences of this person not approving of us. Therefore, we tend to turn a blind-eye to situations which are unacceptable because we fear conflict. This type of fear is debilitating.

These are both mindholds which must be broken. The way I see it, fear of man is a term which summarizes our real, deep-seated fear of:

- Failure, imperfection or being wrong
- Not being loved or needed
- Being left out, discounted or isolated
- Financial desolation

What I love about Jesus is his courage to say what everybody else doesn't have the guts to say. He didn't retreat from confrontation because he was afraid of messing up a relationship. He spoke truth in love.

If you look at Jesus's life and teachings in the Gospels, he didn't need to create an impression. His thought process and messages were completely God-directed. He never compromised. He feared no human being. Many people asked Jesus to do things for them, but he always considered what God desired, even if it meant disappointing people (see Mark 1:29-38, John 11:1-6).

When we passively accommodate others, we could very well miss God's best. Meditate on the prophet Isaiah's words:

> The LORD has given me a strong warning not to think like everyone else does....Make the LORD of Heaven's Armies holy in your life. He is the one you should fear.... He will keep you safe.... Look to God's

111

instructions and teachings! People who contradict his word are completely in the dark. (Isaiah 8:11,13-14, 20, NLT).

I Need to Feel I Am Worthy and Valuable

If the devil comes and whispers we're no good or bad, we shouldn't argue with him, instead, remind him, "Regardless of what you say about me, I must tell you how the Lord feels about me. He tells me that I am so valuable to him that he gave himself for me on the cross!" –Pastor and author A. W. Tozer[108]

What do you like *most* about yourself? On a piece of paper make a list of your positive qualities. On the other side, list what you like *least* about yourself? How many points did you list? Which side has more points? I suspect the side listing what you least like about yourself.

For decades my mantra read, "I'm not good enough as I am. There's something wrong with me. I'm a nobody." I built walls no one could penetrate because if you got in you'd see how unworthy I was. I believed the lie that in order to get others to like me I must imitate someone who, in my eyes, is an example of worthiness.

When I got my first beeper (yes, I'm dating myself), I made sure everyone could see it. *Surely they'll think I'm a doctor or an executive!* I wanted people to think "I'm a somebody." We all have the innate need to feel worthy and valuable. Yet, any time we try to be someone else, or let another person dictate who we should be, we are in bondage.

What gives us value? We are made in the image of God. David understood this. He praised God for his artistic handiwork: "Thank you for making me so wonderfully complex! Your workmanship is marvelous—how well I know it" (Psalm 139:14, NLT).

The only way to accept our innate value and break our negative mindset is by, one, seeing ourselves as God sees us; and two, by replacing false beliefs with biblical truth. In Christ we've been given everything we need to live authentically.

Reflect On It

1. In order to develop a more realistic view of other people's approval, write down a belief. Next to it write a more realistic view point. For example, "I believe I will be rejected if I go to this event." Realistic view point: "There will be people there who'll like me and others who won't care to know me. It's impractical to think everyone will like me."

2. Inventory the people in your life you fear. Then remind yourself that each person has their own list of people they fear.

3. Describe in your journal why you're so amazing and valuable. Praise God for making you so wonderful.

Day Three: Our Search for Significance

No one can make you feel inferior without your consent. −First Lady Eleanor Roosevelt[109]

When I show up at our church's youth group I admit I dress differently than when I attend a women's function. You could say I'm a chameleon, adapting to the social milieu around me. Do you tend to dress, speak, and act the way you do in order to fit in?

It is natural for us to transform ourselves into what a situation calls for. We don't even notice we're doing it. Sadly, chameleons don't know their real selves and how significant they really are. We have a choice: let society determine our worth, or let God.

The dictionary describes a chameleon-like person as "changeable, fickle, or inconstant."[110] When we take an honest look inside and figure out what fuels us to do what we do, we are better able to move forward. As we become more like Jesus we can stop changing color.

Our *self* is formed from our perceptions, attachments, life experiences, and the way we interpret those experiences. This begins in childhood and continues to develop through adolescence. We take this information and make value judgments about ourselves, which are positive or negative, correct or inaccurate.

Most children get the message they need to measure up to their parents or other influential adults' expectations in order to receive love and feel accepted by them. Therefore, they learn to attach their worth to what they do. In other words, they believe they can earn significance and worth.

If we're living to make sure others like us or love us, then we give them the power to determine our self-worth. Fixating on skinny models, in my case, exacerbated feelings of low self-worth. When we don't feel we look like or act like the expectations we've set, we will forever be disappointed, possibly depressed. In an effort to fix that cruddy feeling we'll try *doing* something acceptable.

Self-image is the collection of my beliefs and feelings I have about myself. Self-image asks: *Am I beautiful?* Many Christians have more of a negative self-image than a positive one. Far too many look at themselves and see inadequacy and ungodliness rather than their newness and beauty in Christ. This is actually pride because feelings of inferiority and inadequacy keep our attention focused on ourselves.

Self-esteem (or *self-confidence*) is having confidence and satisfaction in oneself. It is shaped by things such as academic and business successes or failures, divorce, trauma, love, and family of origin. It is based on what I do—my competency level; such as my strengths and weaknesses which I develop through personal worldly experiences. I believe I can or cannot do something I set my mind on. Self-esteem asks: *Am I good enough?* How high or low your self-esteem is depends on how you compare what you'd like to be with how you actually see yourself. We should desire *God-confidence:* the belief I can do anything God gives me to do.

Self-hate is an unconscious feeling that I am lower, contaminated, and defiled compared to other human beings. Self-haters degrade and demean themselves because they feel they can't meet the expectations of everybody else around them. They tend to flatter others to get their approval and feel their needs are not important. They cannot love someone else in a healthy way because they don't love themselves.

We must not hate ourselves because of our faults; we must love ourselves in spite of them. We can despise our sin but not ourselves. The Bible teaches us that our lives, including our feelings, opinions, desires, and needs are not less valuable or important than anyone else. It also teaches we're not more valuable or important either. Henri Nouwen, in his book *The Road to Daybreak,* reminds us of what God sees when he looks at us:

> I am your God...I see all of your actions. And I love you because you are beautiful, made in my own image...Do not judge yourself. Do not condemn yourself. Do not reject yourself...Come, come, let me wipe your tears, and let my mouth say...I love you, I love you, I love you.[111]

Self-worth is based on identity. Positive self-worth declares, "I am created in the image of God, I belong to him, and my identity and worth is in Jesus Christ." Our identity is totally separate from what we've done and what has happened to us. It is separate from the guilt, the shame, and all the other defense mechanisms which have defined us.

Understanding this can increase feelings of value and self-worthiness. It comes as we develop an intimate relationship with God. When the apostle John wrote the book of John he referred three times to himself as "the disciple whom Jesus loved" (see John 20:2; 21:7; 21:20). John wasn't a narcissist. He had high self-worth.

The good news is we can change our perceptions of our self. A person with high self-worth believes,

- I am a forgiven, adopted, chosen child of God.
- I am good, valuable, and beautiful because I'm made in God's image.
- God only made one of me. I am God's personal workmanship; therefore, I embrace my individuality.
- I am somebody worth knowing. You'd like me.

David also had high self-worth. Take his words and personalize them as I did:

> How precious it is, Lord, to realize you are thinking about *me* [Kimberly] constantly! I can't even count how many times a day your thoughts turn toward *me* [Kimberly]. And when I waken in the morning, you are still thinking of *me* [Kimberly]!" (Psalm 139:17-18, TLB, *my personalization*)

Never forget that your birth was not a mistake. Your parents may not have planned to have you, but God desired to create you! He made this exciting declaration, "Can a mother forget the baby at her breast and have no compassion on the child she has borne? Though she may forget, I will not forget you! See, I have engraved you on the palms of my hands" (Isaiah 49:15-16).

Commit to a process of self-acceptance. Jesus said you will be blessed when you're content with who you are (see Matthew 5:5). *Pray:* "Lord, today let me accept myself as a beautiful person, inside and out. I make mistakes, but I'm not a mistake!"

Identity Formation

> Somebody stole my identity, but I'm not worried. She's
> probably better at being me than I was. –Cartoonist
> Randy Glasbergen[112]

"Hello, my name is…. I work as a…. I am a…." Our society tells us that our identities are wrapped in what we do, that our role or job defines who we are. There are two dangers in this thinking. One, someday you will fail at what you do. Then who are you? Two, who you truly are, God's child, at some point will conflict with what you do. Then what do you do?

God described himself as, "I Am Who I Am" (see Exodus 3:14). In other words, I'm me, myself and I. Do you know who you are?

If you've been going to church and/or studying the Bible for any length of time, no doubt you've heard it said your "new identity is in Christ." What exactly is *identity*? My identity is the constant and reliable sense of who I am and what I stand for in this world. "I am what I think I am." In the past my sense of self was grossly distorted. I was my weight. In the sorority the girls associated me with an eating disorder which became my identity.

The day Jesus walked into my messed up life and I committed in faith to follow him, my identity changed. When a person is born-again a remarkable thing happens: the new believer is joined to Jesus Christ in an unbreakable spiritual union and bond. Our identity changes because we are now part of him, he is part of us, and we are adopted into his family.

God took my old identity—all my guilty acts and thoughts, and placed them on Jesus. On that day, the sign I wore around my neck, "Contaminated Loser," was replaced with "Beloved, precious, and valuable." What is engraved on your sign? Destroy it. It has been replaced with "Beloved, precious, and valuable." This is your identity.

We all experience tension between our false identity, or false self, and our real, true self. The *false self* is the constructed, patchwork image we've created to deal with our world. It is defensive, self-protective, and selfish, which makes intimacy with God and others difficult. The *real self* is the image of God within us, the part of us made in his likeness. This is the basis of our true identity. When I believe I am stamped in God's image I can enjoy life.

We don't have to live as a tormented false self. Our identity is fluid, not fixed. God showed me through his Word that my personal areas of bondage are not my identity. How could they be as the daughter of the Most High God?

As a new person in Jesus Christ everything is different—the way I see myself, the way I see you. I am the person I want to be. As he fills my soul with his personality I know that old things, including past traumas and emotional hurts, have passed away (see 2 Corinthians 5:17). That old person died and a new one has been spiritually born. The enemy has been disarmed, along with the power of his condemning lies and shameful words.

You may have never lived as your real, authentic self since most people are trying to *be* what their culture values. A question we must wrestle with is, "Do I fear discovering my real self?" If I've created in my mind an image of the ideal self, and I find out I don't match that image, then no doubt, I'll feel angst. Be assured that God will guide you gently through this part of the self-examination process.

Our identity reflects the image of the triune God. How do we define *the image of God*? We take the biblical account of creation and then look for the same attributes in mankind. The creation account in Genesis 1 and 2 describes God's love for beauty, reason and order. Scripture reveals God is creative; he speaks, commands and rules, and has the capacity for relationship. He embraces his created through fellowship and love. These are all attributes God shares with his human creations. The real self has the ability to think abstractly, reason, create, and direct itself towards that which it knows is good, right, and beautiful.

Today I am at peace with my real self (most of the time). I can follow the plan and life goals the Lord has laid out for me. I state my opinion without feeling I have to agree with the other person, or feel I'm in competition with them. I can set boundaries. I don't need substances to deaden the pain. I know what I like and what I don't like. I have a godly, functioning partnership with my husband. What about you?

Dare to be yourself! Submit to God, reject your false self, and unveil the image of your heavenly Father. *Pray*: "Lord God, tear off my mask so my true self is exposed. Help me to change my current identity to that of your precious daughter designed to be and to do what you have created me to do. In Jesus's name. Amen."

Reflect On It

Have you formed your identity around your problem, a relationship, an addiction, diet, or disease? Explain.

Day Four: I Need to Feel I Belong

> …We belong to the Lord. –Paul, speaking in Romans
> 14:8, NLT

Teased, laughed at, put down, lied about. "You do not belong" sums up a chunk of my childhood. I worked vigorously trying to conform to the way I thought others wanted me to be. The core of approval addiction reveals our inherent need to feel we belong—to God, to another person, to a family, to a group and community.

All you have to do is look at the number of social networking sites to see we're creatures who feel a need to belong. Is this the reason we check our cell phones every couple of minutes? It began with God's first human creation, Adam. He needed a mate to belong to.

When we choose to love God and receive Jesus Christ as our Savior, he adopts us into his family. The blessing of salvation is we are connected to Jesus Christ in the closest possible way. We belong to the family of God and are accepted just as we are—faults and all. As Christians we also belong to the body of Christ. We are part of "the church," which has nothing to do with denominations.

Love That Will Never Let You Go

> My choice is you, God, first and only. And now I find
> I'm your choice! You set me up with a house and yard.
> And then you made me your heir! –David, speaking
> in Psalm 16:5-6, *The Message*

In the children's book, *The Red Thread: An Adoption Fairy Tale,* the king and queen both feel a strange pain that worsens every day. Then a peddler's magic spectacles reveal a red thread pulling at each of their hearts. The king and queen know they must follow the thread. They follow its loose end for days, crossing a sea, until they reach a small village in a foreign land. There they find a gurgling, smiling baby. A wise old villager tells them, "This baby belongs to you."

Adoption, by its very nature, is an act of free kindness to the adoptee. If you adopt a child you do so because you choose to, not because you are bound to. Similarly, God adopts us because he chooses to. Our adoption is a picture of the greatness of God's grace. When I grasp I've been adopted, specifically chosen, am unconditionally loved, I feel special.

One pastor said, "God loves you so much he can't keep his eyes off you. If he had a wallet he'd carry your picture in it." When God bragged about his children in biblical times he did so by showing us their pictures and telling their stories. Like a proud papa, God takes out his wallet and says this about you, "Do you want to see the most beautiful child? Look! This is [*your name*]—the delight of my life!"

Adoption is a family idea. God takes us into his family. He establishes us as his children and heirs. Closeness, generosity, and love are the very heart of the relationship. This is no fairy tale. It is a hard, solid fact founded upon God's grace. God has taken us from the gutters and brought us into his own home as his own daughters.

If you've ever adopted a child you recognize you must work to win the child's affection. You seek to be loved by the child. So it is with God. He goes out of his way to make his children feel his love for them. As members of his family, he wants us to recognize our privilege and security.

A good father, God knows what we need before we ask. He gives us bread each day. He forgives us and delivers us from the evil one. He assures us that we're not only loved and are valuable, but destined for a special purpose. We also receive correction because we are under royal training!

> For he [God] chose us in him before the creation of the world to be holy and blameless in his sight. In love he predestined us to be adopted as his sons [his daughters] through Jesus Christ, in accordance with his pleasure and will." (Ephesians 1:4-5; 11)

This is God's love-promise. Before my birth, and before I was even a Christian, God already chose and destined me to become part of his family someday. This is what he wanted and desired to do (see Psalm 139:16). Rejoice in your legacy!

There comes a point when we come to the end of ourselves. God loves you and is waiting for you to say the words, "Papa, I need your love and gracious fatherly care. I want to claim my royal inheritance and status as your daughter. Enable me to live as your beloved child—one who knows without a shadow of a doubt that I belong to you."

I Need to Feel I Have a Purpose

> We can make our plans, but the LORD determines
> our steps. –Proverbs 16:9, NLT

Every person is designed to make a difference. Deep down, we each want to know that our lives have value. I realized the events of my life—the good, the bad and the ugly, had prepared me for the next step in moving towards God's call for my life.

Every person has a divinely ordained purpose. When our Creator designed the universe, he had you and me in mind already. He had already factored in our specific gifts and talents, and he orchestrated events to nurture those abilities.

While God gives us this gift of purpose he grants us the freedom to choose whether or not we want to pursue his divine plan. If we choose to ignore it there's a price to pay. I eventually chose to follow his plan. I wanted every person struggling with disordered eating and addiction to know an abundant free life in Christ is available. Before I could do that I needed more knowledge about God and the right skills. I enrolled in seminary, began diligently studying the Bible, and focused on pastoral care to women.

During this time God exposed other unresolved areas in my life which needed to be healed. Simultaneously, I rolled my sleeves up and began applying my education to ministry work as a pastoral counselor and teacher. Then I felt the tug to work on the mechanics of public speaking and writing. The capstone of this ministry, Olive Branch Outreach, is to teach and encourage others what God has taught and revealed to me.

All this to say: God doesn't waste anything. He is able to bring beauty out of dust and ashes in every person's life. I am an exhibit of God's craftsmanship and grace. My reward is knowing I've been able to help you.

Reflect On It

- What does God mean when he says, "I will be your Father, and you will be my sons and daughters" (2 Corinthians 6:18, NLT)?
- Do you truly own your real identity and destiny? Why or why not?
- When do you feel most doubtful that you are God's adopted child?

Day Five:
I Need to Feel I am Spiritually Secure

> Two blind men were sitting by the roadside, and when they heard that Jesus was going by, they shouted, "Lord, Son of David, have mercy on us!" Jesus stopped and called them. "What do you want me to do for you?" he asked. (Matthew 20:30–32)

This seems like a crazy question. Naturally they answered, "Lord, we want our sight" (Matthew 20:33). *Lord, we want out of the dungeon. We want freedom!* These blind men personally entrusted themselves to Christ for their healing. Jesus showed them favor, "Jesus had compassion on them and touched their eyes. Immediately they received their sight and followed him" (Matthew 20:34). He told one of the men, "Receive your sight; your faith has healed you" (Luke 18:42). These men passed out of darkness and into the light.

Imagine being the blind man whose first sight was the smiling face of the Healer. Think of looking into the face of Christ himself. They received healing grace through their faith. God calls every person to personally trust in his Son Jesus Christ. These blind men believed and called directly to Jesus for their salvation. When they did Jesus freed them from their personal captivity, and they became spiritually alive. Faith in Jesus Christ is saving faith.

Every person who does this is saved. Until we come to Christ, we're like spiritual zombies—physically alive, but spiritually dead. Until we're reborn by God's Spirit, we cannot hear God's voice nor understand spiritual truth (see Ephesians 2). You must have a personal relationship with Jesus Christ to discover God's divine plan for your life.

Jesus said, "No one can come to the Father except through me" (John 14:6, NLT). The only way to the Father is to profess your belief in Jesus Christ, the Son of God, who died on the cross and rose three days later. In other words, you must be *born-again* and *saved*.

Saved from what? Christians believe that our sin has separated us from God and the consequence of sin is death (see Romans 6:23). Biblical salvation refers to our release from the consequences of sin and, therefore, involves the removal of sin. We are saved from eternal death, slavery, and God's wrath.[113]

If you desire this gift pray*:* "Dear Lord God, I do believe Jesus is your Son and he died on the cross to pay for my sin. Forgive my sin and make me part of your family. I acknowledge I've been living separated from you. I now pledge to turn from going my own way. Thank you for the gift of grace and eternal life, and for your Holy Spirit who has now come to live in me. In Jesus's name, Amen."

If you prayed this prayer God's healing grace has joined you to Christ in a vital, unbreakable, spiritual union. Scripture says, "Through Christ we can approach God and stand in his favor" (Romans 5:2, GW). In God's eyes you are now righteous—perfect before him. You have been forgiven for every past, present, and future sin (see Isaiah 6:7). The chains of your past and compulsive behaviors are broken! *You have a new life ahead of you.*

The news keeps getting better: your faith in Christ has changed your status dramatically. God has given you his name. You belong in a way you never did before. Pack your bags—you're moving to Grace Land! The Bible declares, "You are no longer a slave but God's own child…his heir" (Galatians 4:7, NLT). You are a princess!

Your Father is the great king (see Ephesians 2:6). And your position is permanently guaranteed. This is the highest status you'll ever attain.

This is a free gift of grace—a picture of God showering us guilty sinners with immeasurable love, mercy, and kindness. Now we respond to our new Father with loving faithfulness.

Reflect On It

What a God we have! And how fortunate we are to have him, this Father of our Master Jesus! Because Jesus was raised from the dead, we've been given a brand-new life and have everything to live for, including a future in heaven—and the future starts now! (1 Peter 1:3-4, MSG)

In your journal finish this thought. "These words make me want to ..."

Week Seven

Personal Pain Killers
Addicted to Pain, Stress, and Substances

Day One: Attached to Emotional Pain

"Why would I be addicted to negative emotions?"
you ask. Because pain and negative emotions activate
the reward centers of the brain, causing unconscious
addiction to those negative emotions." –Dr. Ali
Binazir[114]

Have you ever felt like you may not really want to change or recover? Sounds like a dumb question, but it's not. Some people are addicted to pain. We've all heard of being addicted to pain medication, but physical and emotional suffering? Emotional pain can become an addiction.

Dr. David Powlison warns against *hurt hunting*: the endless obsession with one's sorrows, sufferings, and disappointments.[115] A negative feeling, such as anger, guilt, worry, grief, fear, or depression, can become so entrenched and habitual that a person cannot live without it, leading to a paralysis of faith. There are physical as well as mental reasons for *emotional pain addiction* (also called *emotional dependency*). When a person is continuously stressed by emotional pain, there are subtle changes in the body which create a dependency on stress-related circumstances.

Mental health experts say changing habitual patterns of pain can be as difficult as giving up an addictive substance. The emotional pain addict unconsciously seeks out situations that are sure to result in pain.[116] Some people are addicted to pain because of the attention they receive. And I know others who use it as an excuse for a cleaning crew to come in once a month. *Why get well?*

Many Christians believe, "I'll always be a sinner—depraved. I'll be that way until I die." This can be an obsessive mindset. Fully expecting to sin, to be "bad," the person perpetuates the cycle of confession, repentance and forgiveness. She constantly feels shame and guilt for continually messing up. For this person, the anguish associated with this mindset never ends. It is the equivalent of spiritually and mentally flogging oneself.

Addiction to Self-Harm

Today, there are only a few things no one likes talking about. Self-harm is on the list. Daily millions of adults and adolescents harm and mutilate themselves. Tanya cut herself over two hundred times within the last year. She hates what she does to herself. She tries to stop, but can't.

Self-harm (also called *self-injury, self-abuse, or self-mutilation*) is an attempt to deliberately hurt one's own body in order to cope with, or block out, or release built up feelings and emotions. Methods include cutting with razors, glass, knives, and nails; picking at skin, re-opening wounds, hair pulling, head banging, eyeball pressing, bone breaking, and biting. It can be an episodic behavior or a compulsive addictive behavior.

Self-harm is an odd thing: the act of harming oneself creates pain but at the same time the person feels a release of pain. It has a calming effect. A person can become addicted to the euphoric endorphins which are released. The brain tricks her into believing self-harm is comforting. This is one way a person tries to cope and give a voice to the pain of overwhelming emotions, intense pressure, or upsetting relationship problems.

For some who have been abused it is their way of reenacting the abuse which oddly gives them a sense of being in control. It is a way to express strong feelings of rage, sorrow, rejection, desperation, longing, or emptiness. Self-harm is sometimes, but not always, associated with depression, bipolar disorder, eating disorders, drug or alcohol abuse, obsessive thinking, or compulsive behaviors.

After our family moved to London, for a while I compulsively pulled out some of my hair. When we moved back to America I began biting my nails. Apparently, I sought relief from the stress of each move. These kinds of compulsions become difficult to eliminate because they are rewarding to the brain. Although not as invasive or destructive as most self-harm techniques, bad habits such as nail biting may be a red flag an issue needs to be addressed.

If you self-harm, I urge you to do the following:

Tell someone. The first step is often the hardest—admitting to or talking about the behavior. After opening up about it, most feel a great sense of relief. Choose a person you trust, such as a parent, counselor, teacher, pastor, coach, or doctor. If it is too difficult to bring up the topic in person, write a note or send an email.

Identify the trouble which is triggering the behavior. It may be difficult to do this on your own. Pray and ask God to help you pinpoint what feelings or situations are causing you to self-harm. Is it anger? The pressure to be perfect? Relationship trouble? A painful loss or trauma? Malicious criticism or abuse? This is where a mental health professional can be helpful.

Ask for help. Jesus and a network of professionals stand waiting to help you heal.

Addiction to Stress, Worry, and Chaos

Worry is a cycle of inefficient thoughts whirling around a center of fear. –Nazi Holocaust survivor Corrie Ten Boom[117]

The image of the harried overachiever is pervasive in today's stressful society. Consider whether you are addicted to stress, worry, or chaos:

- Do you thrive on living life in the fast lane?
- Are you the employee who obsessively meets and surpasses goals? Or, the one who compulsively stays ahead of the pack and works on weekends and vacations?
- Are you the mom who is fanatical about moving her children ahead, driving them around from event to event seven days a week?

There are also women who are addicted to chaos. They love to be in the middle of turmoil. If there isn't any chaos, they'll create it. I call them drama queens. Creating conflict with family, friends, people in the church, co-workers, and neighbors, provides a level of excitement, a high. The relationship between drug addiction and stress addiction is very real according to psychiatrist Joel Elkes. He said, "Risk-taking and extreme stress produces a pleasurable arousal, followed by a feeling of release."[118]

The term *stress* refers to processes involving perception, appraisal, and response to harmful, threatening, or challenging events or stimuli.[119] Stress is usually associated with something harmful, upsetting, or disturbing to our psychological equilibrium. Yet, it also occurs when we're challenged, excited, or happy. Stress is a byproduct of our illusion of control. The presence of stress in our lives has become so familiar and tolerated we find we are actually uncomfortable without it.

129

Often feelings of stress, worry, and chaos come out of fear. Pray about your personal fears. Do you fear losing control, or being hurt, or rejected, or of disappointing people, or of facing your past, or achieving success? Give all your anxieties and pain to God. You can be confident that you are safe with him. [We will examine fear in Week Eleven].

Reflect On It

- What aspects of stress in your life might you be attached to?
- Do you derive pleasure from strife or anger or violence? If yes, explain.

Day Two: To Get Well…or Not

I am the LORD, who heals you. —God, speaking in
Exodus 15:26

Life. We've each got our own personal challenges. It is normal to get frustrated, impatient, resentful, and bitter. We worry about finances and our marriages. We grieve over losses and agonize over rebellious children. We face uncertainty. We carry the baggage of abuse.

We get so accustomed to the familiar toxic thoughts and feelings that we fail to recognize an abiding sickness which resides within our own souls. One day Jesus came across a lame man around the pool. He asked him, "Do you want to get well?"(John 5:6).

What did this man deeply desire? Wellness would mean a significant life change. Could he handle those changes? Would he be willing to learn how to live differently? After all, he'd no longer be eligible to beg for his provisions. He'd have to find work.

The invalid responded by making excuses, which is human nature. Many of us get comfortable in our pit. We really don't want to get out of it. Jesus commands the man, "Get up! Pick up your mat and walk" (John 5:8) Notice the exclamation point. At once the man was cured. He picked up his mat and walked. With Jesus's command came enablement. He doesn't ask us to do something which is impossible without enabling us to do it.

God has given each of us a powerful gift—our freedom to choose. He wants every one of his children to be whole and happy—to choose life. When we look at what we've lost then God's guidance is easier to accept. The Bible declares, "Your old life is dead. Your new life, which is your *real* life—even though invisible to spectators—is with Christ in God. He is your life" (Colossians 3:3, MSG).

Later Jesus came across this man at the temple. He said something interesting. "See, you are well again. Stop sinning or something worse may happen to you" (John 5:14).

Does this mean sickness and sin are linked together? I don't believe so. In those days sickness was often associated with punishment for sin, and still is in some Christian circles. Sickness is not invariably linked to sin, though it may be a consequence. For example, if a person abuses alcohol it is not uncommon to have medical problems with the liver. A compulsive overeater risks developing diabetes.

It appears that in the case of this lame man his physical condition was a result of sin. This is a reminder that physical healing in itself is not a guarantee of spiritual healing. After being freed from my affliction of bingeing and purging I did not live a godlier life because I wasn't ready to give my pain to God.

Ask God, "Am I ready to give this pain to you?" God continually invites us to move forward. We can accept or decline his offer. If we accept, his grace will enable us to make life changes and to continue to nurture those changes.

Pray as David did, "Finish what you started in me, God. Your love is eternal—don't quit on me now" (Psalm 138:8, MSG).

Day Three: Drunk and Stupid

Society's Myth: If I'm feeling anxious or am in pain the only solution is to dull it with a substance.

Friday night…Barney's Bar & Grill…downtown Cedar Rapids… that's where you'd find me. Barney's was my *Cheers;* a place where I belonged; a place where I could sing and laugh; a place where I could get smashed and not be judged by other drunks.

On this particular night a parental figure, concerned for my safety, gave me twenty dollars and told me to take a cab home. He made me promise. *Of course I will!* Take one guess where the money went.

The lights flickered on and off to the sound of, "We're closing. Time to go!" I staggered to my car, a brand new Olds Cutlass which belonged to my employer. Unfortunately, unlike many other Friday nights, I located the car, got in, started the engine, and aimed for home.

A light turned red. I failed to stop. *Crunch! Bang!* I hit the truck in front of me. A man in his thirties emerged and appeared fine. His bumper took the brunt of the impact. However, the entire front end of my new company car was damaged extensively.

A police officer arrived on the scene…and he wasn't in a pleasant mood. He had come from another alcohol related accident which involved a fatality. Sobbing, I pleaded, "I live only two blocks away. You can take me home. …Please!" He didn't accommodate my request.

I went through the usual booking process and was then led to my cell for the night. I cried myself to sleep. When I woke in the morning I met two young women in the next cell who also were charged with DUI. They placated my guilt and shame for the moment. Then the time came to stroll next door for arraignment. Hand cuffed and completely humiliated, I conformed to the rules so I'd be released as quickly as possible.

A first time offender, I was riddled with guilt and anxiety—guilt about what had happened and anxiety about my future. Trouble had only begun. A whole assemblage of stressors waited in line ready to wreak havoc.

As I look back to the countless times I drove drunk, I am truly blessed I never killed or severely hurt anyone. God had been very gracious. There is no such thing as karma, luck, or coincidence in the Christian life. If God is in control of everything, then what appears to be karma, luck, or coincidence is really a divine appointment made by God. It is no accident that today I teach and minister to women in a federal prison.

My soul-hole was deep and stressed out. Because I chose not to fill it with Almighty God, I continued to live in the dark and in bondage. I drank in a futile attempt to self-medicate. Over the years friends called me on my bad behavior. My response, "I was drunk." In other words, *I'm not accountable for my actions!* Addiction alters the brain chemistry affecting the process of thought and decision making. Denial, minimization, and justification are common.

There was no joy, no hope; only fear and self-condemnation. The shame kept feeding every destructive behavior: the bulimia, drunkenness, and promiscuity, which continued to feed the shame, fueling a never-ending cycle over which I had no control. Asking for help meant admitting I failed. People would see me as a phony. It felt safer to wear a mask of secrecy and deception.

The apostle John said, "People who do what is wrong hate the light and don't come to the light. They don't want their actions to be exposed" (John 3:20, GW).

Long term recovery is possible with our great Physician. After surgically repairing my heart and mind, I eventually healed after twenty years of substance abuse (to alcohol, laxatives, diet, caffeine pills). Never give up, "For nothing is impossible with God" (Luke 1:37).

Temptation and Disgrace

Facing temptation is unavoidable. Even Noah, a God-fearing man, wasn't immune. We find in Genesis 9:20-25, Noah, the man who walked with God and did all he commanded, laid drunk and uncovered in his tent.

After the account of the Flood and the divine promise given through a rainbow, why did the author include a story of drunken stupor, sexual immodesty, family shame, and a curse? Why didn't the writer take a red pencil and "x" it out. What I know is, "All Scripture is God-breathed and useful for teaching, rebuking, correcting and training in righteousness, so that the man of God may be thoroughly equipped for every good work" (2 Timothy 3:16-17). There must be a moral and spiritual lesson for us.

In this story we're reminded of mankind's heart condition toward dysfunction. God saved Noah and his family, but salvation is not the same as transformation. Believers still fall into sin. We are not guaranteed of instant holiness when we say yes to Jesus Christ. It is the beginning of a journey into spiritual growth and godliness called *sanctification*.

Noah reminds us that we're all sinners and mortal. Growing certainly involves an obedient response. But the Christian life isn't about God barking orders from on high and we dutifully obey...or else. Rather, we choose to be obedient as our hearts and minds are changed by his grace.

Another reason for including the text might have been to highlight the consequences to Noah's behavior. Noah's grandson, Ham, and his descendants are cursed for his actions. As my life story illustrates, there are always consequences to destructive actions.

We should understand our roots. Some of us inherited our troubles.

Alcoholism frequently recurs in one's children despite evidence that addictive behavior is not inherited. Children of alcoholics, for example, often become alcoholics because their parents modeled addictive behavior. "Monkey see, monkey do." Many substance and behavioral addictions are passed on from generation to generation. It will continue until the behavior is stopped permanently.

God is the only one "who forgives all your sins and heals all your diseases, who redeems your life from the pit and crowns you with love and compassion, who satisfies your desires with good things" (Psalm 103:3-5).

Reflect On It

- Is the generational sin of substance abuse flowing rampant through your family tree? If yes, ask God to give you the power to break the curse of addiction so you do not pass it on to your children.
- Name one thing you can do immediately to begin stopping the poison.

Day Four: The Lies We Tell Ourselves

> The perpetual delusion of humanity is thinking we are better off hiding than confessing, avoiding rather than facing, clinging to our sickness instead of taking the remedy that's freely given and readily available.
> –Pastor Mark Buchanan[120]

I am always surprised when perceptive people can't seem to relate to the out-of-control aspect of someone else's addictive behavior. I suppose I'm dumbfounded because they are usually floundering in their own addiction.

According to Dr. Les Carter, the number one trait that hinders individuals from making personal improvements is denial. He wrote,

"We each hate feeling like we are being exposed as inadequate, and none of us likes having to eat humble pie. So in self-protection, it seems easier to simply say our problem does not exist."[121]

I recall justifying my actions: "I'm just a social drinker," "I don't drink and binge to relieve anxiety like other addicts. I'm simply having fun," "My choices don't hurt anyone. I can quit anytime." But I couldn't stop. I didn't pass the test to live one week without my attachments.

Addiction and delusion go hand in hand and breed denial. Perhaps you've said, "My (issue) isn't so bad, especially compared to...." The problem with this thinking is when the issue becomes observable, then it may be at a crisis level or a shameful situation.

Denial is a refusal to acknowledge what is really going on—either within us or in front of us. At the core, denial is a carefully crafted lie we tell ourselves and others hoping the real truth won't be discovered. It is an involuntary reaction to protect oneself. Even family members participate as codependents and enablers. The truth is, denial prevents healing from the original pain. Therefore, *discovering the life God intended for us cannot happen until denial is uncovered, acknowledged, and dealt with.*

Even though evidence had been mounting against my actions, I worked to keep the truth out of my awareness sphere. My imagination reduced the consequences of my actions. I think I knew an addiction existed, but I compartmentalized the reality and seriousness of it. Each experience got shoved into the attic of my unconscious mind (called *repression*). When one is in this state of mind it seems no amount of prayer or meditation or Bible reading can replace the toxic thoughts and behavior.

What's the big deal? If this is the response to a "big deal" situation then the person most likely is in denial. In this society we've become masters of pretending, denying, hiding, or twisting the facts to create a particular impression. A popular acronym for DENIAL is:

D = don't; E = even; N = notice; I = I; A = am; L = lying.

Most professionals agree: denial is the unintentional failure to deal with pain. Ask any kid—if they know punishment is inevitable they are tempted to lie to avoid pain. It is not necessarily all bad because it can be a coping skill which initially numbs us to changes we don't wish to acknowledge due to circumstances such as a loss or death or grave disappointment. It can be a buffer to the psyche. In these kinds of cases, denial is usually the first stage of the grieving process.

While we all use denial to a certain extent to cope with pain, we never do so without risk. It tends to catch up with us when we fail to accept the truth. Denial is a powerful tool the enemy uses to convince us we have control of our lives. Scripture says, "Satan himself masquerades as an angel of light" (2 Corinthians 11:14).

We find it in the workplace: "My job is safe"; in schools: "It's the teacher's fault I got an F"; and most often, in relationships: "The reason he hurts me is I don't show him the respect he deserves." We hang onto the misbeliefs in an effort to soothe the inner anguish. It allows us to avoid coming to terms with what's really going on.

Jesus said, "Why do you look at the speck of sawdust in your brother's eye and pay no attention to the plank in your own eye?" (Luke 6:41) *The Message* paraphrase reads, "It's easy to see a smudge on your neighbor's face and be oblivious to the ugly sneer on your own."

Never underestimate denial's ability to cloud your vision. Remember, facts don't cease to exist because they're ignored. Take responsibility and say, "I have an issue. I want to deal with it now." Confess to God. Then tell one safe person. Ask the person if she or he would be an accountability and prayer partner. It is essential to walk in the light of a Christian community.

Break Free from Delusion and Denial

For years my tagline read, "Tomorrow, tomorrow...I'll change tomorrow." The day came when I knew I could no longer keep hiding and lying. There is one person we can't hide anything from—God. Scripture says,

> For the word of God is living and active. Sharper than any double-edged sword, it penetrates even to dividing soul and spirit, joints and marrow; it judges the thoughts and attitudes of the heart. Nothing in all creation is hidden from God's sight. Everything is uncovered and laid bare before the eyes of him to whom we must give account. (Hebrews 4:12-13)

We cannot deny or justify or rationalize when we come face to face with Almighty God. These verses are here to give us hope. His Word is like a sharp sword cutting its way through our behaviors. It penetrates deeply into the human heart and mind. It can scrutinize our unspoken thoughts and hidden conceptions. It reaches deep down where no other voice can be heard. It goes to the inmost recesses of our spiritual being and brings the subconscious motives to light.

Denial is not only emotional. It has spiritual roots because it breeds in the dark recesses of the soul. Jeremiah the prophet describes a heart encapsulated by denial, "The heart is deceitful above all things and beyond cure." In the next verse God states, "I the LORD search the heart and examine the mind..." (Jeremiah 17:9-10).

God knows how much we need his Word. He probes more deeply than man. He knows our rebellious and stubborn hearts inside out. Everything is exposed. He sees deep into our pain. See how ridiculous it is when we hide and deny and rationalize? How nauseating our hypocrisy must seem to him. Our part now is to hear, believe, obey, and share his Word of abundant life.

Reflect On It

The first step out of any kind of denial is to see truth.

*   In your heart, what do you believe God is asking you to look at and discern?
*   What specific areas of denial does God need to change or touch in your life?

Day Five: Face the Truth

> Then you will know the truth, and the truth will set
> you free. –Jesus, speaking in John 8:32

We can't always get away with, "It's not my fault," or "The devil made me do it!" I alone am accountable for what I do. Based on my own life, and working as a pastoral counselor, I recognize there are five common denials which must be acknowledged, accepted, and dressed with action and truth.

1. *It's not as bad as it looks.* Denial makes a bad or intolerable situation look good, even hopeful. When we admit powerlessness and our need for God over whatever has control over us, our lives begin to become manageable.
2. *It's not me. It's him!* If my husband is addicted to pornography, I'm affected too. The key to healing is to start expressing our feelings. We can start by writing and/or verbally confiding in someone we trust. Joining a support group such as Al-Anon is another way to unload the poison.
3. *I caused this to happen.* "I work long hours and so my husband plays video games in my absence. It's my fault he's addicted to them now." It is common for one person to work to get the other to take full responsibility. As long as that person carries the burden the other won't feel remorse or repent.
4. *I can fix this on my own. I don't need outside help.* In the 1960s

Paul Simon made these words famous: "I am a rock, I am an island. And a rock feels no pain; and an island never cries." Withdrawing is detrimental to our personal growth because it is in relating to others that we grow the most. Moving out of isolation begins with our relationship with God. We learn to trust him first. Only then can we venture out to trust people. With God's guidance, anyone can get off their island.

5. *He makes me do this.* We can't really say, for example, that someone made us angry. They did not inject anger into our hearts. It came from within us, lying latent all along. A person's words or actions motivate our anger, and therefore we react in a negative way (see Matthew 15:19). But the person's not responsible for our angry actions.

Each person has a choice to go one of two ways: we can either deny our problems and become easy prey for the enemy. Or, we can return to what provides an anchor for the soul—God and the church. When our desire is to please God we feel compelled to relinquish all oppressive burdens to him.

David regularly pleaded with God. "Show me your ways, O Lord, teach me your paths; guide me in your truth and teach me, for you are God my Savior. My hope is in you all day long" (Psalm 25:4-5). Like David, we appeal to God, "I want to be the person you want me to be. Help me replace the lies I've believed with truth. Help me heal. I want to fulfill the plan you have for my life."

If you fall down, thank God he will forgive you repeatedly. But I would not use God's mercy and grace as an excuse to keep repeating the behavior.

Reflect On It

- Name at least one denial you speak to yourself regularly.
- Then answer: How can I react differently? How can I bring Christ into my life and situations?

Week Eight
The Battle for Control
Identifying Our Conflict Zones

Day One: Lord, Why Can't I Just Stop?

> ...for the battle is the LORD's. –David, speaking in
> 1 Samuel 17:47

For years I felt defeated because I sensed my struggles were a sign of weakness, and a lack of faith and trust in God. As Aristotle said, "We are what we repeatedly do." What I learned liberated me. I hope it does you.

When we become Christians, I wish I could say life on earth is like living in the Garden of Eden. Temptations and bad habits appear and disappear and reappear. There are periodic walks through the valley of darkness...there is tension. Paul describes it as a war, a battle for control.

We can expect conflict to arise in three areas of our lives:

1. *The world*: A societal system of ungodly and unhealthy sets of values and morals.
2. *The spiritual realm*: Unseen warfare with Satan and his demons.
3. *Within ourselves:* Our carnal nature or sinful flesh.

Our minds and hearts are the battleground where conflict with these enemies are either won or lost. It can be very hard to discern when our struggles are a result of the devil's intervention, us acting in our flesh, environmental and cultural pressures, or even abnormal brain physiology or hormonal changes.

These three negative influences commonly work together to lead us away from God. Most often we aren't even aware this is happening. We go about our business believing all is fine, but deep inside something doesn't feel quite right.

Conflict with the World

If I walk with the world, I can't walk with God.
–Evangelist D. L. Moody[122]

Ever wonder what artifacts archeologists will dig up after we're gone? Barbie dolls, Super Bowl rings, Bibles in hundreds of different translations, gold statues of Oscar, roach clips and bongs, The Beatles and Elvis Presley memorabilia, basketballs, pornography films, BMW emblems; and millions of laptops, cell phones, empty booze bottles, movies and music videos.

Every age has its own ideas, thoughts, values, and idols that influence the culture. Paul called this corrupting influence "the world." He said that until a person becomes a follower of Christ, he or she cannot help but pursue the world's godless values (see Ephesians 2:1-3). The world can be described as a system of values, traditions, and ideas that cultivate a lifestyle independent of God. To be "worldly" is to have an anti-God spirit which places idols, self, or things at the center of one's aspirations and activities.

Our disposition, temperament, and habits are manipulated through worldly influences such as the workplace, media and entertainment industries, advertising, the education system, peer groups, world views, and philosophies. These influences contribute to not only toxic thinking and behavior, but to the breakdown of the family, and often trigger abuse and aggression.

Scripture tells us the world is guilty of having "exchanged the truth of God for a lie, and worshiped and served the creature rather than the Creator" (Romans 1:25). Jesus's disciple John warned us, "Don't love the world's ways. Don't love the world's goods. Love of the world squeezes out love for the Father" (1 John 2:15, MSG). Another disciple, James, spoke out against befriending the world because to "be a friend of the world is to become an enemy of God" (James 4:4). God doesn't want to share us with the world!

How do we explain, "For God so loved *the world* that he gave his one and only Son" (John 3:16)? The "world" in this text is translated in Greek to mean "the earth." God's love is so high and so wide he does indeed love every creature that inhabits this flawed, evil earth. He loves the entire world—not the just the nation of Israel, not only the loveable and lovely, but every person.

Jesus intends for us to live in the world (see John 17:15). He also knows we cannot spend day after day in it without it affecting our minds, hearts, and souls. They become unguarded and start to imperceptibly shift away from God. This is why he has given us his Word—to permeate our thinking so we do not become conformed to the world. As we walk in God's power and spend time studying the Bible, God gives us strength to resist the influence of the spirit of the age, and live according to kingdom values.

Reflect On It

- Carefully assess where "the world," or an anti-God spirit, might be influencing your values and behavior in a negative way. In what ways are you (and your children) being shaped by the secular spirit of the world? Name three ways the world usurps your devotion to God. Talk about this as a family.

- Equally, in what ways are you being shaped by the Spirit of God?

Day Two: Conflict with Satan

Don't let us yield to temptation, but rescue us from the evil one. –Matthew, speaking in Matthew 6:13, NLT

There are many popular ideas about this evil being. Some think Satan's not real but rather a personification of the wickedness which abides in the world. Others believe we can be under the power of spiritual forces such as demons. Many believe because they are Christian, they cannot be affected. If Satan doesn't attack Christians, we wouldn't be instructed to put on the armor of God in order to stand against all Satan's strategies and tricks (see Ephesians 6:10-18). He is a very real force. He is working to enslave and bind Christians every day.

Satan is described in the Bible as the ruler of an unseen world—where good and evil collide, where angels and demons wage war (see Ephesians 2:1-2). He is the destructive presence behind this godless age. The world, this earth, is his domain (see Job 1:7).

I don't know how, but he works to control our minds and hearts, and influences us to disobey God. Satan will use forces of nature, sickness, financial crisis's, plagues; and not only wicked people, but deceived godly people, to pull us away from God. We see this in the book of Job in the Old Testament.

Those who have read the Book of Job often misunderstand the purpose of the spiritual warfare Job experienced (see chapters 1 and 2). Satan's motive was not to destroy Job or ruin his life by destroying his family and property. Satan hoped Job would curse and turn away from God for letting such bad things happen to him. Job's wife fell right into Satan's trap. Infuriated, she cursed God (see Job 2:9).

But Job kept his spiritual integrity. He wouldn't blame God for his troubles.

Satan's primary purpose is to make God look bad. He hates God. Yes, he hates us too because we're made in the image of God. But I believe he attacks us in order to tempt us to attack and reject God. Scripture says he will strike us with thorns to our flesh (see 2 Corinthians 12:7). He will attack our self-worth, self-image, families, properties, finances, and health. As a result, we can lose faith and choose to separate ourselves from God. Then Satan wins the battle.

Do not let anything cause you to curse God. We can choose to think as Job did, "Shall we accept good from God, and not trouble?" (Job 2:10)

The mind is Satan's most frequent target of attack because our minds are the part of the image of God where God communicates with us and reveals his will. Satan deliberately attacks our thought process which ultimately affects our emotions and physical body. He shoots malicious fiery darts at our minds in the form of temptation, accusation, and deception.

Unknowingly, we embrace the devil's mind games and accept them as truth. We all have accommodated Satan's lies. When we believe the devil's lies instead of God's words of truth, we are powerless to do what is right.

Our emotions are certainly valid, but they're not always factual. We may believe we're damaged and then become absorbed in a vicious cycle of self-defeat or victimization. Satan's plan is to capitalize on every negative thought, on chemical imbalances, on loneliness, on pain, driving us further into isolation, and away from God.

Jesus said, "The devil was a murderer from the beginning, not holding to the truth, for there is no truth in him." He is no ordinary liar, but "the father of all lies" (John 8:44). Lies are very powerful.

If Satan can get you to believe a lie, then he can begin to work in your life to lead you away from God and into sin.

In addition, Paul warns us, "the work of Satan is displayed in all kinds of counterfeit miracles, signs and wonders, and in every sort of evil…" (2 Thessalonians 2:9-10). I believe he is saying we should avoid every form of contact with the supernatural and demonic,[123] such as: astrology, tarot card readings, psychics, demonic movies and music, séances, Ouija, charms, ghost hunting, supernatural faith healers, Wicca. No human possesses the ability to access knowledge of future events. God is the only omniscient, all-knowing person there is (see Isaiah 8:19-20).

Satan will tempt and take advantage of us if we're not alert to his devices. None of us knows when he will attack, but we know his plans backfire when we turn to God and take our stand on Scripture. In Ephesians 6, Paul tells us to put on the "full armor of God" in order to "stand firm against the schemes of the devil." He records one offensive weapon —the sword of the Spirit, which is the word of God (see Ephesians 6:11; 17-18). Scripture is our weapon to battle the formation of debilitating and controlling thoughts.

Dr. J. I. Packer, considered one of the most influential evangelicals, made the point:

> If I were the devil, one of my first aims would be to stop folk from digging into the Bible. Knowing that it is the Word of God, teaching men (and women) to know and love and serve the God of the Word, I should do all I could to surround it with the spiritual equivalent of pits, thorn hedges, and man traps, to frighten people off… At all cost I should want to *keep them from using their minds* in a disciplined way to get the measure of its message.[124]

We shouldn't take Satan too lightly, for fear we discount the dangers. Nor should we have too strong an interest in him. This parasite is powerful and cunning, but you are more powerful because you have Christ's resurrection power and his Word to draw from. You are empowered to resist Satan's strategies.

Reflect On It

1. Take an inventory of the settings and circumstances Satan is using in your life to push his deceptive messages. Begin by listing the main areas where you believe Satan consistently attacks you.

2. Use your authority as a believer in Jesus Christ to directly deal with him. Confront Satan out loud because he cannot read your mind as God can (remember, he's a created being). Say something like, "Satan, in the name and authority of Jesus, I command you to get away from me. My victory and honor come from God alone. He is my refuge, a rock where no enemy can reach me" (Psalm 62:7).

3. *Pray:* "Lord God, I acknowledge that [*name the areas*] may be empowered by demons. I ask you to send any evil spirits away from me. Help me draw from your power to fight the adversary. Please reveal to me anything else in my life that might give demons a foothold. Fill me with your Holy Spirit so I will be empowered to live in joyful obedience to you and in freedom from sin. In Jesus's powerful name, Amen."

Day Three: Conflict with the Flesh

We often labor under the misguided notion that Satan wants us to do his will. Satan has no will in our lives. He only wants us to do our will. We have met the enemy and he is us. –Educator and author, Mark Rutlan

One day I asked a woman to describe a dream she had for the

future. She answered, "I want to write a book about my life." Have you ever had one of those moments when your mouth sprang into action before your brain could process an acceptable response? I did. I rambled off a list of obstacles every writer faces. In other words, I, the woman who she respected and sought for advice, crushed her dream in one single moment.

There is a mean girl who lives inside all of us—she's rebellious, argumentative, self-centered, prideful, jealous, greedy, judgmental, a people-pleaser, a gossip, and stingy. She can't seem to manage her toxic thoughts and attitudes. This is because of her carnal nature.

As dangerous as the world and Satan are, neither is our greatest problem. Our greatest source of conflict dwells within us, what the apostle Paul called *the flesh*. In the Bible flesh refers to fallen humanity in all its frailty, which includes not only our bodies, but our hearts and minds.

The flesh represents our desires. Desires are good in themselves, such as desires for food, sleep, and sex; desires to achieve and succeed. There are proper ways to satisfy each of these desires. There are also divinely imposed limits. For example, the "lust of the flesh" described in 1 John 2:16 refers not only to sexual sins, but to all our unholy desires and prideful ambitions. This is where our opponent, Satan, strikes. He takes advantage of our bent toward doing precisely what God wouldn't want us to do (see James 1:14-15).

Our flesh works this way with the other two conflict zones. Using temptation as the example, picture a hook with a piece of bait on it. The bait represents what I personally desire—my lusts. Satan knows human nature. He's been watching me. He knows my weakness is shopping and knows what to bait my hook with—a discounted offer. He knows exactly what I want more of—shoes and bags. He will use a worldly device such as an advertisement or coupon to bait me.

On one occasion I devoured the bait...and it was scrumptious! I loaded up my online shopping cart and started to check out. It was pure exhilaration! But the pull of the Holy Spirit was stronger. Suddenly I thought, *I don't have time for this! I don't need these things. I'll only feel guilty.* So I abandoned my shopping cart. Twenty-four hours later the company sent me an email enticing me to return to the shopping cart. The bait: a 20 percent discount. But I resisted. Then 24 hours later another pop-up advertisement suddenly appeared. I couldn't believe it—my abandoned shopping cart popped up! The company attempted to lure me back with an even greater discount.

The tempter knows where to find me and he subtly dangles a specially-designed piece of worldly bait. I am on to him now. I know his strategy and I can take the steps to resist. I choose to abandon my shopping cart and unsubscribe from future mailings—not because shopping is a sin, but because I have a tendency to make shopping an idol. This is a sin because it pulls me away from God. Then Satan wins. How badly do you desire victory?

Freedom over the Conflict Zones

> We...are being transformed into his likeness with ever-
> increasing glory, which comes from the Lord, who is
> the Spirit. –Paul, speaking in 2 Corinthians 3:18

You want to change, to overcome the conflict zones, and live a victorious life free from the power and pollution of sin. You can do it! It is called *sanctification*—the process of growing more into the image of Christ and being increasingly enabled to live rightly, while releasing the reigns of sin. Think of it as getting on a new road that leads to a new spiritual life, a new you. I think of sanctification as the process of God undoing who I've become.

How do we begin? We draw power from Christ himself. Paul told the Ephesians, "...you will understand the incredible greatness of

God's power for us who believe him. This is the same mighty power which raised Christ from the dead..." (Ephesians 1:19-20, NLT).

Dunamis is the Greek word that means "power." The English words *dynamite* and *dynamic* are derived from it. Jesus Christ's resurrection means we have access to his miraculous power when he becomes our Lord. Think about it! That is more power than all the electrical companies in the world combined could possibly put out!

This is important: Our ongoing struggle with the conflict zones doesn't mean we are not saved or permitting sin to control us. Quite the opposite. Our battle to become more and more like Jesus is a sign that sin's dominion has ended and God is on the throne of our lives.

The fact that God tells us sin must be resisted implies sanctification will be a challenge. This is because sin is always trying to get back on the throne, where it reigned in our old life. Even though the old self is dead and buried, the flesh continues to fight for life.[125]

How do we subdue it? God tells us to *live by the Spirit* so we will not gratify the desires of the sinful nature (see Galatians 5:16). The power to live a sanctified life comes only when we plug into God's unlimited power. Daily, we seek his face and ask to be filled more with his Holy Spirit. The Spirit will give us the desire to hear, digest, and obey God's Word.

Amidst all the conflicting voices out there, we must slow down and listen for the voice of God himself. He will continue working in us as long as we walk by faith, make the commitment to live each day guided by the Holy Spirit, and keep plugged into God's Word. If we don't, then we rely on our own wisdom and make wrong choices.

The Bible says where the Spirit of the Lord is, there is freedom (see 2 Corinthians 3:17). Freedom—from living in the blindness and darkness which defines our world; freedom—from the captivity of Satan; freedom—from bondage of the flesh.

Victory over the conflict zones is not based on our ability, but on God. If we put him first in our lives, *we can be certain*, even as we struggle with sanctification, he is changing us from the inside out, giving us new hearts with new godly desires. That is victory!

Reflect On It

- Where in your life do you need to be on guard?
- What bait does Satan repeatedly tempt you with?
- Ask God to show you three ways your flesh usurps your devotion to him. Then confront those areas and devise a specific plan to minimize them. For example, "When confronted with an advertisement for a new diet product, I will pray for and exercise self-control—which God has already given me (see Galatians 5:22). And I will remind myself of Jesus's words (pull up Scripture).
- Power and authority over Satan comes from truth. Study Ephesians 6:10-18.

Day Four: Every Person's Battle

I can resist everything except temptation. −Oscar Wilde, *Lady Windermere's Fan*

A young woman advertised herself on Craig's List:

"I'm a spectacularly beautiful 25-year-old girl. I'm articulate and classy. I'm looking to MARRY a guy who makes at least half a million a year. Where do you single rich men hang out?"

A man who claimed to meet her financial requirements responded, "What you suggest is a simple trade: you bring your looks to the party, and I bring my money. But here's the rub: Your looks will fade and my money will continue to grow. So in economic terms you're a depreciating asset and I'm an earning asset. This is why it doesn't make good business sense to buy you, which is what you're asking, so I'd rather lease. A deal that makes sense to me is DATING, not marriage. If you want to enter into a lease agreement let me know." [126]

This couple turned what was meant by God to be a sacred relationship into an economic transaction. The temptation of money and prestige had more value. We do the same thing whenever we go into any situation which exposes our hearts to temptation. For each person, temptation is different.

Temptation is part of every human being's experience. It is the classic way Satan operates by enticing us into sin, which is why he is called "the tempter" (see 1 Thessalonians 3:5). Who would have thought we'd uncover murder in Moses, drunkenness in Noah, adultery and murder in David? Jesus reminds us hard trials and temptations will come (see Luke 17:1).

The Bible warns Christians not to give Satan a foothold or a grip. The word "foothold" means a small spot or a licensed area. It is an area of our minds over which Satan has jurisdiction. I contend that just by the virtue of our sin nature he already has a foothold. We certainly give him a larger area to dominate every time we entertain or succumb to temptation. Even if the enemy is temporarily given the advantage, we say to him, "Satan, you use evil against me, but God will use it for good!" (See Genesis 50:20)

The moment we're tempted to get our physical or emotional need met in a way which is not conforming to Christ, we're at the threshold of a major decision. The devil's trap doesn't catch you, unless you're first lured by his bait. The question isn't, "Will I be tempted?" The question is, "When I'm tempted will I be on guard and able to resist?"

Temptations come at unexpected moments. Satan watches for distraction, fatigue, anger, hunger, weakness, or loneliness, and then attacks with an enticing offer. At that point we make a choice: to let him in or shut him out. The *existence* of a tempting or sinful thought is different than the *action* of the thought. With each temptation, God provides an escape so we won't have to yield to it (see 1 Corinthians 10:13).

Reflect On It

Jesus said, "Watch out that no one deceives you" (Matthew 24:4). Ask for discernment as you navigate through society's lies and countercultural messages about God.

Pray: "Lord God, I pray for wisdom. I know today I will make a thousand small, consequential, and trivial choices. Help me to choose what I need for a richer, more vital life in you. In Jesus's name. Amen."

Day Five: It is Written!

> I have hidden your word in my heart that I might not
> sin against you. –Psalm 119:11

Jesus can teach us how to beat the devil at his own game because he was tempted by him too. When he was 30 years old Jesus left his life as a carpenter behind—the memories, the conversations, and the laughter he shared with his family. He then headed alone, on foot, to the Jordan Valley.

After being baptized in the Jordan River by his cousin John the baptizer, God's voice invaded earth and introduced Jesus as his Son— the Son whom he loved and was very pleased with (see Matthew 3:17). Jesus must have needed to hear those words before he faced the upcoming temptations. Then he was tossed out into the wilderness for forty days to be tempted by the devil (see Matthew 4:1-11).

I can't help but notice the dissimilarity between the setting in Genesis 2 and Matthew 4. The same tempter who first entered God's life-giving garden now ushers the God-Man into his turf—the dangerous and barren wilderness. The wilderness is an image of life dictated by the world and Satan. It is where we face the strongest and most seductive temptations, and the Tempter himself. Any struggle with addiction and compulsive behavior is a desert because it is the place we are the most vulnerable—it involves deprivation, and can lead us further away from God.

Jesus's First Temptation
Matthew 4:1-4

The air was hot and dry, as was Jesus's skin and mouth; his body dehydrated. He hadn't eaten in forty days so food was an obvious powerful temptation tool. The tempter came to him and said, "If you are the Son of God, tell these stones to become bread."

Satan intended to impede Jesus's dependence on his Father by causing him to use his own resources to meet his need for food, thereby depending on himself. Jesus discarded the bait and fought back by quoting Scripture, Deuteronomy 8:3, "It is written: Man shall not live by bread only, but by every word of God." Jesus would not use his great power to please himself.

Jesus faced the enemy as a man. He never used divine powers to overcome Satan, which is what Satan hoped for. He used the same weapon we have available to us—the Word of God. He could have turned the stones to bread. Although he was hungry and faint, he chose to feed on his Father's Word.

Satan used Scripture to tempt Jesus, quoting the Bible accurately (see Psalm 91:11, 12). He knows the Bible far better than we do. Satan always masquerades his lies as God's truth. He enjoys taking verses out of context to prove his false beliefs. This is why it is so important to have a proper grasp of Scripture if we're to detect and defeat him.

As a believer, we have the power of the Holy Spirit within us to teach us the truths of God's Word (see John 16:13-15). How are you doing at making the time to read and study the Bible? Do you find you need help? Don't fear asking for support.

The Second Temptation
Matthew 4:5-7

Satan realized he couldn't cause Jesus to yield to this particular temptation, so he changed his strategy and the scenery. He led Jesus to the pinnacle of the temple. "If you are the Son of God," he said, "throw yourself down. For it is written: "He will command his angels concerning you, and they will lift you up in their hands, so that you will not strike your foot against a stone." *If you really believe God is going to take care of you let him prove it—and prove it publicly.*

The temple was the center of religious activity for Israel. The majestic jump would have been seen by key leaders. The rescue would have convinced them indeed Jesus was the Son of God. He could have won over every skeptic and avoided years of conflict with the religious establishment. What a tempting offer!

Jesus saw right through it. Without hesitation he replied back using Scripture again (Deuteronomy 6:16), "It is also written: 'Do not put the Lord your God to the test.'" Rather than use God as a magician, he trusted his Father to take him through the desert.

Scripture is brutally honest about life—the good, the bad, the ugly. It can also be taken out of context very easily. Paul warned us, "Let no one deceive you with empty words" (Ephesians 5:6). When we study the Bible it is important that we learn from reputable pastors and teachers. We must also memorize Scripture. Jesus didn't have a concordance with him. He reached into his memory bank and selected Deuteronomy, quoting the most applicable verses to silence Satan.

The three words we use to fight temptation are: "It is written." Memorization is our sword of the Spirit. If we don't have God's Word in our memories then the Holy Spirit is unable to bring it to our minds when we're under attack.

Satan first appeared in the Bible as a serpent. Scripture doesn't say how he appeared to Jesus in the desert. However, today he's pushing his lies and propaganda through cults, the Internet, social networking sites, novels, magazines, music, movies, politics, and television programming. Living in an age of technology, media, and advertisement, how better to subtly assault and devour us!

Ask God to give you a personalized reading plan and to enable you to bring his Word to your mind exactly when you need it. Here are a few personal examples:

1. When I feel pulled toward investing in more anti-aging products I pull up two Scriptures: "It's your life that must change, not your skin! …What counts is your life" (Luke 3:8, 10, MSG); "Man looks at the outward appearance, but the LORD looks at the heart" (1 Samuel 16:7). *I must focus on internal change, not external. In all honesty, who am I really trying to impress—the Lord or man?*

2. When I have a judgmental or critical attitude, and get distracted by focusing on issues which really aren't my business, I pull up Jesus's words to Peter, "…what is that to you? You must follow me" (John 21:22). *You're right Jesus, what is it to me? If I keep focused on you, I won't be distracted by anyone else.*

3. When I feel a tug of war beginning, I remind the devil and my flesh of Galatians 2:20: "My old self has been crucified with Christ. It is no longer I who live, but Christ lives in me." *I'm no longer that woman who needs to control every situation.* Being chosen and adopted by God means I'm to live a "new self" life. *Christ in me is my only hope.*

4. I directly battle the enemy's lies with Scripture, "Hey Satan, I'm going to fix my thoughts on what is true, good, and right. I'm going to think only about things which are pure and lovely, and dwell on the fine, good things in others. And I will praise God and be glad in my circumstances!" (Philippians 4:8) *If I change my thoughts I can change my life.*

5. Quotes can be inspirational too, such as, "Many of life's failures are men (women) who did not realize how close they were to success when they gave up" by Thomas Jefferson.

The Third Temptation
Matthew 4:8-11

Former Prime Minister Margaret Thatcher said, "You may have to fight a battle more than once to win it."[127] It wasn't over for Jesus. As a kid or parent you may have watched the *Roadrunner Show*. In each episode, the coyote (Wile E. Coyote) comes up with absurd, complex contraptions and elaborate plans to catch the roadrunner. The roadrunner outsmarts him time and again, yet the coyote never gives up. He's determined to catch his prey.

Think of Satan as that coyote. He regrouped and came up with an even greater offer. Since Satan desires worship, the third temptation of Jesus was in regard to power and wealth—the ultimate invitation to idolatry. Satan took Jesus to the top of a high mountain and caused him to see all the kingdoms of the world. "All this I will give you," he said, "if you will bow down and worship me." *You can be a super power through me if you let me be your god!*

Satan could give Jesus all this because he is the ruler of this domain. Jesus said the whole world is under the reign of the evil one (see 1 John 5:19). He described Satan as the prince of this world (see John 12:31). When bad things happen I remind myself I shouldn't be surprised since Satan is the ring leader.

For the third time, Jesus lambasted Satan with Scripture, "Away from me, Satan! For it is written: 'Worship the Lord your God, and serve him only'" (Deuteronomy 6:13; 10:20). The words snapped like a whip and Satan recoiled, which is what snakes do when they are threatened.

Scripture continues, "When the devil had finished all this tempting, he left him until an opportune time" (Luke 4:13). At that moment, Satan could find no way to tempt Jesus's pure heart. But

Satan would be back. He always comes back. He would study Jesus and when the time was perfect—when Jesus would be the most vulnerable, the weakest, he'd attack again. This is exactly what he does to us.

Jesus stood firm. He endured the wilderness and claimed victory on Satan's turf before starting his public ministry. Most importantly, none of his retorts to Satan came from his own self-directed will. He relied upon God's Word. He didn't listen to the great deceiver. He acted with strength and faith. Therefore, he was empowered to move forward with God's mission.

This world delivers an appealing message, "You don't have to go through the desert. Take this...buy that...drink this...do that." Walking through the wilderness in the face of temptation and adversity is how God develops our character to be more like Jesus's. Every temptation is an opportunity to do what is right, to run to the God who has been running to you. Thank and praise him that absolutely nothing can get between you and his love, his grace and the plan for your life.

Reflect On It

"Be self-controlled and alert. Your enemy the devil prowls around like a roaring lion looking for someone to devour. Resist him, standing firm in the faith..." (1 Peter 5:8-9).

- What is God telling you to do in these two verses?
- How will you accomplish this?

Week Nine

Everyone Has a Hurt
Finding Purpose in Pain

Day One: Life is About Choices

Pain is inevitable but suffering is a choice. –Unknown

Life is about choices. In every woman's life there are memorable moments which dramatically change the rest of her days.

Pregnant, the home pregnancy test kit read. My doctor's office confirmed it. I had a choice: to bring the baby to term or abort it. There was no doubt in my mind abortion was the answer. After all, I wasn't married, I had an established career and lifestyle, and the father wasn't a significant other.

My family physician gave me a handful of resources. In this country we have a choice to abort or not. I simply replied, "I've made up my mind. Give me the abortion clinic information. I'll take care of it." I did take care of "it." This little baby had no choice. After the procedure I erased the incident from my memory bank.

Two years later Jesus Christ became my Lord and Savior. As a Christian I became keenly aware of the sin I had committed—murder; a sin God graciously and mercifully forgave. *Thank you Lord!*

I promptly shoved the incident back down there in my personal hell with all the other secrets.

Many years later, in a Bible study, my abortion experience surfaced. I felt pressured to make a choice. I could re-bury this dark memory or I could turn to God and ask him to shine his bright healing light on it. I chose the latter. With God's guidance, I began to retrieve the buried memories.

Praying about the abortion I cried, "Father, I'm so sorry I aborted your child. I now see I was sold a bill of lies. What happened to my baby?" Then I got a vision of this little child under the Father's robe. There were thousands of pairs of eyes in the background. He showed me in such a kind, loving, fatherly way that he had his hand on my child, and all the other aborted children.

In this vision my child is happy and waiting for me in heaven. Tears of joy and remorse gushed out. What a beautiful picture of love, mercy, and grace. I thought the whole ordeal was finished, but I was wrong.

As my relationship with the Father grew, he granted me another choice. I could close the book or allow him to show me more. I trusted God and chose to re-open this wound. I signed up for the post-abortal Bible study and support group *Healing Encouragement for Abortion Related Trauma* (H.E.A.R.T.). The class required making a commitment to do the difficult work: navigating through denial, then grief, then anger, then forgiveness.

I began questioning the choices I made seventeen years earlier. Several questions plagued me. "Father, tell me, what was I feeling when I was pregnant for those eight weeks? I don't have any memory of my thoughts or the state of my heart; nothing. But you know. Please show me." I got my answer—an answer I didn't anticipate.

At the time of the pregnancy the monster bulimia dominated my life. I made a choice that day—to purge my baby. This is what the baby felt like to me—a blob of tissue which could be purged away, like the food I ate. I obviously didn't value myself, so how could I value my baby's life? You could say this monster took two innocent lives.

I couldn't get this thought out of my mind. I needed to know more. A few days later I recalled the father's name (also buried away) and had a very strong sense my baby was a boy. As God started revealing small details I put together the story.

I justified my actions. Single and extremely self-centered, I couldn't tell my family for fear of disappointing them. And the father wasn't in my life. I thought, *Those are good enough reasons, right? God understands. I mean, what would I tell this kid about his dad? I'm actually saving him from a lot of pain! God will excuse me.*

The truth is I was more concerned about my body and what other people would think of me, than for a human life. The woman at Planned Parenthood told me it was a blob of tissue, only an inch long. It was an inch long. But I learned this developing life was already termed a fetus, Latin for *young one.*

Everything was present in this fetus which is found in a fully developed adult. The heart had been beating for more than a month, the stomach produced digestive juices, and the kidneys functioned. Forty muscle sets had begun to operate in conjunction with the nervous system. The fetus body responded to the touch from the physician.[128]

God had a great plan and legacy for this little person's life. No, I wasn't justified! Then I became angry, then deeply sad. My sin had cost me in many ways. Now it cost my firstborn.

The last exercise in the H.E.A.R.T. class was to write a letter to our babies. That was tough and emotive. I asked my son for forgiveness. Being set free by God himself melted the guilt and remorse away. And I forgave myself. Through this process I learned the value of not minimizing or invalidating personal pain.

God declares, "Though your sins are like scarlet, I will make them as white as snow. Though they are red like crimson, I will make them as white as wool" (Isaiah 1:18, NLT).

Abortion does not fall under the category of addiction. It was the consequence of binge drinking and living an addicted party girl lifestyle. Bad choices have consequences. Yet, it is in these moments that our loving, compassionate Father draws us close and whispers love, forgiveness, and hope into our hearts and souls.

Minimizing painful circumstances and suppressing the memories only makes things worse. Putting life events in perspective can be a positive coping mechanism. First acknowledge, then accept the fact that [*name your hurt or violation*] happened and resulted in significant pain. Start to listen to the Spirit who guides you. "Give your burdens to the Lord. He will carry them" (Psalm 55:22, TLB).

Feeling like an Outcast
John 4:1-42

> ...whenever hurt is present, it must be embraced as an opportunity to enter more richly into the reality of a world in need of redemption. The effect of pain can be to increase our thirst for God and our desire to live for Him. –Psychologist Larry Crabb[129]

The eating disorder, drunkenness, sexual sin, the abortion, denial and codependency, the feelings of rejection and dejection—I can say for almost thirty years I felt like an outcast—a shame filled castaway.

Jesus introduces us to a Samaritan woman who felt the same way (see John 4:1-42). This unnamed woman, familiar with shame, came to Jacob's well at noon, all in an attempt to avoid the stares and whispers. It was too hot for most people to be outside. The other women would band together when it cooled off, not only to draw water, but to revel in companionship. Not this woman. She had three strikes against her: she was a Samaritan, a member of a hated mixed race. She was living in sin, and she was in a public place.

Shunned by the other women and her own accusatory thoughts,

162

she braved the sun's scorn each day. For the span of five husbands, maybe longer, this woman came to the well, always at noon and always alone, her empty jar a symbol of her life. Upon seeing Jesus she likely thought, *Darn! There is a man at the well today—a Jew! Perhaps he won't notice me. I'll fill my pot quickly and leave.*

This man noticed her. He crossed every boundary and spoke. No respectable Jewish man would talk to a woman, let alone such an outcast. He asked her for a drink. *He can't be talking to me?* This was quite unusual. Feeling undeserving of his acknowledgment, she reminded him of her ethnicity.

Bracing for rebuke from him, nothing came from his lips. Instead he gently said, "If you knew the gift of God and who it is that asks you for a drink, you would have asked him and he would have given you living water."

What did Jesus mean by living water? In the Old Testament many verses speak of thirsting after God as one thirsts for water. God is called the fountain of life (see Psalm 36:9) and the spring of living water (see Jeremiah 17:13). Only Jesus could give this woman the gift which would satisfy and quench her soul's desire.

The woman at the well confuses the two kinds of water. Most likely no one had ever spoken to her before about spiritual thirst. Jesus answered her, "Everyone who drinks this [well] water will be thirsty again, but whoever drinks the water I give him will never thirst. Indeed, the water I give him will become in him a spring of water welling up to eternal life."

I've never heard this before. I want to hear more. If she could have what this man offered, she'd have joy. She asks for some of the water. Jesus redirects her, "Go, call your husband and come back."

"I have no husband," she replied.

Jesus responded, "You are right when you say you have no husband. The fact is, you have had five husbands, and the man you now have is not your husband."

Did she drop her bucket or just her mouth? I wonder how long

163

that pause continued for. *How could he have known this? Was this a setup to shame me?* No. Not with Jesus. He saw right into her soul. He already knew every detail about her past. He knew before she spoke. We don't have to go into the dirty details of our shameful moments if we're uncomfortable. Jesus already knows. He won't reject you, expose you, or pull back to avoid being tainted by you.

Then she went to tell the good news. Many of the Samaritans from that town believed in Jesus because of her testimony. Despite her reputation, many came out to meet Jesus. Scripture says, "They begged him to stay in their village. So he stayed for two days, long enough for many more to hear his message and believe." The Jewish rabbi hung out with the Samaritans. How can you not love Jesus!

Noteworthy is what Jesus didn't say. He made no reference to her sin. He didn't call her to repent, although she did when she aligned her lifestyle with his kingdom. Instead, he showed her a reflection of herself. Jesus drew out the details of her situation in a nonjudgmental way. He wanted her to be both reflective and receptive to his offer of forgiveness and a relationship with God. Jesus brought her face to face with his remarkable gift—living water and eternal life.

Jesus esteemed sinners. He gave every one of them his love and his time. He deliberately went out of his way to meet this woman from Samaria. He didn't follow man's rules or prejudices. He reached out with a message of hope and new life, which he still does today.

I know how she felt; worthless, ashamed, abandoned. Jesus knew her pain and heartache. He knew mine, and he knows yours. No matter what you've done, you can go to him and come to know him as your Savior. Jesus gives us himself—the living water, the armor of God.

As others see change in you they become curious, which is your opportunity to introduce them to Jesus. Don't stay silent. Take what you've learned and teach your loved ones. Look for opportunities to tell them what great things Jesus has done for you (called a *testimony*). Then you bless them with living water.

Pray: "Thank you Jesus for your living water. Forgive me for searching for other things to fill my life. How could anyone who has tasted your water and goodness drink from any other well? Yet I confess I have. Jesus, help me keep your living water pure by removing the impurities I tolerate in my life. Keep my faith pure and deepen it. Give me zeal like this Samaritan woman. My desire is to be bold and tell everyone about you. Amen."

Reflect On It

- What do you have in common with the women in these two stories?
- In what ways do you feel their shame, their feelings of unworthiness?
- Describe how you view Jesus now.

Day Two: From Ugly to Beautiful

Every human soul houses innumerable secrets. Every human soul has its own style in safeguarding those secrets as well as a different degree of ease with which those secrets are allowed to step out from behind the curtain. –Speaker and author, Marilyn Meberg[130]

After the fourth flush I grabbed the near empty bottle of *Windex,* then ripped off three squares of paper toweling and proceeded to clean up around the toilet bowl. After tossing the residue of a gaping emotional wound into the garbage I reclined on the couch, numb and oblivious. *I feel like garbage…but tomorrow will be different,* I promised myself. *Today is the last day.*

Despondent, that is what I had said every day for the previous fourteen years. Driven by shame, it never was the last day. It has been said that evil thrives in our pain. I have seen it in my own life, and see it in others—the weight of shame. How deep do you believe your shame runs?

- Do you feel unworthy and wonder why God would love you?
- Do you regularly berate yourself over minor happenings?
- Do you struggle to overcome memories of verbal, emotional, or physical abuse?

If you said yes you may be suffering from unhealthy shame. What is shame? Psychologist Edward T. Welch, author of *Shame Interrupted* wrote,

> You are shunned. Faces are turned away from you. They ignore you, as if you don't exist. You are naked. Faces are turned toward you. They stare at you, as if you were hideous. You are worthless, and it's no secret. You are of little or no value to those whose opinions matter to you.[131]

Shame is an uneasy topic. It is a universal experience but we choose to ignore it because of the deep sense we are unacceptable because of something we've done or associated ourselves with. Shame is not the same as guilt or embarrassment. Guilt means feeling bad for something we have or haven't done: "I am wrong." Shame means feeling bad for who we are: "I am unacceptable."

Guilt often leads to shame if the feelings of guilt are based on actions deemed by the person to be morally wrong. It is not the same as embarrassment. Embarrassment doesn't afflict a person's soul. You eventually laugh about it. With shame you never laugh. Shame magnifies defectiveness and sin. It makes us feel less than human.

As long as I could keep my bulimia and sexual promiscuity a

secret I could slow down the cycle of shame. If my actions were exposed then my worst nightmare would come true. I'd be seen for who I truly am—a defect.

Eventually my secrets got out when I lived in a sorority. You might as well have embedded a scarlet "S" for "shame-filled" on my chest. The tarnished stain on my soul got larger and larger as the gossip spread throughout the house. Harsh judgment from others only strengthened the erroneous core belief I was irreparably flawed.

My senior year was coming to a close. In the sorority, the junior class had a tradition of roasting the senior class with a "special gift." I feared what toxic tribute waited for me. My gift was a box of laxatives. Mortified, my face turned scarlet red. I wanted to run, to cry. Instead I laughed with the rest of them, "Ha, ha. You're so funny!"

With shame, everybody else is in on the "the joke" except the person who is going through it. As I anxiously sat through rest of the roasting I prayed another girl would be crucified, since misery loves company. No such luck. I died alone. Like a play, the curtain parted and my neurosis appeared center stage for all to see. I felt naked and mortified.

Since we all have a compelling, God-given need to be loved, to feel accepted and worthy, most of us will go to virtually any lengths to meet these needs. If we didn't long to be wanted and loved, then we wouldn't care. If we didn't care, then we couldn't be shamed by other's rejection or attacks.

Shame's only positive purpose is to lead us to the healer. The Bible's teaching on shame is redemptive and encouraging. The feeling of shame which shouts that we have no value runs contrary to God's voice which declares we have immense value—so much value that his only Son went to the cross for me and you. *No, I don't deserve to wear the scarlet "S"! I'm not contaminated!*

Shame Reduction

> What do you do…After you've cried till you're numb.
> After you've replayed the failure over and over in your
> mind. After you've run yourself down and can't think
> of any more names to call yourself. What do you
> do then? You find some way to hold back the pain.
> –Author Ken Gire[132]

We all construct walls of emotional scar tissue to cover our
unhealed wounds. These protective barriers lock us in and others out,
inhibiting our ability to develop close connections. The degree of
this self-protection is equal to the severity of our perceived wounds
of shame.

Jesus too felt shame as he hung naked and despised on the cross.
But he never lost sight of where he was headed. Focused on God, he
put up with the pain and ignored the shame created by his tormenters.
His example can help us find a way to diminish pain.

> Let us fix our eyes on Jesus, the author and perfecter
> of our faith, who for the joy set before him endured
> the cross, scorning its shame…" (Hebrews 12:2)

There are four messages for us in this one verse:

1. To *fix* means to trust. Set your mind and heart on Jesus who,
   for you, has defeated shame and fear and guilt. He won't let
   you down. He will always be there to help you through.
   Fixing our eyes on Jesus will make it easier to take our
   thoughts captive. Then we're not so tempted to focus on our
   personal problems.
2. Looking up to Jesus describes an attitude of faith, not just
   an act. The word *author* in Greek means "one who takes the
   lead." The fact that Jesus prayed is evidence he lived by faith.

We follow his lead. In faith we pray our heart's needs and desires. He alone makes everything perfect.

3. We wonder, "What is so joyous about being crucified?" This is not what the verse is saying. "For the joy set before him..." means Jesus fast-forwarded to the salvation plan and eternity. He knew he'd come out of the tomb alive in three days. He knew he'd be exalted to heaven in glory.

   We're being asked to follow his lead and look ahead in faith. The heroes of faith listed in the book of Hebrews (Chapter 11) lived for the future. This is what enabled them to endure. The author emphasized the importance of future hope. When you're in a difficult place, fast-forward and in faith anticipate the great work God is going to do. Don't ask "why," ask "what."

4. Jesus "scorned" or despised the shame of the cross. Before he was crucified, he underwent a merciless beating, a public mocking meant to inflict maximum pain and humiliation. The enemy tried to keep Jesus down by the weight of shame, but he lost that battle. Jesus had no shame. It was our shame, our scarlet S's, he suffered on the cross, and then buried once and for all. *The burden of shame is not yours to bear any longer!*

Reflect On It

Acknowledge the secrets you have been hiding. Ask God to help you begin to identify your personal scarlet S's.

- How have you been safeguarding your secrets? Did you grow up in a house where family secrets were buried?
- What abuse, damage, or beliefs do you keep hidden?
- How is your shame affecting your relationship with God and others?
- What do you need to bring to the light to begin the healing process? Name one step you can take today.

Day Three: The Leprous Man

When we are the most wounded, we find ourselves
nearest the Wounded One. –Unknown

When I think of an ancient wounded people I think of lepers. In
the Old Testament, leprosy, like AIDS today, was a terrifying disease.
There was no known cure for the debilitating illness. Untreated,
leprosy causes permanent damage to the skin, nerves, limbs, and
eyes. Body parts become numb or diseased as a result of secondary
infections, which can result in tissue loss causing fingers and toes to
become shortened and deformed.[133]

Today leprosy can be treated successfully. In Biblical days it
represented a physical, emotional, and spiritual death sentence.
Levitical regulations required lepers to tear their outer garment
like a mourner's, to dishevel their hair, and keep their face partially
covered.

As the leper passed others on the streets they had to call out,
"Unclean! Unclean!" (see Leviticus 13:45-46) They had to keep
at least six feet away when they passed. If either person broke that
boundary the "normal" person jeopardized their reputation. Rejected
and treated like garbage, they were forced to live in an isolated leper
colony, far away from humanity.

Living with leprosy must have been similar to the 1980s AIDS
crisis when the public, in general, wouldn't go near anyone diagnosed
with this fatal disease. Can you imagine the shame? To be shunned
by society around-the-clock. Little children ran away in fear. *Mommy,
there's a monster over there!* The older kids threw stones and objects at
them and shouted, *Leper! Leper!*

All the things we take for granted were barred from their life.
When was the last time someone shook their hand, patted them on
the back, put an arm around their waist, or gave them a hug or kiss?
They lived without hope or love or joy; without the simple dignities
of life. Unlike the rest of the community their deep needs were never

met. And in a leper colony, no tabernacle existed, which meant no presence of God.

One leprous man heard about Jesus's miracle healings. He found him and begged, "If you are willing, you can make me clean." Filled with compassion, Jesus reached out his hand and touched the man. "I am willing," he said. "Be clean!" Immediately he was cured" (Mark 1:40-42). Jesus broke the boundary and risked his own reputation because he knew this poor man needed his touch. He didn't seem to care.

Studies show people develop very slowly and even die if they are denied touch.[134] Conversely, if a person is touched in a bad way it can traumatize their soul. Touch is the earliest sense to develop and the last one to leave at the end of life. God created our bodies and minds to crave touch. Touch tranquilizes the nervous system by increasing endorphins.

What breaks a stronghold of shame? Being touched in the right way by the right person.

Deprived of touch, undoubtedly, this man experienced depression, maybe even suicidal ideations. But on that day he had hope. Risking everything, he gathered enough courage to seek Jesus. Both fearful and excited, he dared to approach the rabbi. This leprous man believed. When Jesus touched him he showed his unity with every other outcast. The man's life of shame ended. Jesus healed him and he belonged once again.

The sight of this precious man filled Jesus with compassion. Jesus could see the glimmer of faith left in this man's sunken eyes. He reached out and touched him—the same man no other human being would dare draw near to. His gestures vowed, "I love you. I care. I understand. I want to help."

Isolation. Shame. Ridicule. Rejection. The same compassion Jesus felt when he came across those deemed untouchable, standing on the outskirts of humanity, is the same compassion Jesus feels for us. He is saying to you: "I love you. I care. I understand. I want to help." In prayer, tell him exactly where you desire spiritual and emotional cleansing.

Break the Stronghold of Shame

> Shame should be reserved for the things we choose to
> do, not the circumstances that life puts on us. —Ann
> Patchett, *Truth and Beauty*

If we touch someone who is sick or dirty or bloody, we can get sick, dirty, and bloody. If we're regularly touched by a person who spews lies, we can spew lies. If we're touched by Jesus Christ, God sees us as holy because we are covered by Jesus Christ's holiness.

Are you ready? This is huge. The moment we believe in Jesus Christ and accept that his death paid for all our sins, we are set apart as God's children for a sacred purpose. This means in God's eyes we stand in front of him as holy creatures. Yes, holy!

Scripture says, "For he [God] chose us in him before the creation of the world to be holy and blameless in his sight" (Ephesians 1:4). The Greek word for *holiness* means sanctification.[135] God chose us to be conformed to the image of his Son, and set apart (see Romans 8:29). Blameless does not mean perfect or sinless. It means that in every situation, we completely trust God and do what our minds and hearts tell us is the correct thing to do.

Holy is from the same root as the word pure. *Vine's Complete Expository Dictionary* defines *pure* as "free from defilement; not contaminated." Any contamination or defilement of ourselves can *only* come from what *we do*—the stuff that comes out of our own hearts and minds (see Matthew 15:18); not from what others do to us.

What Jesus basically said is that nothing outside a person can render him or her unclean. Food can't; people can't; the sins of your family can't; perpetrators can't. Nobody can make you an untouchable outcast. Get out of your mind that you're dirty, or can be contaminated by coming into contact with someone you define as unclean, or by not measuring up to society's standards.

According to Scripture, evil thoughts, murder, adultery, sexual sins, stealing, lying, and cursing come from within ourselves (see Matthew 15:17-19). When we do sin, God is quick to forgive when we turn to him. No one else has the power to make us sin. This is why we are counseled to transform our minds, which ultimately translates into purer actions. When our insides are clean, then our outsides are clean.

Reflect On It

Meditate on each verse. What is God personally saying to you?

- "Those who trust in me will never be put to shame" (Isaiah 49:23, NLT).
- "The Sovereign LORD will wipe away the tears from all faces; he will remove the disgrace of his people from all the earth. ...you will never be put to shame or disgraced, to ages everlasting" (Isaiah 25:8; 45:17).

Day Four: A New Life Free From Shame

Shame is the lie someone told you about yourself.
–Anais Nin, *Why Men Fall Out of Love*

A common thread runs through each story: every person discovered they desperately needed Jesus's touch and had to put their faith in him alone. Too many of us have been trying to scrub away our guilty and shame-filled consciences. We deny we're really broken. It is far easier to act strong than admit we need help. It is time to put the soap away and come out of hiding.

Jesus said it is the poor in spirit who inherit the kingdom—those who know their desperate need for him and don't try to deny it (see Matthew 5:3). You might unconsciously put up a fight, but recognize God is leading you away from shame. If you want to break all strongholds of shame here are a few things you can start to do:

1. *Give yourself permission to feel the pain:* A therapist said, "Pain creates suffering only when you refuse to accept the pain." On the pain scale it may feel like a ten. The intensity is normal and will slowly begin to subside. Depending on the core issue, the pain may not completely disappear, but it will become bearable. Give yourself permission to feel sadness, but not shame.

2. *Begin to put words on the shameful event.* Describe it: write or talk about it.
    *   What happened?
    *   How do you still carry the incident with you?
    *   How do you feel exposed, dirty, like an outcast?

3. *Talk with God and another person.* Express to God what is on your heart. Then ask him to lead you to a safe person or group. Those things that shame us the most, the things we most fear to tell, don't set us apart. They can bind us together if we take the risk to speak about it.

4. *Forgive yourself, even if you weren't the offender.* Forgiveness is unique to Christianity. No other place can take our shame and guilt and wash it away. [We will study forgiveness in Week Twelve.]

5. *Consider:* How does your shame affect your relationship with other people? If you are not sure, ask God to show you.
    *   Whom do you avoid?
    *   How do you cover up: physically and/or emotionally?
    *   How do you attempt to make up for feeling dirty or bad?

6. *How does your shame affect your relationship with God?* Do you avoid him because you think you're not good enough to

come to him? If yes, what would it feel like to know God is not ashamed of you?

7. *Affirm yourself.* Say out loud: "Today I receive God's grace in place of my shame. I believe I'm completely worthy and acceptable before God. Therefore I accept myself."

Day Five: Redeemed, yet Living with a Thorn

There is a legend about a bird which sings just once in its life, more sweetly than any other creature on the face of the earth. From the moment it leaves the nest it searches for a thorn tree, and does not rest until it has found one. Then, singing among the savage branches, it impales itself upon the longest, sharpest spine. And, dying, it rises above its own agony to outcarol the lark and the nightingale. One superlative song, existence the price. But the whole world stills to listen, and God in His heaven smiles. For the best is only bought at the cost of great pain... Or so says the legend. —Colleen McCullough, *The Thorn Birds*

The apostle Paul, I'm convinced, understood compulsive behavior. Before meeting Jesus Christ on the road to Damascus, Paul was a man obsessed with killing Christians. A divine encounter with Christ changed him dramatically (see Acts 9:3-6). With the same conviction and drive which fueled his opposition to Christ, he became passionate about being his disciple.

Then he had a second supernatural encounter (see 2 Corinthians 12:3-10). In order to keep Paul from being prideful and boastful, God permitted Satan to afflict Paul with a "thorn in his flesh," which is used to describe a chronic infirmity, annoyance, or trouble in one's life. He asked three times for it to be removed. God reserves the right to say no—"No, this isn't good for you. Have this instead."

God responded to Paul: "My grace is sufficient for you" (2 Corinthians 12:9). I imagine Paul pled, "But Lord...," and God replied, "I've given you sufficient grace. It will be more than enough for whatever you face."

Paul hoped God's grace would include the removal of the suffering. God showed him where his true sufficiency laid. Power came through seeing weakness as the very vehicle for manifesting the power of Christ. Only in his weakness did Paul trust implicitly in God. God didn't answer Paul's request, yet he met Paul's needs.

God gets our attention through our thorns. We've all got them. Some come in the form of consequences. Like with Paul, some thorns may never go away. But God's grace is sufficient to handle them for life. Paul courageously pressed on in spite of personal infirmities, frequent rejection, emotional distress, and bodily injury. He showed resilience through trials. He modeled ceaseless perseverance and passion.

A thorn or our downfall may be necessary for it is in failure and helplessness we can most honestly turn to and receive God's grace. Grace was all Paul needed. He didn't care what men thought of him, only God. No amount of conflict could break Paul down or make him turn back. This is the work of God's grace.

The great paradox is, the weaker we are, the more obvious the need for God's power and grace. It is possible you may come to see your thorn as a kind of gift. By the grace of God, we no longer are destined to live as slaves to the mistakes, addictions, and pain of the past. We are presently being transformed and can look toward the future with hope.

Redeemed, yet Living Forever Scarred

Despite horrendous obstacles and deep scarring, you can shine in the corner of the world God has called you to. After the crucifixion and burial of Jesus, the Bible says the disciples were together. Then Jesus appeared among them and showed them his hands and side (see John 20:19-20).

His scars were infallible proof he was the same person. The imprints of the nails were visible on his hands. In his side there appeared a scar from the spear. When Jesus rose from the dead, he could have erased from his body everything that pointed to what he had suffered and endured. But he didn't. Secondly, he means to show us suffering is oftentimes necessary.

Today Christ wears these bodily scars as ornaments of his hard fought battles. How important is it for our needy, hurting generation to recognize Jesus by his scars? Very important; they tell his story. He will wear his scars forever as a reminder of the sacrificial price of salvation—not as a reminder of the shame he endured.

Our scars are part of our stories. Halie used to cut herself with a razorblade regularly. One day she methodically carved the word "misfit" into her forearm. Then Jesus rescued her. As part of her recovery and to show the world an image of God's grace, she tattooed the word "Beloved" over the misfit scar. Like Jesus, she wears her scar proudly.

I believe God values our scars over our accomplishments. Grace is an expression of God's love which gives us the ability to live extraordinary lives beyond our natural ability, scars and all.

Reflect On It

- Identify and list your scars and thorns. Some will be physical, others emotional. Describe how each one is part of your story.

- How do you think God might be trying to use you, scars and all, at this point in your life?

Week Ten

Transformation of Desire
Lord, I Give In to You

Day One: Radical Acceptance

When we are abandoned by the things we value, when we discover that no matter how much we have gathered we do not have enough, when we realize that even in the currency we value we are very poor, we are ready to start talking to God. Not before. Faith means betting our lives on the grace of God. —Pastor and author M. Craig Barnes [136]

Deep wounds and sin are like rotten foods in our refrigerator. We smell the loathsome odor, but we don't know where the stink is coming from. Accepting and admitting our own sinful state is step one towards transformation. Only when we face the truth about what is really going on inside of us can freedom from suffering and spiritual transformation occur. Only as we allow God to fill us with him will we find where the odor is coming from. Only then can we accept our immeasurable worth and be truly set free.

We are human beings, living on this earth, with our own sets of frailties. Even when the Holy Spirit woos us and opens our eyes to our pathetic condition, we still have a tendency to seek our own solution instead of yielding to God's terms. Deep down, we don't want to lay down our arms.

The opposite of denial is acceptance—*radical acceptance.* For many of us home decorating is a creative outlet. For others it's an addiction. We must ask, "What place do I give it in my life?" Radical acceptance proclaims, "I've depended on redecorating my home to make me feel good and feel valued. I admit I've believed that newer, bigger, and better would bring pleasure."

Acceptance is acknowledging reality for what it is. There is nothing bad about these things. They only become bad when they feed our human desire to be in control. These soul stuffers are no different than substance soul stuffers. They are illusions and confirm that God is not number one in our lives.

Radical acceptance is admitting we are not following God's plan and we have a problem. In the Twelve Step program this is considered the first step—admitting we are powerless over our attachment, and therefore, our lives have become unmanageable. It is not about judging ourselves bad or justified. "The reality is I admit I have an eating disorder—period." This is the starting point for change.

I found it difficult to admit I'd been hiding in a cave with my abductor for so long. My gut said the emotional pain would only increase. Little did I know this was good! When we come to grips with our hurts then God, the great physician and transformer, can help us. Then our faith grows. And don't forget this is merely one part of your story. It is not your complete story. It is not *all* of you.

I finally admitted I made my own choices and then took responsibility for those choices. God knew the areas in my life which needed to be confessed, accepted, and changed to bring completeness and mind renewal. I don't know what yours are, but he does. Transformation begins when we prepare our hearts and minds to accept the truth and consequences of our behaviors, no matter how unpleasant. Are you ready?

Break the Power of Your Secret

> To confess your sins to God is not to tell him anything
> he doesn't already know. Until you confess them,
> however, they are the abyss between you. When you
> confess them, they become the Golden Gate Bridge.
> –Author Frederick Buechner[137]

Everyone has at least one dark secret. Every day millions of people hide things from friends and family. Many people go their whole lives keeping them hidden; or will deny, hide, justify or minimize them. Fear of exposure is powerful. Given we long to be accepted and admired, disclosure feels like all our sins are displayed on a highway billboard. Yet, if we continue to hide our secrets, the roots only get stronger, hence the term strongholds, and Satan wins.

If we want to grow and move ahead we must get familiar with the attribute of confession and repentance. To *confess* means we simply agree with God that our behavior is wrong. It gives us a sense of accountability to God. Step five in the Twelve Step program states that we "Admitted to God, to ourselves, and to another human being, the exact nature of our wrongs."

Real confession means humbly telling the entire truth about our actions. It begins the process of breaking the toxic cycle and represents the first step in mending the soul. As Mike Wilkerson said, "We must admit that our own hands have built the idols of our heart."[138] It is in brokenness and confession that our cover is blown, our burdens are lifted, the truth is released, and joy powerfully rushes in. Why? God's mercy is birthing a renewed mind and a pure heart.

We have all heard the saying, "Confession is good for the soul." There is healing power in confession. It is a process of becoming open, real, and honest with God, with others, and ourselves. Both James and Paul counseled that we not only tell God, but at least one other person (see James 5:16; Romans 10:10). Those who've embraced radical acceptance find healthy and safe outlets to release

181

their secrets. Some confide in a friend, others to a therapist, and some to a pastor or priest.

We must be willing to ask for help and share honestly about what's going on. We talk about our feelings and concerns. We don't defend our actions. This kind of connecting brings about healing and wholeness. Confession lets in the light and destroys Satan's grip (see John 8:12).

Confession is *always* followed by God's instant and complete forgiveness—grace. It clears the obstacles out of the way which hinder our relationship with him and others. When we come clean then troubling feelings of guilt and shame are removed. We can breathe again because confession cleanses and purifies.

Confession opens the door to making amends with others. We can only change ourselves, not another person. But the amazing thing is, when we change, we change the equation. The other person is forced to change in a positive manner. A healthier (not perfect) relationship is possible.

Our willingness to leave our attachments and insatiable desires behind shows God we're committed to him. Let your desire to please God compel you to relieve oppressive burdens. Be aware, it will be the sting of denial or shame or guilt or pride which will discourage you from confessing.

Reflect On It

We can't recover from a compulsive behavior of any kind unless we first see it, and then admit we have it. Answer these questions honestly. Remember, God knows the truth.

- What habit is driving either you or somebody else crazy?
- What are you addicted to?
- Do you see yourself as a codependent or a perfectionist?
- Are your attempts at being in command out of control?
- Are you ready to talk to someone else? If not, what do you fear?

Day Two: Consecration to God

The chief end of man is to serve God and enjoy him
forever. –Shorter Westminster Catechism

Consecration. What comes to mind when you hear that word?
Probably something really religious or ritualistic. True, consecration
in the Old Testament meant the Israelites were to undergo purification
rites. The definition for us is pretty simple: "dedication to God."
Consecration happens when we claim that our deepest desire is for
God, beyond everything else.

Consecration requires our willingness to trust in God's mystery
instead of complete comprehension. If I'm solely dedicated to
overcoming my behaviors on my own, I can't be consecrated to
God. Consecration is built on faith.

The opposite of consecration is self-sufficiency and pride. Oswald
Chambers stated in *My Utmost for His Highest,*

> He [God] can do nothing for us if we think we are
> sufficient of ourselves; we have to enter into His
> Kingdom through the door of destitution. As long as
> we are rich, possessed of anything in the way of pride
> or independence, God cannot do anything for us.[139]

Human beings were made for many things, but we have only
one primary purpose—to live consecrated to God. In fact, evidence
now shows human beings may be born with a desire for a relationship
with a "Transcendent Other." This longing begins to reveal itself in
children as young as three years old.[140]

Detoxify Thyself

The human personality is a reservoir of the most
incredible feelings and ideas. But in many circles,
especially Christian ones, the message seems to be:

183

Ignore it, keep it out of your mind, focus on Christ
in a way that blots out any deep self-awareness.
–Psychologist Larry Crabb[141]

When we hear the word *detoxification,* alcohol and drug detox
is what usually comes to our minds, or some sort of body cleansing
ritual. *Detox,* for short, is the removal of toxic substances from the
body, which includes our minds.

Repressing toxic feelings is how many of us deal with our
negative and pessimistic legacies. Painful memories are toxic to the
soul. They are stored up in multiple centers in the brain. If those
memories are about past events, they remain alive in the present and
effect what we do and who we are. We need to detox them. This is
recovery—recovering God's purpose for our lives and uncovering
our real selves.

Reverend Hiram Johnson said, "We all come out of childhood
wounded because of imperfect parenting. Termites are found in
virtually all of our family trees."[142] Even the family tree of Jesus
Christ reveals a closet full of dysfunctional skeletons. Yet these people
recovered God's plan for their lives.

Our family legacies are part of us. There is no burying them. And
God will use them to further his kingdom in some mysterious way.
They make up our kaleidoscopes. Often called *breaking the generational
curse*, we have the power to make the decision and say, "This is what
I want to keep alive. This is what I want to get rid of and not bring
with me into the next generation."

When we experience problems God stuns us into a state of self-
examination which is crucial to transformation. He can help us
become aware of beliefs shaped by our past. Our beliefs are those
things we believe to be truth. Digging them up, with the help of God,
and perhaps a professional, enables us to see those beliefs as faulty. We
detoxify them so we can develop new thoughts and beliefs.

Secondly, seeing sin as sin is necessary to the detox process. We
can be convinced we're okay or we're doing God's will when in

reality we're not. Sin is one thing God hates. One reason is because its capability to pervert is so great. The Lord said, "If you do not do what is right, sin is crouching at your door; it desires to have you, but you must master it" (Genesis 4:7).

At every moment of conviction, we must choose to master the sin crouching at the doorway of our minds. If we leave it unchecked, it may eventually destroy us. Sin needs to be called out for what it is—a toxic substance.

Pray as David did, "How can I know all the sins lurking in my heart? Cleanse me from these hidden faults. Keep your servant from deliberate sins! Don't let them control me. Then I will be free of guilt and innocent of great sin" (Psalm 19:12-13, NLT).

Reflect On It

- What fears are holding you back from consecrating yourself to God? Ask him to begin to reveal them to you.
- What do you believe is keeping you from self-examination?

Day Three: Lord, I Give in To You

I know, O LORD, that a man's life is not his own; it is not for man to direct his steps. –Jeremiah, speaking in Jeremiah 10:23

Do you think believers can remain in bondage? They can. I had been safely detoured from the road to hell, but unfortunately, for the next fourteen years my old self remained alive and well.

Our old nature and ways don't instantly disappear when we become a believer. We don't automatically think all good thoughts and express the right attitudes. We may still struggle with addictive, obsessive and compulsive behaviors. Fortunately, as we become more like Christ, we struggle less. He gives us the ammunition to fight our battles. Gratefully, God patiently waits for us to choose him over society.

In the opening chapters of Exodus we find God's people in slavery to an evil dictator named Pharaoh. God heard their cries for freedom, stretched out his mighty hand, crushed Pharaoh, and saved his people. After the miracle of delivering his children from Egyptian rule, the same children doubted God's provision for them. They returned to idol worship, grumbled bitterly and repeatedly.

Like the Israelites, we continue to love the wrong things and our worship is distorted. Through his Word and a series of circumstances, God cracked through my tough veneer. Undeniably, I needed to do a lot of healing work. Through the power of the Holy Spirit, God and I continued to work together on restoration and growth. It is the old prideful perfectionist in me that today strives to believe I've been completely healed, eradicating sin and my old ways. This is simply not the case.

God's work isn't over when we receive Christ—it's merely begun. Using the analogy of illness, imagine going to the doctor because you feel extremely ill. He diagnoses you with an infection and sends you home with a large bottle of antibiotics. He instructs you to take three tablets every day until they're all gone. After you ingest the first pill you don't feel any different. But you begin to feel better within a couple days. This is when it's tempting to discontinue the antibiotics declaring, "I'm healed!" If you discontinue the medication chances are great the infection will thrive because it hasn't been totally eliminated.

Our old selves are like that infection. When we become Christians we have the option of either letting our infection continue to fester, or to begin taking our medication, the Word of God, as instructed. Thinking that we are smart enough to navigate through life without our medication isn't wise. Scripture says, "There is a way that seems right to a man, but in the end it leads to death" (Proverbs 16:25).

As a Christian, our past is still part of our present. What many of us fail to realize is we are new in Christ, but our new selves still live in the same world, with the same families, in the same bodies; with all those old memories, desires, habits, addictions, and consequences (see Romans 7:21-25). Becoming a Christian doesn't remove the internal impulse to sin nor does it deter the devil from trying to exploit it. What is new is our ability to draw on the power God offers so we can resist these influences. We are a "new creation" because we are now in Christ and he is in us.

We can give Jesus our past and its memories, and leave our junk at the cross. We may have to deal with the consequences of our past, but they no longer define who we are, daughters of the Most High God.

Here is the key: We must be an empty vessel before we can be filled. We must desire the presence of God himself—not just his blessings. We must allow God to clean out all the cobwebs of our hearts and minds, and allow his grace to fill us up. We can only do this when we submit ourselves wholeheartedly to him.

We can expect a complete restoration in the future in eternity. Today we have grace. What we can expect now is that God will gather up all the broken pieces of our lives, making something beautiful and useful out of them, rather than demolishing us and starting over.

Grace Works through a Submissive Spirit

...Offer yourselves to God as people who have come back from death and are now alive. –Paul, speaking in Romans 6:13, GW

You may have noticed I haven't talked about surrender. We most certainly can come crashing down and finally admit, "I give up! I surrender!" But the flesh is going to be continually coming up with new lies and justifications to stay in the old way of life.

Many of us fear that a lifestyle of complete surrender will cost too much. I believe many of us cannot surrender completely on our own at this stage. What we can do is *submit*.

Have you ever driven your car with the parking brake on? Most of us have at one time. Driving with the brake engaged is potentially dangerous, which is why we only use it in situations where the car might roll. Consider that you are navigating through life with your parking brake on. God is asking you to release it—to release your life to him—to submit.

Submission is different than surrender, although we use the words synonymously. Submission is an act of our will, a purposeful intention. It is accepting what God has ordained as his purpose in our circumstances. Surrender is a total relinquishment of control, a declaration of spiritual bankruptcy. *I've hit rock bottom. I'm spent. I can't do this any longer in my own strength.* When there are no other perceived options, we surrender in complete dependence on God. Often the state of total surrender is not experienced for months or years. What takes place in its absence is *willing submission*.

The Bible says to submit ourselves to God (see James 4:7). Yet, everything in the world teaches us to do the opposite, to lead and be independent. The word *submit* means to line up under another's authority. When we line up under God's authority we are not alone. Submission is giving God permission to work his grace in my life.

Jesus submitted. The night before the crucifixion, he pleaded that God would rescue him. Three times Jesus asked his Father to take away his cup (see Mark 14:36-41). The cup symbolized God's divine judgment and the agony of alienation during the approaching crucifixion. I would have told God, "I really want to fulfill this mission, but isn't there an easier way out?" Not Jesus. He submits, "I want your will, not mine" (Mark 14:36, TLB).

Jesus accepts God's answer. He didn't seek an object of attachment to deal with the pain. He knew his mission would pave the way for eternity for us. We too must learn to submit and focus on God's decisive plan for us.

"Trust in the LORD with all your heart and lean not on your own understanding" (Proverbs 3:5). Trust and submission go hand in hand. Don't allow the devil to discourage you from taking the next step.

Reflect On It

How do you honestly feel about submitting to God? Tell him now.

Day Four: A Supernatural Wrestling Match

> There will likely be a time in our Christian journeys when, like Jacob, we will wrestle with God all night long…But there must eventually come a dawn when we say, OK, God, You win…Not my will but Thine be done. –Author Gary Thomas[143]

If you've ever watched a wrestling match, it's not so pretty. Wrestlers get down and dirty. There is no half-hearted involvement. They give it everything or face loss. Have you ever considered you may actually be in a daily wrestling match with God because you don't want to let go of your favorite things?

If you said yes, you'll empathize with Jacob's story. Jacob and his twin brother, Esau, were born to Isaac and Rebekah (see Genesis 25). Jacob was a self-willed mamma's boy who had all the opportunist instincts of an ambitious business man. God planned that Jacob would have the firstborn's birthright and blessing, even though he was the younger son. He became the bearer of the covenant promise.

As you can imagine, this angered Esau. Jacob fled to avoid a nasty conflict. God's plan for Jacob also included marrying his cousins Rachel and Leah, and becoming the father of the twelve patriarchs.

Jacob's entire attitude about life required changing. His self-reliance had to go. He needed to be weaned away from trusting his own cleverness to dependence upon God. He had to come to see his unscrupulous and dishonest dealings. He had to feel utter weakness and be brought to such self-distrust that he'd no longer try to exploit others.

When Jacob returned with his family back to Esau's country, he sent a polite message telling his brother of their arrival. Jacob misinterpreted Esau's reaction. His own guilty conscience made him expect the worst and Jacob fell into complete despair. God always waits for the right time...the time had come.

That night as Jacob stood alone by the river Jabbok, God met him (see Genesis 32:22-32). A spiritual wrestling match ensued—hours of desperate, agonizing conflict. Scripture says God touched the socket of Jacob's hip and his hip dislocated. Similar to Paul's thorn, from that day forward, every time Jacob took a step it reminded him of his own spiritual weakness and minute-by-minute need to depend on God.

In their struggle, the man [God] said, "Let me go, for it is daybreak." Jacob replied, "I will not let you go unless you bless me." The man asked him, "What is your name?"

"Jacob" he answered. Then the man said, "Your name will no longer be Jacob, but Israel, because you have struggled with God and with men and have overcome" (Genesis 32:26-28).

Jacob finally surrendered and requested a blessing. God blessed him and changed his name. Notice the order: first surrender, followed by blessing. After Jacob's supernatural encounter he knew how it felt to be unable to handle "things." No particle of self-sufficiency remained in him. Left weak and humbled by God, he'd never again trust in himself and author his own destiny. Jacob learned his lesson and never lapsed back into his old ways.

God built into Jacob a spirit of submission. He desired God's blessing so much that he clung to him through all the painful humbling. He was brought low enough for God to raise him up. Then God assured him he needn't fear Esau any longer.

Society's and Satan's motives are to keep us in bondage. Our fears, our self-possessiveness, our self-protection, the desire to avoid pain—all the stuff we hold onto, cause a struggle when we're faced with giving every part of ourselves to God. There are moments when God must break our self-confidence in order that we submit to his plan and methods. God's motive is to break us of our attachments and grow us into the likeness of Christ.

God demonstrated his strength and perfect love in the midst of Jacob's weaknesses. He gave him a thorn as a reminder of his sovereignty. Wrestling with God will bring victory when such struggling is done by means of a submitted heart, prayer, and sincerely seeking his favor.

As you contemplate which direction you want to go, remember God's directives are for our own good—to keep us from doing a great many things which may be perfectly right for everyone else, but are not right for us. When we realize we're truly broken we can reach for his mercy and grace. Then an honest relationship with him begins.

Say "Goodbye"

I can't change the direction of the wind, but I can adjust my sails to always reach my destination.
–Unknown

My college roommate refused to say "goodbye." Pulling out of our house's parking lot in her Mustang convertible, she'd yell, "Later!" The time has come to go one step further and lay our favorite thing down. If we truly desire to diminish the power of our flesh and submit to God, then we must make a commitment to begin the process of detachment, of saying "Goodbye," not "Later!"

Detachment means we stop finding meaning and security in our soul stuffers—in people, substances, things, positions, money, and power. We need to learn how to adjust to change and flexibly adapt. When we first submit to God and ask him to take over, it will feel like we're giving up our very soul. Yet, if we don't bend, the addiction will break us. This is why it is essential we pray and ask the Holy Spirit for self-control and guidance.

My name, *Sucker,* is on many retail marketing lists. Almost every day I receive juicy enticing email offers. I'd be lying if I said I didn't glance through them. The dopamine in my brain begins to excrete and I begin getting excited. God spoke to me clearly through his Word: "No one can serve two masters. Either he will hate the one and love the other, or he will be devoted to the one and despise the other" (Matthew 6:24).

No question, letting go of what is pleasurable and familiar is difficult. Those nasty habits resurface. The toxic thoughts recur. Sin keeps climbing back onto the throne. The attitude, "I'll stop the behavior and replace it with something else (and ignore the root cause)," isn't usually effective. To stop the cycle we must work to free ourselves from the root desires. We need to look at the internal cause rather than focus only on the action. It is great if we can replace a toxic obsession with a healthy passion. But if we don't find out why, then most likely we'll end up playing musical addictions.

Presently we have something tangible we can hang onto, something we perceive brings us pleasure. When we let go we don't have anything tangible in our hands. What I want you to realize is when you let go you open the door to freedom. I cannot show you scientific measurable results. It is called faith. What Jesus is asking us to do is give him all our tangibles. What he gives us in return is immeasurable love and purpose.

Reflect On It

Consider that some of the wrestling matches with God reveal selfish motives, rather than a desire for God's glory. Have you pushed God away because perhaps you feel hurt or feel he didn't give you what you wanted?

Day Five: Biblical Detachment

> Our Lord never insists upon obedience; He tells us very emphatically what we ought to do, but He never takes means to make us do it. We have to obey Him out of a oneness of spirit. That is why whenever Our Lord talked about discipleship, He prefaced it with an *if*. –Oswald Chambers, *My Utmost for His Highest*.

This is our season of truth. Ecclesiastes 3 tells us there is a time for everything. This is our time to search, to throw away, and to rebuild. Jesus said, "If any of you wants to be my follower, you must put aside your own pleasures and shoulder your cross, and follow me closely" (Mark 8:34, TLB).

I think too often this is one of those biblical truths which have been misapplied. Taken out of context it results in a narrow and faulty doctrine that basically says, "If you really want to follow Christ you must give up your comfortable life to suffer and be miserable. The more you suffer, the more God will love you."

Jesus meant we must accept the death of our own self-directed life. In the process we must be willing to face whatever physical, emotional, or social harassments ensue—being ridiculed for our beliefs and losing certain friends (they were probably not real friends to begin with), swapping happy hour for serving the homeless, or giving up expensive cosmetic procedures. This is what exchanging our old selfish life for a new selfless life in Christ looks like.

Far too many Christians are living a life they weren't meant to live. They assume that if they do something they don't like or feel comfortable with, it is what God wants. They don't understand that God desires for them to live an abundant life. Someone once said, "Life isn't about finding yourself; it's about discovering who God created you to be." As we discover our God-given purpose and live in accordance with that, joy is imminent.

Are you living spiritually like a person who is on a diet but leaves a pack of frozen pizzas in the freezer? It is hard to deny ourselves what we truly desire with temptation banging at our door each day, maybe every minute. With the help of the Holy Spirit we can learn to let go of sinful, insatiable desires. To do this we must grow in the spiritual virtue of attachment—attachment to God alone.

A Radical Change of Mind

The only way to dispossess [the heart] of an old affection, is by the expulsive power of a new one.
–Puritan Thomas Chalmers[144]

Emily lived next door to Anna. The kids in the neighborhood liked tormenting Anna, calling her names because she was a girl "of color." It hurt her deeply. One day Emily wanted to go skating but her skates were broken. The only girl she could borrow a pair from was Anna.

"Okay, you may borrow them," Anna answered. When Emily returned them, she found Anna sitting by the fireplace reading the Bible. Emily thanked her and recalled, "She looked at me and with tears in her eyes, said, "Emily, don't ever call me names again." Then she left the room. Emily said, "Those words pierced my heart. I resolved to never again abuse a member of a minority group."

This story is an illustration of *repentance*. Repentance literally means *change of mind,* which leads to a complete turnaround of motivations. It goes hand in hand with confession. It means acknowledging you have been relying on your idols for security, significance, and hope.

You say, "I've been doing life my way. It's not working. I have to change and go in God's direction." Frederick Buechner said we come to our senses when we repent.[145] If our confession doesn't come out of a true desire for godly repentance, it's merely counterfeit repentance. Our minds and hearts won't change.

Looking at denial straight in the face and admitting our offenses is the start to changing our mind and heart. Repentance requires we choose to nurture a love relationship with God rather than our object of attachment. Genuine repentance also means we make amends with the people we've hurt (called *restitution*).

Two of Jesus's disciples, Judas and Peter, betrayed and denied him. Torn apart with self-loathing, guilt and shame, Judas the traitor committed suicide. Peter, however, repented and became a powerful leader. They both had entirely different fates. True repentance doesn't look back—it looks forward. Instead of saying, "But this happened..." We say, "I have a whole new beginning ahead of me!"

Pray: "Lord God, I am weak. Today I call upon you for help to follow you faithfully. Forgive my excuses, my sins of willfulness and selfishness. Forgive my grasping idols. I agree to listen to the voice of the Holy Spirit. Enable me to turn my life around. Restore me as only you can. In Jesus's name, Amen."

Reflect On It

- What form does counterfeit repentance presently take in your life?
- What specifically must you commit to Jesus and say goodbye to so you aren't continually recaptured by your object of affection?

Week Eleven

Transformation of Mind
Lord, Renew Me Wholly!

Day One: An Authentic Make-Over

Charles H. Spurgeon, an influential preacher in the 1800s, recounts:

> I was walking one day, while I was seeking the Savior. All of a sudden the most fearful oaths that any of you can conceive rushed through my mind. I had not, that I know of, ever heard these words; and I am certain that I had never used in my life... the most fearful imprecations would dash through my brain. Oh, how I groaned and cried before God. That temptation passed away; but ere many days it was renewed again; and when I was in prayer, or when I was reading the Bible, these blasphemous thoughts would pour in upon me more than at any other time....[146]

If this godly man regularly fought toxic thinking, then we

shouldn't feel too defeated. God never gives up on his creation. To be renewed—to revive the image of God within us—to restore what has been lost—is part of God's plan. Look at how often the state of renewal is referred to in the Bible:

- "God satisfies your desires with good things so that your youth is renewed like the eagle's" (Psalm 103:5).
- "When doubts filled my mind, your comfort gave me renewed hope and cheer" (Psalm 94:19, NLT).
- "Don't be conceited, sure of your own wisdom. Instead, trust and reverence the Lord, and turn your back on evil; when you do that, then you will be given renewed health and vitality" (Proverbs 3:7, TLB).
- "Though outwardly we are wearing out, inwardly we are renewed day by day" (2 Corinthians 4:16, GW).
- "...be transformed by the renewing of your mind" (Romans 12:2).

God has made each of us special, extraordinary, and maybe a little peculiar. We are all different on purpose. As Christians, we've been raised to a God ordained new life, not to excel in our old life or to copycat somebody else's.

The Bible says we are God's amazing workmanship (see Ephesians 2:10). I am *his* masterpiece. Yet I have to admit there are days I desire what the world has to offer and want to create my own masterpiece—which is countercultural to God's plan:

> Don't copy the [*sinful and compulsive*] behavior and customs of this world, but let God transform you into a new person by changing the way you think. Then you will learn to know God's will for you [*you will recover God's plan for your life*], which is good and pleasing and perfect. (Romans 12:2, NLT, *my interpretation*)

Have you ever noticed that many elderly Christians tend to be more thoughtful, kind, patient, and loving? Through years of imitating Christ they've grown more and more into his image. Their physical health may be failing, eyesight growing dim, hearing waning, but they rarely lose heart. Why? Their inner nature and minds continue to be renewed every day.

The good news is we can partake of a powerful kind of freedom— freedom of the mind. God transforms us by renewing our minds, which he does when we ingest his Word, truth.

Changing Our Mental Tracks

> If you want to know where your heart is, look where your mind goes when it wanders. Work on refurbishing your mind because it affects everything you do. –Unknown

"You could stop if you really tried or really wanted to!" The assumption is that by exerting willpower and trying hard in our own strength, we can stop compulsive behavior. Perhaps you've promised yourself you'll read the Bible more, or relax on your cleaning rituals, or quit spending so many hours on Facebook, or stop obsessing about food and exercise. I used to think I could stop my obsessive behaviors with mere willpower, but was wrong.

Willpower can produce short-term change, but it also creates constant internal stress because the root cause hasn't been dealt with. And when you do fall, those nasty feelings of shame rise back to the surface again. The change doesn't feel natural, so eventually you give up and quickly revert back to old patterns.

"Once an addict, always an addict. I'll never change because compulsive behavior is in my genes." Perhaps this is your belief or what you've been told. A saying goes, "Don't believe everything you think!" Research does indicate some people are more prone to addiction. But susceptibility does not mean inevitability. Social and environmental factors make up a large part of addiction risk.[147]

For the most part, we learn how to think, feel, and act. Therefore, we can unlearn many actions. Here is a good metaphor. Think of your brain like a snowy hill. Characteristics of the hill such as the slope, rocks, consistency of the snow, are like our genes, a given. When we slide down the hill on a sled, we steer it. We create a path determined both by how we steer and the characteristics of the hill. We can't predict where we end up because of the factors in play.

The second time you slide down the slope you'll most likely find yourself near the path you made the first time. It won't be the exact path, but close. If you spend your entire day sledding up and down, at the end you'll have some paths which have been used a lot and others which have been used very little. With every slide down the hill, you'll find it becomes increasingly difficult to get out of those well-worn paths.

We all have laid down mental tracks or paths. They can lead to good habits or bad habits. It is possible to get out of those old tracks and start new ones. It can be difficult because once we've created these tracks they become fast and very efficient at guiding our thoughts down the hill.[148]

To take a different path becomes increasingly difficult unless a roadblock is put in the path to help us change direction. When that new iPhone® calls out, *Buy me! You need me!* I choose to put up a roadblock. I realize this is my flesh speaking. I say, "I don't need a new phone." Truth be told, I want a new iPhone® to impress my peers. I remind myself that God is the only person I need to impress. Therefore, I will use the money (which is really God's money) to either pay down my debt or use it for God's Kingdom. Now I'm beginning to create a new, and soon well-worn, track.

God designed humans to adapt. Dr. Norman Doidge, in his book *The Brain that Changes Itself,* said if we learn to refocus, we will not get sucked in by the content of an obsession but can work around it.[149] Already formed habits will resist. The flesh will fight, but will be bridled by the Holy Spirit. The devil will trouble you, but prayer will send him away.

The Mind of Christ

> May the words of my mouth and the meditation of my heart be pleasing to you, O LORD, my rock and my redeemer. –David, speaking in Psalm 19:14, NLT

Get ready for this: Paul declared, "we have the mind of Christ" (1 Corinthians 2:16). He isn't saying we are brainiacs or perfect and cannot fail. He is telling us we can experience a powerful mind change. We can think spiritual thoughts because Jesus is alive within us. His mind is active in our minds! This gives us hope, especially when we tie it into God's other promise that we can be transformed by renewing our minds. God wouldn't have told us this if he didn't give us the ability to do it.

This is exactly what Paul meant when he wrote Philippians 4:8. *The Message* paraphrase reads, "I'd say you'll do best by filling your minds and meditating on things true, noble, reputable, authentic, compelling, gracious—the best, not the worst; the beautiful, not the ugly; things to praise, not things to curse." The mind of Christ directs us to think about the constructive—not the destructive.

When we feel love and think positive thoughts our bodies release the hormone DHEA. Our brain releases positive chemicals and our brain cells look like beautiful, lush, healthy trees because healthy chemicals are released.[150] If we choose to think positively then we're that much closer toward developing a good habit.

On the other hand, ongoing negative behavior eventually wreaks havoc on our entire being. When we think negative, stressful thoughts our body releases the hormone cortisol. Prolonged cortisol secretion results in significant physiological changes, such as weight gain, and also weakens the immune system. Negative emotions release toxins. Brain cells look like dark, ugly, mangled thorn bushes.[151]

DHEA is cortisol's enemy. Research indicates DHEA has an anti-depressant effect and protects from cortisol over-concentration long term. When we train ourselves to think positively instead of negatively, our tolerance for pain is higher, our recovery from illness or surgery is quicker, and our blood pressure drops.[152] No wonder God tells us to think on good, positive things.

The first attribute Paul talks about is truth. We must evaluate what is going on in our minds and ask, "Does truth occupy the high ground in my mind?" If not, then we can expect negative consequences to happen. We know untruths come out of wrong or bad beliefs. This is why we must learn how to address errors in our thinking and replace them with truth.

We have a great responsibility to watch and guard what we believe we're responsible for. If our thoughts are in line with the mind of Christ, in line with Philippians 4:8, we will be successful. The key is empowering the Holy Spirit with the spiritual discipline of studying the truth. This means every day ingesting the Word of God and spending time with him.

Reflect On It

1. Examine your thoughts. On a piece of paper create two columns. Label one "Lies or Misbeliefs." Label the other "Truth." Write your typical negative expression under "Lies." Then write a positive affirmation, preferably using Scripture, under "Truth."

2. Every day your brain is engaged in an activity called *choosing*. Instead of, "I *need* to check my phone messages and Facebook account every fifteen minutes," say, "I *choose* to switch

tracks and will do something better, like give my struggling girlfriend my undivided attention for one hour."

3. For example, after much prayer you agree, "In order to function effectively I must commit a significant amount of time living outside the virtual world." Good. At first concentrate on switching tracks in thirty-minute segments until it becomes a habit.

As you engage in these exercises remember God's Words, "Be strong and work. For I am with you" (Hagai 2:4).

Day Two: Take an Honest Look and Practice Interrogation

Why are you thinking these things? –Jesus, speaking in Mark 2:8

With a lump in her throat, Jenny confided to her Bible study group, "When I'm at work and around other people, I don't desire to eat a lot. But when I get home and I'm all alone, that's when I lose it. I'll sit for hours, numb, eating junk food. Why do I eat like a normal person around other people, but not by myself?"

Jenny openly confessed her battle with food. This was the starting point to breaking her addiction. She asked *why*. Many professionals simply recommend, "Stop your negative self-talk," without telling you how to do it.

This reminds me of the popular Bob Newhart skit titled, "Just stop it!" (Newhart played a psychologist in the TV series *The Bob Newhart Show*.) His solution to every problem is simple: just stop it! Don't like your weight? Stop eating so much! Irrational fears? Stop being afraid! Careless with money? Stop spending!

As pop psychologist Dr. Phil says, "How has that worked for you?" Not so good? The next step is to ask God, "Why the insatiable cravings? What am I trying to cover up?" I call this *interrogation*—the process of exploring the reasons why we do what we do. You may need to seek guidance from a Christian counselor who can help you break down large barriers.

Life began shifting when I made the commitment to understand the shape my thoughts had taken by examining them regularly. When prisoners are taken captive, they're interrogated. When we take a thought captive, we do the same. *"Why* am I thinking this way?" We ask God for information. *"Why* am I feeling so fearful and rejected today? This is the third time this week!" *"Why* do I keep doing what I don't want to do?" "Where is this coming from?" Jesus asked God an agonizing question from the cross, *"Why* have you forsaken me?"

Don't be afraid to ask God *why.* A problem cannot be solved until it is honestly faced and opened up. Dig up specific fears. Begin to pay attention to any anxiety. Notice any apprehension. To merely send your thought away is to leave an opening for another negative thought to take hold. Rather, interrogate it. We ask God to reveal toxic memories and agreements we've made with ourselves. Once I started interrogating my thoughts and actions instead of blowing them off, God began to expose and clean out a lot of old hurts.

God began to reveal to Jenny the source of her battle with food. She was terrified to be alone. So she ate. The fear came from the fact her dad left Jenny and her mom when she was three years old. Jenny had a choice: either, in faith, she could get to the source of her feelings of abandonment and inability to be alone. Or, in fear, she could leave the wound alone, living in pain and denial, and eat herself to death. If she follows her faith, God will begin opening and redressing the wound, possibly through counseling.

Many women fear confronting memories of the past. Why do we need to do this? To know *the why* opens the door to seeing the seriousness of a problem and the need for more than "Stop it!" or "Go away thought!" Often mere behavior modification isn't the answer. Discovering the motivation behind the thought or behavior is important.

Christ in us means he is the Lord of our memories. When we understand the memory or the thought, the soul heals because we're freed from unnecessary guilt, anxiety, and shame. We claim our identity as God's daughter and move toward permanent Christlikeness. We reject any agreements or claims that have been given to the enemy. Denial disappears. Satan has no more power.

Pray: "Lord God, thank you for continuing to free me. Reveal that which needs to be broken and restored by you. Help me to recognize and stand strong against my enemies, standing firm in who I am in you. Deliver me today from any yoke of bondage. Help me to keep moving forward so I won't be drawn back into those things which have kept my mind enslaved to the world's, Satan's, and my own flesh's ways. In Jesus's name. Amen."

Reflect On It

When I take each toxic thought captive in obedience to Christ, it means I ask the Holy Spirit to clarify whether the thought will help me or hurt me. When your next problematic thought pops up ask:

1. What is the source? Where did the thought come from? The devil, the flesh, or the world? Yes! Toss it out.
2. Can I defend this thought from the Word of God? Is this thought scripturally sound? Is it truth? No! Toss it out.
3. If I follow this thought will this get me where God wants me to go? No! Toss it out.
4. Will this thought build me up or tear me down? Jealousy, greed, shame, anger, fear, and pride will tear you down. Toss it out.
5. Does it bring life (freedom and joy) or death (bondage)? Death! Toss it out.
6. Does this thought make me feel shamed or condemned or unworthy? Yes! Toss it out.

7. Does this thought fit who I am: the daughter and a follower of Jesus Christ? No! Toss it out.
8. Does this thought bring glory to Jesus? No! Toss it out.

Day Three:
Pursue Contentment

> It is not our circumstances that create our discontent or contentment. It is us. —Inspirational artist Vivian Greene

A bumper sticker reads: "Contentment is *not*: a faster car, a handsome husband, a million dollars, plastic surgery, a huge house, or winning a popularity contest. Contentment is: Knowing who you are, why you are here, and where you are going!

What I propose now is we pursue the attribute of contentment. Our culture certainly discourages it since we are constantly bombarded with messages to make more, get more, and have more, which only fuels our insatiable appetites. Yet, our lives will be transformed if we choose to develop an appetite for contentment instead of over-stimulation.

Contentment is a state of being characterized by not desiring more than we need. Another word is *satisfaction.* A content person is generally satisfied with life. If cultivated, contentment can produce feelings of serenity, pleasure, and stress reduction. The apostle Paul is a great example of a person who pursued contentment. He said, "I have learned to be content..." (Philippians 4:11).

Notice Paul said he "learned" contentment. This was a big deal. Because of his zeal for communicating the Good News, Paul spent years in prison and was beaten frequently. I would guess a spirit of contentment didn't just happen one day. Most likely it was years in the making. If it were me I'd be wailing, "Get me out of jail first. Then I'll be content Lord!"

Paul's writings highlight that contentment, astonishingly, has nothing to do with our circumstances. He endured due to his faith. He knew God was in the middle of his circumstances and would provide his daily bread. He trusted him solely.

I can honestly say that today I'm content, a far cry from the state of my soul just ten years ago. When I began replacing worldly, selfish thoughts with God's thoughts, I began to feel content. For example, I used to think I had to sell hoards of books and have a powerful speaking platform in order to be successful. Through consistent Bible study, the power of prayer, and Christ in me, today I know this isn't true. Those ideologies don't define me. I give those worldly desires to God. He knows what he's doing. He defines each person's effectiveness. He is the one with the divine plan, not I. I will succeed at being myself only as submit to him.

Like Paul, if we embrace our Savior wholeheartedly, we can learn to be content with our lives. I believe we must first have a strong foundation of contentment before we feel happy on a consistent basis. Without that grounding we'll merely live craving more. If I seek God more than anything else, I will eventually seek more of what God wants for me...and be satisfied with that.

When we feel content we become others-directed instead of self-seeking. Focus on loving and helping others. It is an effective remedy for any compulsive behavior because it breeds pleasure and satisfaction. *Choose contentment.* Spend time with God. Ask him to help you transform your attitude to one of satisfaction. I am convinced if we don't, we'll always be at risk for addiction because discontentment is a destructive force.

Reflect On It

- On a scale of one to ten, ten being the most content— feeling gratitude, satisfaction, and submitted to God, where do you fall on the scale? Explain.
- Name two things you can incorporate into your daily schedule to begin to increase your level of contentment.

Day Four: Fear, Faith, and Recovery

Take courage! It is I. Don't be afraid. –Jesus, speaking
in Matthew 14:27

We are nearing the finish line of this particular journey. The
last part requires examining the three most common roadblocks to
healing and breaking toxic habits: fear, grief, and unforgiveness.

We each have two important groups of mindsets: positive faith-
based emotions and negative fear-based emotions. I believe all of
our addictive behaviors are disguises for fear. If I substitute the word
"fear" for addiction it makes sense. When we live in a constant state
of fear [addiction] most of life passes us by because we're physically,
emotionally, relationally, and spiritually unable to focus on anything
else. We lose all ability to concentrate and, therefore, are unable to
consume truth. Our goal is to understand fear, and then turn it into
faith.

Satan's plan is to instill deadly, incapacitating fear because it
makes us dependent upon our attachments. The illusion of control,
dishonesty, negativity, denial, dependency, and defensiveness is born
out of fear. I feared truth. Who would I be? How would I function
without my dependencies? It felt easier to escape into my world of
addictive behaviors.

Fear is a reaction to an event which we interpret as a threat to our
well-being. There are two types of fear: positive fear and toxic fear.
Positive fear is God-given. All people have an instinctual response to
potential danger, which is important to survival. It motivates us to
buy home insurance (fear of fire), to follow the law (fear of prison),
and to obey (fear of discipline).

Toxic fear is from Satan. Phobias and negative emotions such as
anxiety, worry, panic, and anger, evolve out of fear. Toxic fear can
lead us to feel powerless, which often triggers anger, and/or a frantic
attempt to fix the situation. When we let go of fear these toxic

emotions can dissipate. Fear can even be disguised as an addiction to danger and risk-taking; the kind we feel before we bungee jump, watch a horror movie, or shoplift.

Toxic fear can be paralyzing. When we start to feel like this, we typically begin to isolate to decrease feelings of guilt and shame. We practice denial or defeat or escapism. It prevents transformation and recovery because it breeds hopelessness and despair. It is rooted in the belief that God's Word isn't real, and therefore, becomes a hurdle in our relationship with God.

There are three roots of fear which threaten healing. Fear about haunting past experiences, fear of lack of control in the present over something upsetting, and fear of the unknown. Each contributes to the desire to relieve tension. It is interesting that fear most often relates to future events. We are not fortunetellers. There is nothing we can do about the past or the future.

Scripture says perfect love—love from the Father, drives out fear, because fear has to do with punishment (see 1 John 4:18). God did not give us a spirit of fear (see 2 Timothy 1:7). Yet, our greatest crises come from toxic fear. The solution: we admit to God we can't fix our problems ourselves. We put our confidence in him alone.

Faith, on the other hand, is like a cool breeze on a hot day, refreshing us and giving us the strength to continue to fight. Scripture says, "Faith is being sure of what we hope for and certain of what we do not see" (Hebrews 11:1).

Recognize that our experiences aren't characterized by either fear *or* faith; rather, fear *and* faith. Faith doesn't wipe out fear. It has been said that if we didn't experience fear, then we wouldn't need faith. Jesus experienced both human fear and spiritual faith at the same time. He prayed and agonized over his forthcoming crucifixion.

Fear is an opportunity to cultivate faith. One way we cultivate faith is by creating new faith–based mental tracks. Begin to identify toxic fearful thoughts such as, "This situation can't get any better," or "I've always been a loser and always will be," or "Addiction runs in my family. There's no hope." We capture these thoughts. In faith we give them to Jesus. We know through the power of Christ we can overcome. Faith shouts back to fear (Satan):

- "I'm not going to be in this dark valley forever. I have hope!"
- "I've been gifted by God. I'm not a loser."
- "I can break the generational curse of perfectionism and addiction in my family with God's help and grace."
- "I belong to God, therefore, have overcome evil because Jesus, who is in me, is greater than Satan" (see 1 John 4:4).
- "I'm not going to think this way because I'm God's daughter."
- "I'm in God's family we don't do this."

Reflect On It

- Circle the destructive choice you are most likely to make in the midst of a fear-producing situation: *Denial. Defeat. Bitterness. Escape.*
- Are you willing to allow God to do whatever is necessary in order to free you from fear?
- Are you afraid to step out in faith, to do what God is asking you to do? If so, remember who's sending you. Take one step forward. God's right there and will catch you if you fall.
- One overarching message of the Bible is "fear not." Experience God and cultivate faith through specific verses. Write them out. Put them somewhere visible. Tape some on your mirror or refrigerator. Put some in your phone. Memorize them.

- Use your Bible concordance and pick a bible verse which speaks about courage and strength. Use it to fight fear-based feelings. For example, "The LORD is my light and my salvation—whom shall I fear? The LORD is the stronghold of my life—of whom shall I be afraid?" (Psalm 27:1)

Day Five:
Heal Your Soul by Healing Your Grief

> God is our merciful Father and the source of all comfort. He comforts us in all our troubles...—Paul, speaking in 2 Corinthians 1:3-4, NLT

When Ariel, a self-confessed Internet addict, began the self-examination process she came to the conclusion, "I'm a complete failure as a Christian." What Ariel never realized was that in order to mend her soul she needed to grieve a loss. Grief is intense emotional suffering caused by a loss. It is not always about death. It happens with divorce and relationship breakups, in business and life transitions, with disaster or misfortune. Grief involves a complex set of emotions, all of which are perfectly normal.[153]

Ariel lost her mom at the young age of fifteen. In her family you "bucked up" and moved on—no time for tears. Overnight she became Mom to her three younger siblings. Her dad buried his grief in his work. Ariel worked relentlessly to keep the family connected. She felt unworthy and believed God gave her what she deserved.

Through counseling she eventually came to understand she had been created in the image of a loving God who built her to share her emotions. She grieved and let herself cry over losing her mother. There may be no greater window to the soul than our tears. In order to heal, sorrow must be acknowledged and accepted. Jesus openly wept (see John 11:35; Jeremiah 9:1-11). He can help us mourn over what we've lost or done.

Did you know God keeps track of all our sorrows and collects each tear? He does. Each one is recorded in his book (see Psalm 56:8). Most people say they feel better after a good cry, which is no surprise. Tears which come from sorrow have a different chemical composition than tears that come from joy. There are no toxins in joy tears.[154] When you cry, it appears, stress hormones released by the brain are flushed out of your system. You begin to feel calmer, even refreshed.

My brother and I have talked about how distressing moving multiple times had been for us. Moving stresses both parents and children, especially if the move is resented. The loneliness and loss of friendships hurts. Research shows many are at risk for depression. Relocating may also increase the risk of teen sexual activity as the teen seeks social acceptance.[155] I had no control over what happened in my life. Since I could choose what I ate and weighed, bulimia is how I chose to deal with loss.

Sometimes our behavior is due to a memory of an earlier loss which was never fully grieved. If someone has died or left, an addiction may be due to intense feelings of guilt for aspects of the relationship which were never acknowledged. Other times addictive behavior only surfaces during certain times of the year, such as the month the person left or died, on family holidays, or a birthday or anniversary.[156]

In this society we're very good at downplaying our anguish. Our culture values the ability to stand strong in times of grief. Weeping is often seen as a weakness. *Be self-controlled!* We stuff our grief because we're so good at denial and minimization. We generally don't value, or give permission for the open expression of grief or pain. Even the abused tend to downplay their pain.

Mental health experts say the rule is: if *you feel* a significant loss, regardless of the world's definition, it is a loss. Every person grieves differently. The goal is not to get life back on track the way it was before. The goal is to find and accept *a new normal.*

Grieve the Loss of Your Past

> The past isn't your past if it is still affecting your present. –Psychologist Tim Clinton[157]

Read these two verses slowly. Truly, they are powerful and comforting. However, Paul leaves out something—something that can separate us from God. Can you see it?

> For I am convinced that neither death nor life, neither angels nor demons, neither the present nor the future, nor any powers, neither height nor depth, nor anything else in all creation, will be able to separate us from the love of God that is in Christ Jesus our Lord. (Romans 8:38–39)

The answer: our past. God knows the wounds and lies of our past can distort our view of him, and of life, and ultimately separate us from him. This is why it is important to grieve the loss of our pasts. Grieve whatever season of life you were in when you feel you lost your innocence and soul. I needed to grieve my adolescence and young adulthood because I could never get it back.

Scripture says, "It is better to go to a house of mourning than to go to a house of feasting" (Ecclesiastes 7:2). Doctors Robert Hemfelt, Frank Minirth, and Paul Meier list four areas we should grieve:[158]

Grieve for our original family pain if there was a high level of abuse or dysfunction within it. We may need to detach and disengage from a parent, and then grieve the loss. Or, when we come to terms with the fact we'll never have the loving parent we desired, we should grieve the loss.

Grieve over saying good-bye to Mom and Dad if this act has been deferred. Many adults and codependents are still living in their parent's home or striving to meet their parent's approval. We must learn to focus on God and stop looking to our parents for things they cannot give us. This doesn't mean we ignore them and antagonize the situation.

Grieve over the addictions, codependencies, and other coping mechanisms we are abandoning. Our attachments have become an important part of our lives. We need to mourn their loss. In the Sermon on the Mount, Jesus said, "Blessed are those who mourn, for they will be comforted" (Matthew 5:4). He is speaking of grieving over our personal sin. Notice he said that if we did this we'd be blessed.

Grieve over the losses accrued over the years. The truth surfaced: I'd been gravely deceived, lost my virginity, wasted precious years, destroyed priceless friendships, and chose to kill my unborn child. I made grave errors and threw away thousands of dollars. I cried. I hurt. I needed to forgive myself. First I grieved my baby's death. Then I took time to grieve the passing away of my old self. I wept over the death of this pitiable young woman who, like Hamlet's Ophelia, lost her innocence and the essence of her soul.

God too grieves for our losses. He is a God who restores and takes every tear, every mistake, and works them into a new vibrant plan. He told the Israelites if they returned to him he would repay them for the years the locusts ate and never again would they feel shamed (see Joel 2:25-26). God *will* make up for the lost years—the years that sin and dysfunction devoured.

Reflect On It

Which of the four areas of grief mentioned above do you feel moved to mourn? Here are two things you can do immediately:

1. *Express your grief in a prayer to Jesus (in voice or in writing).* Jesus cried openly. His tears give not only dignity to your grief but freedom to your emotions. He knows and feels your pain.
2. *Make a list of a few good friends to call.* Share your grief with others. Let them comfort you and hold you up in prayer. You may want to consider joining a grief support group.

Week Twelve

Radical Forgiveness
Let it Go and Discover Healing

Day One: The Intruder

I, even I, am he who blots out your transgressions,
for my own sake, and remembers your sins no more.
–God, speaking in Isaiah 43:25

Chatting about the plans for the weekend came to a screeching halt as we approached the home we recently moved into. The front door stood wide open. I felt the blood drain from my body when I saw kitchen items spewed across the floor. *We've been robbed!*

Nothing prepares you for that sight. At first I felt fearful—some mysterious weasel slithered in and violated our space. Then I became angry because it took our stuff. The police suspected the neighbor kid. We upped the security and eventually the fear subsided.

Three years later we received a blank envelope tucked within the daily mail. It contained a one-hundred dollar bill with a note which said something like, "I'm the person who stole from you years ago. I want to pay you back. Please forgive me. I don't want to tell you who I am in case you want to beat me up. I'll pay you back as I can."

Beat you up? I want to hug you! We were convinced it was the neighbor kid, Brian. We got two more envelopes, each containing a one-hundred dollar bill, devoid of any notes. My husband started to talk to Brian regularly. One day, with great hesitancy, Brian said, "I need to tell you something." My husband responded first, "I already know and you've been forgiven."

Given the nature of his past relationships, he looked shocked. Brian found it hard to forgive himself. No one forgave or loved a person who is "bad." We did. We loved Brian because God first loved us (see 1 John 4:19). And in return, God loved Brian through us. This young man felt valuable for the first time in his life. He could begin the process of forgiving himself and move forward.

Once we've been forgiven, it is unnecessary to continue the self-torture, feeling guilty about what our sins have done to others or to ourselves. We can be grateful for forgiveness. Forgiveness is not so much about those who need to be forgiven, but rather about facing our personal demons head on. God knows how difficult it is.

Think about the forgiveness Jesus offered. It has been said that Judas took his own life as a form of self-punishment. He never knew Jesus forgave him for turning him over for arrest, which led to his crucifixion. Jesus forgave Peter for disowning him. He forgave the woman who committed adultery. He forgives you. Now it's your turn to own the forgiveness God has given you. Let go of the shame and self-condemnation permanently!

God said, "Their sins and lawless acts I will remember no more" (Hebrews 10:17). However, Satan will continue to bait us into self-sabotage by leading us away from working on forgiveness. If God forgets our sins, we can let them go.

Unlock a Life of Freedom

If the child of the past and the adult of the present
are to integrate fully into the person of the future,

215

there comes a time when both must release the hurts of the past. This doesn't mean that you forget what has been done to you, but that you forgive those responsible, whether they deserve your forgiveness or not. Forgiveness is the final destination on your healing journey. The road that lies beyond is one of health. –Psychologist Gregory L. Jantz[159]

God's grace is the miracle which causes transformation. It changes angry, hurt people into forgiving and loving people who come to understand "hurt people hurt people." I knew if I was to grow and trust again then I had to release the hurts of my past. This meant I first had to ask God to forgive my sinful actions, and then ask him to empower me to forgive those who hurt, teased, rejected, and assaulted me—whether they deserved it or not.

I hurt and let down other people. I asked for my mother's forgiveness. I confessed stealing money from her to support my addiction. She answered, "What you did hasn't changed the way I love and think of you. We've all done things we aren't proud of. There isn't anyone to judge you except God. And we know how forgiving He is."

There are perceived benefits to holding onto our anger. It makes us feel powerful and in control. However, we do great damage to ourselves when we hang onto an unforgiving spirit. Physically, the emotion unforgiveness releases toxins. Relationally, when we fail to forgive, our bitterness slowly poisons our other relationships since we create division, conflict, and turmoil. Spiritually, when we don't forgive, we block God's mercy.

Forgiveness is a powerful tool which can transform feelings of anger and bitterness into feelings of neutrality, and for some, into positive emotions. Someone said, "You can either be right or you can be happy, but you can't be both." It has been documented repeatedly, and I have seen it personally in ministry, forgiving provides a reduction in symptoms associated with a traumatic or shameful experience. It promotes improved well-being and enhanced relational skills.

Forgiveness means we let go of what was done to us, or should have been done for us. We give up our rights for revenge or retaliation. We no longer define ourselves by what has happened to us, but by what God is presently doing in us. Why should we forgive?

- God forgave us. Out of gratitude to him we choose to forgive.
- We are made in his image and created to reflect him. Telling somebody, "I forgive you because God forgave me" is to reflect Jesus to an unforgiving world.
- God commands us to.[160]
- It has personal benefits as a healing agent and it frees the soul.

Peter asked, "Lord, how often should I forgive someone who sins against me? Seven times?" "No, not seven times," Jesus replied, "but seventy times seven!" (Matthew 18:21-22, NLT) That is 490 times!

In other words, *keep forgiving until it becomes a new habit.* This requires ongoing cultivation. Understand you will go through difficult moments. Setbacks are normal. Remember, God has the power to make *all* things new.

Reflect On It

The Bible is filled with practicalities and instruction. It often gives us a petition followed by a consequence. Jesus said, "For if you forgive men when they sin against you, your heavenly Father will also forgive you. But if you do not forgive men their sins, your Father will not forgive your sins" (Matthew 6:14-15).

- Apply this statement to your situation: "If I will [...] then God will [...]" This exercise can be applied to other life situations, not just forgiveness.
- If you're having a hard time asking God for forgiveness talk about it with him and a trusted friend, especially if you need to forgive God for not rescuing you from your pain.
- How have you hurt others?

Day Two: Two Kinds of Forgiveness

> It [forgiveness] may be the most costly gift you ever give; yet, precisely because it is so costly, it is also one of the clearest ways you can show God's love as his image bearer. –Pastor Mike Wilkerson[161]

How would you feel if you got this note from your mother: "I wish you had never been born. You were one of the biggest mistakes I've ever made."

Author and speaker Sheri Rose Shepherd did. She tells about the time she became pregnant with her first baby. Wanting to put aside her estranged relationship with her mother, Sheri Rose wrote her a letter expressing her joy. Then she received a package from her mom. Thinking her mom sent a gift for the baby, she was surprised to find her own baby things, her birth certificate, and that heart breaking note.[162] She opened the box with joy in her heart, only to have it turn to grief, then bitterness.

You may have a parent like this. This is an example of unforgivable pain because someone we love and trust has betrayed us. We may not be able to avoid bad circumstances, but God gives us the ability to choose how we will react.

There two concepts or types of forgiveness: *decisional* and *emotional*. Dr. Neil Anderson sums them both up in this statement: "Don't wait to forgive until you feel like forgiving. You will never get here. Feelings take time to heal after the choice to forgive is made."[163]

Decisional Forgiveness

The *decisional forgiveness* process usually comes first. I choose to obey God: "Be kind and compassionate to one another, forgiving each other, just as in Christ God forgave you" (Ephesians 4:32). I say, "You hurt and wronged me but I choose not to hold it against you. I trust God to judge you fairly."

Decisional forgiveness is not a feeling but an act of my will to obey God. I choose not to hold this injustice against you or seek revenge. I want to put this behind me and move on. I may have to put a safeguard or boundary into place so this event doesn't happen again. I am making a decision about my behavioral intentions. We also tell Satan, "I'm not giving you a foothold in my mind any longer!"

Meanwhile, what do we do with emotions such as anger, worry, and sadness? Many therapists suggest we learn to schedule them into our lives. Once we decide to forgive and accept our negative emotions, we can make conscious and informed decisions about how much time we want to spend with them.

Pray: "Lord God, As you know, I'm having difficulty forgiving [*name*]. I know I'm not following your commandment to forgive. Thank you that in your blood there is cleansing and forgiveness. However, right now, drawing on your strength, I'm making a decision to forgive [*name*]. I take [*name*] off my hook and place [*name*] on your hook. I thank and praise you for forgiving me, and being patient and understanding."

Talk to God in your own words. Reaffirm your faith and trust in him by getting right back into his Word.

Emotional Forgiveness

The second type, *emotional forgiveness*, is the process of replacing negative emotions with positive emotions. With decisional forgiveness I choose to forgive you, but I cannot manage my negative emotions. I continue to hang onto bitterness, anger, hatred, and fear. We often need the help of a professional counselor or pastor, along with the support of friends.

Decisional forgiveness takes place instantaneously, while emotional forgiveness can be a recovery process. It may take years to heal depending on the depth of the wound. It could also happen quickly depending on the event. It is the process of emotionally releasing and forgiving, perhaps time and again. And let us not forget, forgiving and escaping consequences are not synonymous.

Paul said one reason for forgiveness is to keep from being beaten by Satan. Satan knows bitterness and anger are weaknesses. He will exploit those emotions. God casts our sins into the depths of the sea (see Micah 7:19). We should do the same with the sins of others, in so doing, casting Satan down with them.

Sheri Rose Shepherd knew she had to forgive her mother. She knew if she didn't she'd remain in bondage. She wrote,

> That day I experienced a pain I could not escape. Through a bucket of tears, I sat down and wrote her a real letter—a letter that cut through the bitterness and loneliness that I know we both felt for years. It was a letter asking forgiveness and it paved the road to healing.[164]

Forgiveness begins with our will. We can either choose to forgive and heal, or not to forgive; to hurt and hate. Whatever choice we make, we'll be changed. Jesus is our model. Submissive as a lamb, he was led to slaughter. His words carried no hate towards his accusers and torturers—only sadness for a child of God bent on their own path of destruction.

We will always remember the painful situation or loss, but we choose not to play the tape repeatedly. We choose to take our eyes off the offender and focus on God. Then we move into the healing phase. You have to ask yourself, "How bad do I want it?"

Is the forgiveness journey easy? No! It is hard work. It can be costly. Yet, choosing to heal is the best phase to be in. Choosing to offer a kind word in exchange for a deceitful one is healing. Once the process starts we begin to experience freedom. This freedom moves us back into relationship with God and others.

Reflect On It

What might scheduling your feelings into your day look like? Think about what time of the day you are free to explore your emotions with God. Say what needs to be said. Start the process of forgiving those who have hurt, shamed, embarrassed, or belittled you in the past. How long do you feel you might need—15, 30, 45, or 60 minutes? Schedule it!

Day Three: Part One
What Forgiveness Is Not

Kerri said, "He did horrible, abusive things to me. He thinks he's justified and shows no remorse. He doesn't deserve to be forgiven!"

The Bible counsels us to "make every effort to do what leads to peace and to mutual edification" (Romans 14:19). But if your addiction is the result of a traumatic or tragic event, forgiveness will most likely be difficult. It is normal to feel that forgiveness is impossible. It is still necessary if you want to be victorious over your dependencies. With God it is possible.

It is common to want the person who has hurt us to show remorse or confess their guilt before we forgive them. Often, this

221

never happens. Some have argued that since Christ forgives us, we should not only forgive others, but fully relinquish them from the consequences of their actions. I don't believe this is what God intends. [I will be sharing Scripture to support this.]

We need to mentally separate the act of forgiveness and the act of reuniting. They are not the same. Forgiving the person is about changing us…not the offender. If they sincerely repent and ask for forgiveness, and then give ample evidence of changed behavior, then a reunion may be possible. To freely forgive is the biblically correct position. But it is an altogether different matter to suggest that once forgiven, a person is free from any consequences. Let's look at what forgiveness does *not* do.

Forgiveness Does Not Let the Person off the Hook

Often an offender's actions destroy lives. This doesn't mean you do not hold the person accountable for their actions. God does: "I, the LORD, search all hearts and examine secret motives. I give all people their due rewards, according to what their actions deserve" (Jeremiah 17:9-10). Forgiveness involves mercy and grace, but it also involves accountability.

God's love is two-sided—mercy and judgment—which deals with accountability. Many women struggle with this because it means setting boundaries and following through with consequences. Part of this process is coming to understand that God sets consequences. Therefore, we must too.

In 2 Samuel 11 and 12 we meet King David and are given a recap of his disturbing escapades. Considered a man after God's own heart, he committed adultery and then murdered a man in a last-ditch effort to cover his own sin. He refused to admit what he'd done. David's adultery with Bathsheba was a sin of passion, a sin of the moment which overtook him. But having Bathsheba's husband, Uriah, killed was premeditated, deliberate, and a disgrace against God.

Scripture says the "Lord considered David's actions evil" (2

Samuel 11:27, GW). Other versions say the thing David had done displeased God. Notice God is angry with David's actions, not David the person, his child.

At this point in time Bathsheba and David were about to have a baby. God sent in the prophet Nathan to confront the guilty king about his actions. By telling a story about someone else's crime, Nathan prepared David for dealing with his own sins. David finally sees the truth and confesses.

God judged David's sins and he paid dearly for his deceit for the rest of his lifetime. "Because you despised me and took the wife of Uriah the Hittite to be your own. ...Out of your own household I am going to bring calamity upon you" (2 Samuel 10-11).

These verses came true: their first baby died, murder was a constant threat in his family, his household rebelled against him, his wives were given to another in public view, and David missed out on building the Lord's temple. The consequences were irreversible. *Sin which has been forgiven and forgotten by God may still leave human scars.*

Despite David's actions, God still used him. In fact, his virtues were found worthy enough to generate from his seed the forthcoming Messiah. We know David truly repented because he wrote Psalm 51 during this event. His words give us valuable insight and hope.

Forgiveness Does Not Excuse, Condone, Deny, Minimize, or Justify the Behavior

When my sister-in-law stole from me she made me mad. When she apologized I said, "That's okay," even though it wasn't alright. When someone apologizes, often the other person answers, "That's okay," because she has been told to "forgive and forget." Yet, she still hurts and is distrustful.

Forgiveness is *not* saying, "It's not a big deal." If it truly is no big deal, then there's nothing to forgive. If it is a real offense against you—a child of God, it is a big deal. It is so big that Jesus Christ died for it.

Many offenders want you to take responsibility for their behavior. If you're ever confused about who the victim is, or if you find yourself apologizing for how you caused the person to offend you or others, you're playing into the devil's hands.

As human beings created in the image of God, he calls us to account for our moral choices. Invariably we mess things up and need to be honest about the part we played in the situation. For example, if I leave money in plain sight knowing my sister is a kleptomaniac, then, I have facilitated the theft.

When God forgives our sin he's not saying our past behavior is disregarded. What if somebody has a history of abusing children? Although they experience God's grace and forgiveness, the laws of our land demand they be held criminally responsible for their crime. Even after they've served their sentence, prudence still dictates the person not volunteer in children's ministry.

Reflect On It

Ask God to show you if the material in today's reading applies to you. Pray and ask him to forgive you for the ways you have hurt others, and to help you forgive those on your list.

Day Four: Part Two
What Forgiveness is Not

Forgiveness Does Not Forget

There are two words which shouldn't be associated with forgiveness: forgive and forget. The fact is, we don't forget. Brain studies reveal whatever is important to us is stashed away in our long-term memory. Unless an accident or disease damages our brain warehouse, those memories never disappear. This doesn't mean we can always access them. Sometimes we have psychological resistance to remembering because recalling certain incidents is too painful.

The memory doesn't disappear; it is merely laying low which makes us feel safer and in control.[165]

Paul told the Philippians, "I forget what is behind, and I struggle for what is ahead..." (Philippians 3:13-14). The biblical word *forget* in this context does not mean to "put out of one's mind." It has the meaning of letting go. It means we're not going to allow the experiences of the past to dominate our future and prevent us from becoming all God has purposed. There are memories we can't put out of our minds. But we choose not to allow them to dictate our attitudes and behavior in the future, even toward those who may be responsible for those memories.

Furthermore, if someone is taught to be a "good Christian" and to forgive and forget, the offender, and others involved, may get the message this behavior is acceptable. Whether we have forgiven the person depends not on whether we remember the incident, but rather it depends on our attitude. We know we have truly forgiven when we're no longer controlled by the pain...and no longer wish the person dead. We still remember what happened, but that memory no longer has power over our thinking and behavior.

Forgiveness Does Not Mean Reconciliation

People are generally reluctant to forgive because they don't understand the difference between forgiveness and trust. Forgiveness is not an expectation of a future relationship with the person. It doesn't mean letting the offender back into your life. Forgiveness is your gift. But you're not commanded to trust them. They must prove they've changed over time.

If a relationship with *any* person is not healthy, it is appropriate to distance yourself from the person. Jesus always withdrew from a situation if it was about to become violent or unhealthy (with the exception of the crucifixion).

Forgiveness Does Not Deny We Hurt

Forgiveness is not promising to never talk about the wrongdoing or hurt feelings. If there ever was a tragic victim, it was Tamar. A beautiful, royal princess, the daughter of King David, her life should have been a fairy tale. Instead, it became a nightmare. Her spoiled and deceitful half-brother, Amnon, raped her. Then his lust changed to hatred. Scripture says,

> Then Amnon hated her with intense hatred. In fact, he hated her more than he had loved her. Amnon said to her, "Get up and get out!" "No!" she said to him. "Sending me away would be a greater wrong than what you have already done to me." But he refused to listen to her. He called his personal servant and said, "Get this woman out of here and bolt the door after her." (2 Samuel 13:15-17)

In that culture the law mandated that when a man raped an unmarried woman he had to pay a dowry, marry, and never divorce her (see Deuteronomy 22:28-29; Exodus 22:16-17). Tamar was telling Amnon that by sending her away and not marrying her he was destroying her future.

Grieving, Tamar tore her robe (a symbol of her virginity) and wept loudly. Absalom, another brother, appeared to deny Tamar her grief and discounted her emotions by saying, "Be quiet now, my sister, he is your brother. Don't take this thing to heart" (2 Samuel 13:20). Apparently David was furious, but he did nothing.

What happened to Tamar? Scripture says she lived in Absalom's house a ruined and desolate woman. *Ruined. Desolate.* Tamar lost hope. She had every reason to feel anger, hurt, shame, and grief—even hate. It doesn't sound like she ever found another person to pour her wounded heart out to, or forgave those who hurt her. Did she ever find the comfort of God?

Forgiving the person doesn't mean your healing process is

finished. The wound must be cleaned up. We need to talk about the pain and have our feelings validated. Otherwise, we may live a ruined and desolate life.

Forgiveness Does Not Wait For an Apology

Some say, "I will forgive him as soon as he says he's sorry." The truth is some people will never apologize. There are people who will continue in their destructive, rebellious, and foolish behavior. Others will be stubborn and never confess or admit their sin. Some will move away, and others will die before they ever repent. We choose to forgive them because we know this is God's desire.

Reflect On It

Lewis Smedes wrote in his book *The Art of Forgiving*, "Only a free person can choose to live with an uneven score." The essence of forgiveness is the surrender of our expectations, emotions, rights, and pride to God's will. This is repentance.

Many of my prayers to God have been, "Help me change my mind toward this person and to try to see her/him as you see her/him. She/he hurt my feelings, but I want to forgive them because they probably didn't realize what they were doing or saying." I remind myself, "hurt people hurt people."

Forgiveness is a choice—our choice alone. It is a gift from God to the forgiver. It is also a gift from the forgiver to the person who doesn't deserve this gift. It is the hardest call of a Christian. Every day you must make the *decision* to forgive. Every day you must take your *emotions* to God.

- What is your greatest battle with forgiveness today?
- What lack of forgiveness or bitterness is still attached to you?

Day Five: Your Story is Only Beginning

> Give thanks to the LORD, for he is good! His faithful
> love endures forever. Has the LORD redeemed you?
> Then speak out! Tell others he has redeemed you
> from your enemies. –Psalm 107:1-2, NLT

Your story of redemption doesn't stop here. Before you were born God created a plan specifically designed for you (see Ephesians 2:10). You can do something amazing with the rest of your life if you choose to follow him.

When God created us in his image, he intended that we pour ourselves into one another. Our faith and healing are not complete until we take what we've learned and experienced, then give it to others in need. God wants you to make his name known. This is part of total health.

You are designed to be different. You have the potential to do something great. Scripture says that what God opens, no one can close; and what he closes, no one can open (see Revelation 3:7).

The 28th President of the United States, Woodrow Wilson said, "You are here in order to enable the world to live more amply with greater vision, with a finer spirit of hope and achievement. You are here to enrich the world."

Make your life extraordinary! Live chosen, loved, and submitted. Thank you for taking this incredible ride with me. God bless you!

About the Author

Kimberly Davidson received her MA in specialized ministry from Western Seminary, Portland, Oregon; a BA in health sciences; food and nutrition from the University of Iowa. She is a board certified biblical counselor and spiritual development coach, helping women mend their souls.

Kimberly is the founder of Olive Branch Outreach, a ministry dedicated to bringing hope and restoration to those struggling with body image, abuse, and food addiction. She has ministered to women for over ten years, from within prison walls to youth centers, inspiring others to empower God to meet their emotional and spiritual needs.

Kimberly is the author of four books, a contributor to five books, and she has penned numerous articles. She lives in Oregon with her husband and numerous critters.

If you enjoyed this book by Kimberly, you'll want to connect with her through either her website at *www.OliveBranchOutreach.com* or on Facebook. She'd love to hear your story or meet you at a future event.

Notes

1   Gerald May, *Addiction & Grace,* (New York: HarperOne, 1988), 3.

2   The Holy Bible is considered "God's Word" because he speaks to us in its sacred pages. Inspired by the Holy Spirit, the writers declare is from God himself; therefore to be true and binding upon us. This word is infallible, because written under the guidance of the Holy Spirit, and therefore free from all error of fact or doctrine or precept.

3   W. E. Vine, *Vine's Complete Expository Dictionary,* (Nashville: Thomas Nelson, 1996), 547.

4   David Jeremiah, *Turning Point,* "When You're Floundering," November 8, 2012.

5   David Hawkins, *Breaking Everyday Addictions,* (Eugene: Harvest House, 2008), 9.

6   Stated by Dr. Archibald Hart, *Healing Life's Hidden Addictions,* (Ann Arbor: Servant Publications, 1990).

7   Read more: *Woman fears she is addicted to Internet shopping* - Mywesttexas. com: West Texas Living http://www.mywesttexas.com/life/article_28091eaf-171c-5590-a4d0-008e12077c6c.html#ixzz1vuZPLXxY; Accessed August, 2012.

8   See http://thinkexist.com/quotation/just-cause-you-got-the-monkey-off-your-back-doesn/761553.html; Accessed November 24, 2012.

9   See: http://www.brainyquote.com/quotes/keywords/addiction. html#oqSo6rsRG30qEsul.99; Accessed November 30, 2012.

10 See: http://www.quotegarden.com/habits.html; Accessed March 31, 2012

11 Drs. Michael A. and William Mitchell, "Habits—They Can Make or Break Your Child," *ParentLife,* March 1998, p. 6.

12 See: http://www.quotegarden.com/habits.html; Accessed March 31, 2012

13 Dictionary.com Unabridged; Based on the Random House Dictionary, © Random House, Inc. 2012.

14 Tim Clinton, *Turn Your Life Around,* (New York: Faith Words, 2006), 115.

15 Lance Dodes, M.D., *PsychologyToday.com,* "The Heart of Addiction," March 23, 2012

16 See http://www.goodreads.com/quotes/tag/addiction; Accessed March 31, 2012.

17 C. S. Lewis, "The Trouble with X," in *God in the Dock: Essays on Theology and Ethics* (Eerdmans, 1970) 155.

18 Elizabeth Cooney, *The Boston Globe,* "Miracle Grow," June 28, 2010; Reprinted in *Brain In the News,* July/August 2010.

19 J. Keith Miller, *Compelled to Control,* (HCI, 1998).

20 Larry Crabb, *Finding God,* (Zondervan, 1995). 41.

21 C. S. Lewis, *Mere Christianity,* (San Francisco: HarperSanFrancisco, 1980), 56.

22 John Eldredge, *Beautiful Outlaw,* (New York: FaithWords, 2011), 54.

23 David Jeremiah, *Turning Point,* "Blood Brothers," July 10, 2012.

24 David Jeremiah, *Turning Points,* "The Garment," August 2012, 23.

25 Daniel G. Amen, M.D., *Healing the Hardware of the Soul,* 6, New York: The Free Press, 2002

26 *60 Minutes,* "Hooked," Aired April 29, 2012; See http://www.cbsnews.com/8301-18560_162-57423321/hooked-why-bad-habits-are-hard-to-break/?pageNum=2&tag=contentMain;contentBody.

27 Spear, "The Adolescent Brain and Age-Related Behavioral Manifestations," *Neuroscience and Biobehavioral Reviews* 24 (2000) 4:424-25.

28 Steven Stiles, M.D., *Thorns in the Heart* (eBook Edition, 2011), 202.

29 Daniel G. Amen, M.D., *Change Your Brain, Change Your Life,* (New York: Three Rivers Press, 1998), 6-7. Amen Clinics: See http://www.amenclinics.net/conditions/Addictions.

30 Stated by Dr. Linda Mintle in her presentation, "Make Peace with Your

Thighs: Overcoming Food Addiction," *AACC Counseltalk;* October 16, 2012.

31 *60 Minutes,* "Hooked," Aired April 29, 2012; See http://www.cbsnews. com/8301-18560_162-57423321/hooked-why-bad-habits-are-hard-to-bre ak/?pageNum=2&tag=contentMain;contentBody.

32 Joe S. McIlhaney, Jr., M.D. and Freda McKissic Bush, M.D., *Hooked,* (Chicago: Northfield Publishing, 2008), 31, 61.

33 James K. Childerston and Debra Taylor, *Christian Counseling Today,* "The Brain and Sex," 41, Vol. 17, No. 2, 2010.

34 U. Schjodt, H. Stodkilde-Jorgensen, A. Geertz, and A. Roepstorff, "Rewarding Prayers," Neuroscinece Letters, 443 (2008): 165-168.

35 Augustine, *Confessions,* trans. R. S. Pine-Coffin (New York: Penguin, 1961), 177.

36 Derek Tidball, *The Message of the Cross,* (Downers Grove: Inter-Varsity Press, 2001), 74.

37 Linda A. Merchadante, *Victims and Sinners,* (Louisville, Westminister John Know Press, 1996), 20.

38 See Ezekiel 28:12-17; Isaiah 14:12-15; Luke 10:18

39 Timothy Keller, *The Reason for God,* (New York: Riverhead Books, 2008), 168, 171-172.

40 Stated on www.AddictionInfo.org: See http://www.addictioninfo.org/ articles/4198/1/Is-Everyone-Addicted-To-Something/Page1.html; Accessed March 13, 2012.

41 Similarly stated by Timothy Keller, *The Reason for God,* (New York: Riverhead Books, 2008), 81.

42 Mike Wilkerson, *Redemption,* (Wheaton: Crossway, 2011), 49.

43 Derek Tidball, *The Message of Salvation,* (Downers Grove: InterVarsity Press, 2001), 254.

44 Melissa Healy *Los Angeles Times* "Pain and heartache are bound together in our brains," March 29, 2011.

45 *Science,* October 10th issue, http://mentalhealth.about.com/b/2003/10/16/ rejection-feels-like-pain-to-the-brain.htm.

46 *National Geographic;* http://news.nationalgeographic.com/ news/2011/03/110328-romantic-rejection-pain-brain-scans-mri-health-science.

47 See: http://www.goodreads.com/quotes/tag/addiction; Accessed March 31, 2012.

48 Steven Stiles, M.D., *Thorns in the Heart* (eBook Edition, 2011), 166.

49 Dwight L. Moody Quotes: http://thinkexist.com/quotes/dwight_l._moody/3.html; accessed June 2, 2008.

50 Larry Crabb, *Becoming a True Spiritual Community,* (Nashville: Thomas Nelson, 2007), 91.

51 See Deuteronomy 4:15-19; Exodus 34:16; Isaiah 57:7-8

52 According to Tim Kreider, "The Busyness Trap," quoted in *BreakPoint Daily: We Could Use Some Rest;* 7/10/2012.

53 *SoulCare: New Every Morning;* October 17, 2012.

54 Augustine, quoted in Hughes, *The True Image,* p. 65; Accessed September, 2012.

55 Tim Clinton, *Turn Your Life Around,* (New York: Faith Words, 2006), 127.

56 National Eating Disorders online: http://www.nationaleatingdisorders.org.

57 According to a study published in the journal *Sex Roles*: Medical News Today, "Only The Beautiful Need Apply," March 3, 2010; http://www.medicalnewstoday.com/articles/180941.php.

58 Timothy Keller, *The Reason for God,* (New York: Riverhead Books, 2008), 80.

59 Gerald May, *Addiction & Grace,* (New York: HarperOne, 1988), 153.

60 John Eldredge, *Beautiful Outlaw,* (New York: FaithWords, 2011), x.

61 Diane Langberg, :Self-Deception: A Supporting Column of Addiction," CCCF Annual Conference, 2008: The Addict in Us All.

62 Gregg A. Ten Elshof, *I Told Me So,*(Grand Rapids: Eerdmans, 2009) 25.

63 John Eldredge, *Beautiful Outlaw,* (New York: FaithWords, 2011), 130.

64 Caroline Leaf, *Who Switched Off My Brain* (Switch On Your Brain Organisation Pty; Ltd., 2007), 113-114.

65 Don Miguel Ruiz, "The Four Agreements," posted on Facebook August 10, 2012.

66 Oswald Chambers, *My Utmost for His Highest,* March 25.

67 *The Serenity Prayer* is the common name for an originally untitled prayer by twentieth century American theologian, Reinhold Niebuhr.

68   Realistic Recovery; see http://realisticrecovery.wordpress.com/2009/02/21/list-of-character-defects.

69   Drs. Tim Clinton and Ron Hawkins, *Biblical Counseling,* "Perfectionism" (Grand Rapids: Baker Books, 2009), 189.

70   Anne Wilson Schaef, *When Society Becomes Addicted,* (San Francisco: Harper & Row, 1987), 68.

71   See http://christian-quotes.ochristian.com/Oswald-Chambers-Quotes/page-2.shtml.

72   *SoulCare: New Every Morning;* December 6, 2012

73   This checklist is quoted in: Allen E. Mallinger, M.D. and Jeannette Dewyze, *Too Perfect* (New York: Ballantine Books, 1992), 3.

74   Frederick Buechner, *Wishful Thinking,* (New York: HarperOne, 1973, 1993), 104.

75   Bruce Larson, *There's A Lot More to Health Than Not Being Sick,* (Fleming H. Revell Co; 2nd edition, 1991).

76   See http:// www.answers.com/topic/physicality#ixzz2FRhcOgAr.; www.merriam-webster.com/dictionary/physicality.

77   *PR Newswire;*http://www.prnewswire.com/news-releases/first-impressions-are-everything-new-study-confirms-people-with-straight-teeth-are-perceived-as-more-successful-smarter-and-having-more-dates-148073735.html; Accessed November, 2012.

78   *Business Wire,* "The Future of Haircare: Consumption Trends and Product Preferences," April 20, 2012.

79   *Market Wire,* "Market Research Forecasts U.S. Retail Sales of Cosmeceuticals at $11.9 Billion by 2016," May 9, 2012.

80   See Romans 8:11;1 Corinthians 15:45; 2 Corinthians 3:18; 5:17; Colossians 3:9-10.

81   See: http://www.challies.com/reading-classics-together/if-we-have-died-to-sin-why-do-we-still-sin; Accessed November, 2012.

82   See John 4:6; 19:28; Luke 4:21, Mark 14:49, John 19:28

83   J. I. Packer, *Knowing God* (Downers Grove: InterVarsity Press, 1973), 103.

84   *Christian Counseling Today,* Gregory L. Jantz, "Addicted to Love," Vol. 17, No. 2, 2010, 37

85   Stated by: Drs. Robert Hemfelt, Frank Minirth, Paul Meier, *Love is a Choice* (Nashville: Thomas Nelson, 1989), 25.

86   Leo Booth, *When God Becomes a Drug;* See http://www.lexpages.com/SGN/paschal/religious_addiction.html; Accessed November 5, 2012

87   Quoted by Archibald Hart, *Healing Life's Hidden Addictions,* (Ann Arbor: Servant Publications, 1990), 132.

88   Adapted from: Melody Beattie, *Learning To Live And Love Again. Codependent No More* (New York: Harper/Hazelden, 1987), 211.

89   Quoted by Dr. David Jeremiah, *Turning Points,* August 17, 2012.

90   Robert Whitcomb, *Psychology for Living,* "Trapped by Relentless Hope," Summer 2012 Vol. 54 No. 2.

91   See Isaiah 49:14-15, 18; Jeremiah 24:7; Matthew 23:37; Mark 12:29-30; Matthew 22:36-38

92   Polner, M, "Divine Relations, Social Relations, and Well-being," *Journal of Health and Social Behavior* 30: 92-104, 1989.

93   Francis Chan, *Crazy Love,* (Colorado Springs: David C. Cook, 2008), 95.

94   See Matthew 3:17, 26:53; John 5:30, 8:38, 15:15; 16:32b; Hebrews 5;8

95   Stated in *Our Daily Bread, Day 18,* "Herd Instinct," April 17, 2007; http://odb.org/2007/04/17/herd-instinct/

96   See Psalm 100:3; Isaiah 53:6; Matthew 9:36.

97   John Ortberg, *The Life You've Always Wanted,*(Grand Rapids: Zondervan, 1997, 2002), 158.

98   Ibid, 162.

99   Ibid, 163.

100 Archibald Hart and Sylvia Frejd, "The Digital Addiction Invasion," *Christian Counseling Today,* p. 25, Vol. 19 NO. 3, 2012.

101 Colleen Moore and Tesh, "Moms at Risk for Internet Addiction," *Impact Publishing,* 2012.

102 "The Role of the CHRNA4 Gene in Internet Addiction: A Case-control Study," http://www.ncbi.nlm.nih.gov/pubmed?term=internet%20addiction%20chrna4; "New research offers clues to Internet addiction," See: http://www.smartplanet.com/blog/smart-takes/new-research-offers-clues-to-internet-addiction/28804; Accessed November, 2012.

103 Linda Mintle, "The Altered Self," *Christian Counseling Today,* p. 21, Vol. 19 NO. 3, 2012.

104 See: http://scottjeffrey.com/2009/06/digital-addiction; Accessed October, 2012.

105 Archibald Hart and Sylvia Frejd, "The Digital Addiction Invasion," *Christian Counseling Today,* p. 25-26, Vol. 19 NO. 3, 2012.

106 *PRWEB*: February 29, 2012; Concerned About Internet Addiction? Cognitive Behavioural Therapy Could Be the Answer, Says Counselling Directory.

107 John Ortberg, *The Life You've Always Wanted,* (Grand Rapids: Zondervan, 1997, 2002), 169, 172.

108 A. W. Tozer, *Tozer Topical Reader,* comp. Ron Eggert, 2.185, Camp Hill: Christian Publications, 1998.

109 Justsell.com; June 9, 2010.

110 Dictionary.com Unabridged; Based on the Random House Dictionary, Random House, Inc. 2012.

111 Henri Nouwen, *The Road to Daybreak* (New York: Doubleday, 1988), 29.

112 *Today's Cartoon,* November 17, 2012; See http://www.glasbergen.com.

113 See Ephesians 2:1-3; Romans 5:9; 1 Thessalonians 5:

114 Dr. Ali Binazar, *Huffington Post,* "Addiction Recovery: Why We're Addicted to Negative Behaviors," June 15, 2010.

115 David Powlison, "In the Last Analysis," 2007 Leadership Conference, Sovereign Grace Ministries.

116 See: http://www.thepositivemind.com/tpm/aboutpainanddullnessarticle.html; Accessed July, 2012.

117 Corrie Ten Boom, *Clippings from My Notebook,* (Minneapolis: World Wide Publications, 1982), 33.

118 *New York Times Science*, "Stress addiction: 'life in the fast lane'," July 26, 1983.

119 Lazarus RS. *Stress and Emotion: A New Synthesis* (Springer Publishing Company; New York: 1999); Cohen S, Kessler RC, Gordon LU. Strategies for measuring stress in studies of psychiatric and physical disorders. In: Cohen S, Kessler RC, Gordon LU, editors. *Measuring Stress: A Guide for Health and Social Scientists.* Oxford University Press; New York: 1995. pp.

3–26; Levine S. Developmental determinants of sensitivity and resistance to stress. *Psychoneuroendocrinology.* 2005;30:939–946.

120 Quoted in: *Mary E. DeMuth, Beautiful Battle: A Woman's Guide To Spiritual Warfare,* (Eugene: Harvest House, 2012).

121 Les Carter, "Anti-Growth Trait," e-newsletter February, 2009; www.drlescarter.com

122 Quoted by Dr. David Jeremiah, *Turning Point,* "Walking and Pleasing," August 1, 2012.

123 See: 1 Thessalonians 5:21-22; Leviticus 19:26, 31; 20:6; Deuteronomy 18:9-13; Acts 19:18-20

124 J. I. Packer, foreword to R. C. Sproul, *Knowing Scripture,* (Downers Grove: InterVarsity Press, 1979), 9-10.

125 See Ephesians 4:22-24; Colossians 3:9-10; Galatians 5:17; 1 Peter 2:11.

126 Quoted by Mark Earley, The *Breakpoint* email newsletter, Oct. 22, 2007.

127 Quoted in Robert J. Morgan, *Nelson's Complete Book of Stories, Illustrations, & Quotes,* "Temptation" (Nashville: Thomas Nelson, 2000), 728.

128 Focus on the Family. 1997. *The First Nine Months,* Colorado Springs, CO, 80995.

129 Larry Crabb, *Understanding People,*(Zondervan, 1987) 174.

130 Marilyn Meberg, *The Zippered Heart,* (Nashville: Thomas Nelson, 2002).

131 Edward T. Welch, *Shame Interrupted,* (Greensboro: New Growth Press, 2012), 6.

132 Ken Gire, *Moments with the Savior,* (Grand Rapids: Zondervan, 1998), 39.

133 Wikipedia: See http://en.wikipedia.org/wiki/Leprosy#References

134 Pam Leo, "Reach Out and Touch Somebody," see: http://blog.babesinarms.com.au/2009/09/04/reach-out-and-touch-someone; Accessed November, 2012.

135 W. E. Vine, *Vine's Complete Expository Dictionary,* (Nashville: Thomas Nelson, 1996), 307.

136 M. Craig Barnes, *When God Interrupts,* (Downers Grove: InterVarsity Press, 1996), 75.

137 Frederick Buechner, *Wishful Thinking,* (New York: HarperOne, 1973, 1993), 18.

138 Mike Wilkerson, *Redemption,* (Wheaton: Crossway, 2011), 132.

139   Oswald Chambers, *My Utmost for His Highest,* "The Bounty of the Destitute," November 28.

140   Justin Barrett, *Why Would Anyone Believe in God?* (Walnut Creek: Altamira Press, 2004).

141   Larry Crabb, *Understanding People,*(Zondervan, 1987), 100.

142   Hiram Johnson, *Tragic Redemption* (Austin: Langmarc Publishing, 2006), 70.

143   Gary Thomas, *Seeking the Face of God I* (Eugene: Harvest House, 1999), 84.

144   Thomas Chalmers, *The Expulsive Power of a New Affection,* (Amazon Digital Services, Inc.)

145   Frederick Buechner, *Wishful Thinking,* (New York: HarperOne, 1973, 1993), 96.

146   C. H. Spurgeon; *Heartwarming Bible Illustrations;* Accessed October, 2012.

147   *Genetics Science Learning Center,* "Genetics Is an Important Factor in Addiction," http://learn.genetics.utah.edu/content/addiction/genetics/; Accessed April 28, 2012.

148   Norman Doidge, M.D., *The Brain That Changes Itself* (New York: Penguin Books, 2007), 209-210.

149   Ibid, 173.

150   Caroline Leaf, *Who Switched Off My Brain* (Switch On Your Brain Organisation Pty; Ltd., 2007), 113-114.

151   Ibid.

152   Stated by Marilyn Meberg, *I'd Rather Be Laughing* (Nashville: Word Publishing, 1998), 101.

153   Drs. Tim Clinton and Ron Hawkins, *Biblical Counseling,* "Grief and Loss," (Grand Rapids: Baker Books, 2009), 130.

154   Katherine Wollard, *Body/Mind,* "Go Ahead, Cry Yourself A River," from William Frey II, *Crying: The Mystery of Tears.*

155   Walt Larimore, M.D., *God's Design for the Highly Healthy Teen,* (Grand Rapids: Zondervan, 2005), 250.

156   Drs. Tim Clinton and Ron Hawkins, *Biblical Counseling,* "Grief and Loss," (Grand Rapids: Baker Books, 2009),131.

157   Tom Clinton, *Hunger and Thirst Weekly Devotional*, August 2, 2012.

158   Drs. Robert Hemfelt, Frank Minirth, Paul Meier, *Love is a Choice* (Nashville: Thomas Nelson, 1989), 216.

159   Gregory L. Jantz, *Hope, Help, and Healing for Eating Disorders*, (Wheaton: Harold Shaw Publishers, 1995), 125.

160   See Colossians 3:13; Matthew 6:14-15; 18:21-35; Mark 11:25; Luke 6:37; 11:4; 17:3-4; Ephesians 4:32

161   Mike Wilkerson, *Redemption,* (Wheaton: Crossway, 2011), 80.

162   Sheri Rose Shepherd, *Fit For Excellence*, (Lake Mary: Creation House, 1961) 23.

163   Neil Anderson, *The Bondage Breaker,* (Eugene: Harvest House, 2000, 2nd Rev.), 69, 72.

164   Sheri Rose Shepherd, *Fit For Excellence*, (Lake Mary: Creation House, 1961), 23.

165   Stated by Marilyn Meberg, *I'd Rather Be Laughing* (Nashville: Word Publishing, 1998), 128.

CPSIA information can be obtained at www.ICGtesting.com
Printed in the USA
LVOW051321220213

321192LV00002B/159/P